A MESSAGE FROM GOD

What can there be for those locked behind bars? Whether you are locked in jail literally, or are in a figurative prison of a destructive illness, relationship, or situation, this devotional will show you how to tap in to the unfailing hope that comes from knowing Jesus in a personal way.

For licensing/copyright information, for additional copies or for use in specialized settings, contact:

Connie Blanchette
PO Box 220
Holly Springs, GA 30142-0004
bcblanc@aol.com

ACKNOWLEDGEMENTS

I thank the Lord for giving me His love for prisoners. He has led me every step of the way to prepare the writing of this book.

I have been inspired and challenged to bring this devotional to completion, and I couldn't have done it without the professional help of my designer, Juli Phillips. Juli understood my heart's desire to do a work that would bring glory to the Lord, and her designs and layouts have accomplished that.

God gave my friend, Marcia Jawara, new and fresh ideas relating to the Christian life and the struggles of prisoners in today's world. I am most grateful for her insights.

My husband, Bob, has been patient with me and has prayed for this book to bring glory to our Lord. I am so blessed to have him as a partner in my adventure of life!

—*Connie Blanchette*

Acknowledgements

This book is dedicated to my family and friends who have stuck by me on my long journey.

I especially want to thank my three wonderful sons, McKoy, Latoy, and Romaine for their love and understanding during the time of my incarceration. I am so blessed to have sons who do not leave when the going gets tough.

My mother and father have been faithful to me during the years, and I praise God for them. Thank you, Mom and Dad, for your unconditional love and care for me.

My friends, Ms. Williams, Ms. Davis, and Connie Blanchette have helped with prayer efforts, the editing, the typing, and the publishing of this book, and to them I am so grateful.

—*Marcia Jawara*

Introduction

After searching extensively for devotionals for prisoners, we came up with only one, and it was inferior and not relevant to most prisoners. God impressed on us the need for a devotional that was simplistic and relevant to the problems which prisoners daily face.

A Message from God: Daily Devotions for Prisoners came through the ideas impressed on us by the Holy Spirit of God from our personal experiences.

As you read these daily meditations, be assured that we know whereof we speak. We have been where you are and feel what you feel. There is hope for every person who is incarcerated. God loves each of us with the same love.

Pass this book on and let others share the comfort and understanding it brings.

We love you and praise God for the plan He has for your life!

Connie and Marcia

ABOUT THE AUTHOR

Connie Blanchette

For ten years Connie Blanchette has watched the marvelous transformation that takes place as prisoners turn their lives over to Jesus Christ. She has mentored several prisoners who are now leading productive and Christ-honoring lives. She enjoys writing and speaking for God's glory.

Connie and her husband Bob live in the Atlanta area where Connie serves as a volunteer Southern Baptist Convention chaplain, taking every opportunity she gets to love and minister to the incarcerated.

About the Author

Marcia Jawara

Growing up in Jamaica was a daily struggle, but God knew that Marcia Jawara would need that experience to face an even greater struggle.

She left her native country and her family to marry a man in the United States. She didn't know where life was taking her, but she would find out in later years that God had a plan that was created before the foundation of the world.

Her life was still a daily struggle in the U.S., and because of being in the wrong place at the wrong time, she ended up in prison, facing years of confinement. During this time, she accepted Jesus Christ into her life and started growing in her knowledge of God and His Word.

Marcia's future is bright because of Jesus!

x

JANUARY

January 1 – Pray, Pray, Pray

Pray without ceasing. (I Thess. 5:17)

This is a new year with new opportunities and new challenges. We do not know what the future holds; but as the old saying goes, "We know Who holds the future."

Every new year for a prisoner is another year closer to release. Sometimes our eyes only look at our incarceration instead of Jesus. This year, look unto Jesus, the Author and Finisher of your faith and things will go better. The time will even go faster.

Memorize I John 5:14, 15 and let it sink deep down into your spirit every day. It says, "And this is the confidence that we have in him, that if we ask anything according to his will, he hears us; and if we know that he hears us, whatever we ask, we know that we have the petitions that we have desired of him."

God loves to answer prayer, and He does answer if we ask according to His will. If we say, "Lord, please save my mother's soul," is that according to God's will? Yes, indeed! Be assured that God will answer your prayers if they line up with the Bible and His sovereign will in your life.

The message for today: Prayer is the very best gift you can give or receive. There is no cost, but wonderful rewards. Continue praying for one another.

Prayer: Dear Heavenly Father, I ask You to bless my friends and family. Thank You for teaching me to pray with Your will in mind.

January 2 – A Good Place to Live

He who dwells in the shelter of the Most High
will abide in the shadow of the Almighty. (Psalm 91:1)

Are you in prison and need someone to encourage you today? If you are lonely and sad, I have a remedy. No matter how difficult your situation seems, there is always a scripture that you can turn to that will give you encouraging answers to your problem.

Read Psalm 91 today. As you read, grab hold of the verses and make them personal to your own life. David writes in Psalm 91:5, "You will not be afraid of the terror by night; or the arrow that flies by day".

Psalm 91:11 says, "For He will give His angels charge concerning you, to guard you in all your ways." God cares about you and will help you not to be afraid, because He is protecting you. You don't have to fight your battles. God has been with you your whole life, and He is with you now. He will not leave you or forsake you. You are not an orphan if you know Jesus as Savior.

John 14:18 says, "I will not leave you as orphans: I will come to you." (NASB)

The message for today: Don't just visit the secret place of the Most High God. Live in it daily and be comfortable in God's care of you. Trust Him to be your Protector and Helper in all your trials.

Prayer: Dear Heavenly Father, Help me to live in the secret place of Your presence, knowing that You love me and only want what is best for me.

January 3 – Where's Your Focus?

I will lift up my eyes to the mountains; from where shall my help come? My help comes from the Lord, who made heaven and earth. (Psalm 121:1, 2)

In times of trials and tribulations in jail, we tend to focus on our problems instead of God, our Heavenly Father.

In Psalm 121 He told us to always look up "to the hills" because our help comes from above. God is our refuge and strength, a very presen t help in trouble (Psalm 46:1). If we start applying God's remedy to our wounds, they will be healed.

Psalm 46 tells us that God is in total control of our lives. He is our refuge and strength, a very present help in trouble. He sees how Satan comes to us with temptations, trials and confusion; but He is the Author of perfect peace in the midst of the storms of life. Psalm 46:10 is an admonition worth looking at. It is so simple: Be still and know that I am God. That is more difficult than it sounds, but it works if we can just read the Word of God and trust in His provision for us.

Walk by faith. Walk in the anointing of our God and you will encounter the awesomeness of Jehovah-rapha, the LORD our Healer.

The message for today: Glance at your problems. Gaze at Jesus!

Prayer: Dear Heavenly Father, I thank You for being my Healer and my Helper in times of trouble. I ask You to help me to keep looking up. Help me to focus on Your provision – not my problems. Thank You for being everything I need.

✝
January 4 – Do What God Says

Abraham called the name of that place The LORD will provide (Jehovah-jireh)... (Genesis 22:14)

I grew up poor on the small island of Jamaica. Many families were in the same situation, but we were always dependent on God and trusting in Him so much that we got up each day thanking Him that He is the Great Provider, Jehovah-jireh. Because of His faithfulness, we were never without.

In Genesis (Chapters 12-22) Abram (later called Abraham) was called by God to leave his relatives and go to a land that He would show him. Abraham was obedient in everything God asked, and He rewarded that obedience by giving him a son named Isaac. Genesis 22 tells of the greatest test any father could be given – that of offering his only son to show God that he loved and trusted him. Genesis 22:5 is one of my favorite verses where Abraham said to the young men with him, "Stay here with the donkey, and I and the lad will go over there; and we will worship and return to you." What faith!

Prisoner, what God did back then, He is able to do now for you. He wants to provide salvation, friends, and hope. Let Him meet you where you are today.

The message for today: The Lord will provide for you.

Prayer: Dear Heavenly Father, Thank you for Your faithfulness. Help me to obey You in everything, big or small, to show You that I love you.

January 5 – Help!

Therefore I urge you, brethren, by the mercies of God,
to present your bodies a living and holy sacrifice,
acceptable to God, which is your spiritual service
of worship. (Romans 12:1)

As a prisoner, I had many problems which weren't easily solved. I talked to my friends and I worried, but I didn't go to Jesus until He finally got my attention. I found that He is all powerful, and yet for years I turned to the other things or people instead of the Creator for help. Why was I so misdirected? I realized, almost too late, that it was the way I had been thinking for years.

The Apostle Paul tells us in Romans 12:2 that we should not be conformed to this world, but we should be transformed by the renewing of our minds. This is done by reading God's Word, the Bible, everyday and praying to Him for guidance. Little by little, our minds are changed from doubting the future and being afraid of it to trusting God for all that happens. As our minds are changed, we get to know God better, and that is what maturity is all about.

The Bible says that anything that is not of faith is sin (Romans 14:23). Have faith today that God is working everything out in your life for your ultimate good, even in times of trial.

The message for today: Success begins with Jesus, the Master of all.

Prayer: Dear Heavenly Father, I thank You for the ability to think and make wise decisions. I pray for Your guidance as I read Your Word and pray daily. I pray for You to renew my mind by Your great power.

January 6 – I Didn't Sign Up for This Class!

Casting all your care upon him for he careth for you.
(I Peter 5:7)

Have you ever wondered when things are constantly going wrong why they are prolonged? Why won't this trial end? Doesn't God care?

God knows each of us because He created us. Thus, He knows what we need and when we need it, whether it is problems or blessings.

Our first problem when we are put through a test is that we are impatient. We get frustrated quickly and we do not stop to think how Jesus would handle the situation. Secondly, we keep our eyes on the very thing that causes us to be frustrated.

When things get you discouraged, start praying before you make any quick decisions. Ask Jesus Christ for His guidance; then go to the Word of God, the Bible, and look for a passage that speaks to you. Read until you find something for your situation.

God has told us that we are "more than conquerors" through Him who loves us (Romans 8:37). We like to think that we are more than conquerors until we have something to conquer. Our Father, who knows the end from the beginning, has a solution for every problem you will ever encounter. Trust Him today.

The message for today: God will keep you in perfect peace if your mind is "stayed" on Him (Isaiah 26:3).

Prayer: Dear Heavenly Father, Thank You that You are the answer to every problem I will ever have. Help me to come to You first when I am worried and overwhelmed. Help me to cast all my worries and burdens at Your feet, where they belong.

January 7 – Good Advice

Seek the peace of the city to which I have caused you to be carried away captives and pray unto the Lord for it, for in its peace shall you have peace. *(Jeremiah 29:7)*

This verse says that, as we pray for peace in our place of captivity, we will have peace. Somehow "jail" and "peace" don't seem to go together, but God makes the difference. It is not easy to pray for our place of incarceration and the personnel who run it; but as we pray specifically we can see definite changes in our environment and people's attitudes.

As you pray for your fellow inmates, things also change. Jeremiah 29:11-13 tells us that God thinks thoughts of peace toward His children and that He has a great plan for each of us. He promises us in 29:12 that He listens when we pray for His peace to be in us and around us. "Then shall you call upon me, and I will listen and I will hearken unto you."

God is listening to your prayers. Maybe He allowed your jail time to learn to pray for your fellow prisoners. Take your time of confinement as a daily challenge from God to learn all you can about His peace, His Word, and prayer.

The message for today: Peace is a by-product of knowing God well.

Prayer: Dear Heavenly Father, I thank You for my life and this time of confinement. I pray for this prison, the warden, the staff, and those who prepare and serve the meals here. I also pray for my fellow prisoners to come to know Jesus as Lord and Savior.

January 8 – Exercising Your Faith

Be strong and courageous; do not be afraid or tremble at them, for the Lord your God is the one who goes with you. He will not fail you or forsake you. (Deut. 31:6)

In prison it is common to hear people blaming God for their problems. Where is He when they need Him? Why won't He answer their prayers?

The devil is the author of confusion, fear, and doubt. We should not blame God. Satan knows that you are a child of God, so he puts things in your life to drive your faith away because he is the great deceiver. That is his job.

The book of Daniel is a wonderful example of being strong and courageous, in spite of what Satan tries to do to you. Daniel must have had faithful, godly parents who taught him how to stand firm in the faith, and stand firm he did. In Daniel 6 we read how his faith was severely tested, but God gave him the victory in the end.

God delivered Daniel from the den of lions, and He will deliver you as you trust Him. Memorize today's Bible verse and keep it tucked inside your heart when the devil tries to make you afraid. God's Word works!

The message for today: God is with you. Exercise the faith you have. It is enough to give you victory over everything!

Prayer: Dear Heavenly Father, I thank You that You are helping me to grow in the grace and knowledge of You as I read Your Word and hide it in my heart.

January 9 – Me? Selfish?

But when he came to his senses, he said, "How many of my father's hired men have more than enough bread, but I am dying here with hunger! I will get up and go to my father..." (Luke 15:17, 18).

In our pride, most of us end up in jail because of making wrong decisions and thinking that we won't get caught. The story of the prodigal son gives a good example of what our pride can do to us.

Pride turned the prodigal son's life to selfishness. "Father, give me my share of the estate" (Luke 15:12). Then he had to hit rock bottom before he realized how good he had it before. At first, it probably felt good to be free and not have anyone to answer to; but when he became destitute and was starving, home looked a little better to him. He knew he needed to return home and reconcile with his family.

We often find ourselves in that same position after we have turned away from our Father in heaven, but the greatest thing is that He is always waiting to welcome us back.

If you know Jesus Christ as your Lord and Savior, and sin has come between you and your Heavenly Father, the Bible says that He is "faithful and just to forgive us our sins and to cleanse us from ALL unrighteousness" (1 John 1:9).

The message for today: Pride goes before a fall, but God is always there to pick us up, dust us off, and help us return to the path He has chosen for us.

Prayer: Dear Heavenly Father, I confess that I have been prideful in my life and I ask You to forgive that pride and change my life so that I will serve You forever.

January 10 – True Concern

In a little wrath I hid my face from thee for a moment;
but with everlasting kindness will I have mercy on thee,
saith the Lord thy Redeemer. (Isaiah 54:8)

The Bible says that God so loved the world that He gave His only begotten Son that whoever believes in Him should not perish but have everlasting life. For God sent not His Son into the world to condemn the world; but that the world through Him might be saved. (John 3:16-21)

These verses are such a picture of God's great love. We can't understand that kind of love, but it's real. Would you give up your only son to die for someone you didn't even know? God did.

We surely didn't deserve it because we are all sinners, but that is the unconditional love of God. The Bible says in John 3:17 that Jesus did not come to condemn us but to save us forever. All He wants us to do is to believe on Him and accept that He died for our sins.

The message for today: Accept God's great love and ask Him to teach you to love as He loves.

Prayer: Dear Heavenly Father, I know I have sinned against You. I ask Jesus Christ to come into my life and save me from my sins. I accept Jesus here and now as my Savior. Thank You for saving me, today, _____ (Fill in the date and never forget it.)

January 11 – What Have You Given?

Then took Mary a pound of ointment of spikenard, very costly, and anointed the feet of Jesus, and wiped his feet with her hair, and the house was filled with the odor of the ointment. (John 12:3)

The law of nature tells us that we have to plant corn in order to get a harvest of corn. We have to exercise regularly to get a healthy body. We must work to get paid.

It is the same way with our service to the Lord. In John 12 Mary broke a precious alabaster box of costly ointment (about one year's wages!) and anointed the feet of Jesus. He was so honored by this sacrificial act of love and service to Him that He made sure the Bible would contain this story forever.

As Christian prisoners, we can give Jesus our best by giving Him the first part of our day, every day. The moment we are awakened in the morning, we could give Him 20 minutes of reading His Word and praying. He would be greatly honored by our "first fruits" given to Him, and the rest of our day would be covered with His blessings. In a year, we would have spent 365 days (20 minutes per day) or 122 hours with Him! Talk about honoring Jesus! He would love it!

The message for today: Don't be afraid to break your alabaster box. Give Jesus your best, and the returns will be awesome!

Prayer: Dear Heavenly Father, Thank You for freely giving Your very best to us by giving us Jesus, Your Son. Help me today to give up a few minutes of my time for You to show You that I love You more than this world.

✝

January 12 – Stay Close

If we live in the Spirit, let us also walk in the Spirit. Let us not be desirous of vainglory, provoking one another, envying one another. (Galatians 5:25, 26)

There are times when we are drained, and it feels like the presence of God has departed from us. We know that God's Word says that Jesus will never leave us (Hebrews 13:5b) – no matter what; but sometimes we allow our feelings to tell us differently.

When we feel as if our spirit is not functioning the way it should be, it could be that there is something coming between us and God. Perhaps we are grieving the Holy Spirit of God who lives within us by not reading the Bible, not praying, being angry with someone, or even being angry with God for placing us in prison. We need to get things right between God and us by confessing sin and asking Him to search our hearts and show us our sin.

We all need an extra push sometimes. Romans 8:26 says that the Holy Spirit helps our infirmities and actually prays for us when we don't know what is wrong. He will show you what is wrong if you go to God in prayer and persist until He shows you. Remember the old saying: Pray Until Something Happens (PUSH).

James 4:8 says that we should draw near to God and He will draw near to us. That is a promise that works.

The message for today: Live your life so close to God that He finds nothing to censure.

Prayer: Dear Heavenly Father, I thank You for the Holy Spirit who lives inside of me and prays for me. Help me to live in close fellowship with You and stand on Your promises in the Word of God.

January 13 – What Would Happen?

Rejoice always. (I Thessalonians 5:16)

In I Thessalonians 5:16-18 we are told to give thanks for everything. Does that include going to jail? Let's face it — it's hard to be happy behind bars!

I once met a lady whose uncle was a preacher, who died unexpectedly. All of his family attended his funeral and wept bitterly, but she seemed so happy. During the funeral, she asked everyone the question, "If you died this minute, do you know where you would spend eternity?" Because she was certain that her uncle was in heaven, she could praise God, even in the midst of sadness and tears.

What about you? If you died this moment, do you know for sure that you would go to heaven? You can be sure. Here's how.

- Admit that you have sinned and done wrong things (Romans 3:23)
- Ask Jesus to come into your heart by faith (Romans 10:9, 10, 13)
- Believe that He will save your soul (Acts 16:31)

The message for today: After accepting Jesus Christ into your heart, grow in the grace and knowledge of Him by reading the Bible and praying.

Prayer: Dear Heavenly Father, Thank You for loving me so much that You sent Jesus, Your only Son, to die for me. Jesus, thank You for dying for me, being buried, and rising again to provide my salvation!

✝

January 14 – The Word Works!

Blessed are they that mourn for they shall be comforted.
(Matthew 5:4)

There are many things in jail that can cause us to "mourn", but there is a remedy for sadness. It is the Bible, God's Word. As we read and think about it every day of our lives, we can be comforted. In II Corinthians 4:8 Paul said, "We are troubled on every side, yet not distressed; we are perplexed, but not in despair; persecuted, but not forsaken; cast down, but not destroyed."

Every time you have a problem, a fear, a doubt, a hurt feeling, or a sickness, the Bible has the perfect answer for you. God will show you the answers to all your problems as you go to Him as soon as the problem starts. Start speaking directly to your situation and be comforted by the never-failing Word of God.

When I have a trial starting, I say something like this to Satan, "Devil, I know it's you again, so I command you to leave me alone. I bind you, rebuke you, and banish you in Jesus' Name. God's Word says that I am more than a conqueror through Jesus Christ, my Lord, and I trust Him totally."

It works every time. You put God in control – not Satan.

The message for today: God's Word works. Cast all your cares upon Him for He cares for you.

Prayer: Dear Heavenly Father, I know that You love me and help me through all my trials. I choose to trust You and not my feelings of fear. Help me to love Your Word and learn victory verses, which will overcome Satan.

January 15 – The Perfect Attorney

All My compassions are kindled. I will not execute My fierce anger… (Hosea 11:8)

We have a Heavenly Father who loves us unconditionally. That means that God loves us, even when we are not lovable and even when we sin against Him.

If you are a Christian, you have a Lawyer (an advocate), whose name is Jesus Christ. He says that He will forgive you of every sin you commit when you ask Him. The Bible tells us that if we confess our sins, God is faithful and just to forgive us our sins and cleanse us from all unrighteousness (1 John 1:9).

The word "confess" means that we say the same thing God says about our sin. If we lie, we tell God, "I lied", because He knows everything already. We should not say, "Well, I had to tell a little white lie." We should just admit to God what we did. It is as if God takes a giant pencil and writes our sin across the sky, so He knows what we have done wrong. We cannot trick Him. He knows all. He is omniscient.

By choosing a lifestyle in prison that honors Jesus, we offer God our lives, and that makes Him very happy. Paul told us in Romans 12:1, "I urge you, brethren, by the mercies of God, to present your bodies a living and holy sacrifice, acceptable to God, which is your spiritual service of worship."

The message for today: We have a wonderful Heavenly Father who adores us.

Prayer: Dear Heavenly Father, Thank You for caring about every single thing I do. Help me to please You daily as I live my life.

January 16 – What Do You Look Like?

Examine yourselves, whether you be in the faith...
(II Cor. 13:5)

Can you tell someone to follow your example and be sure that they will see the Jesus in you?

In order to be an example of Jesus, we have to change many things in our personal lives. It would be wonderful to be like the Apostle Paul who told the believers in Philippi to be followers of him and watch for the people who were enemies of the cross of Jesus, because they had him for an example (Philippians 3:17).

Your Christian testimony in jail means more than you could possibly imagine. The Holy Spirit can help you to stand out from the crowd. It's not easy, but it is possible and God will draw people to you who see the difference in your life. I have led three people to faith in Jesus since I got serious about living for the Lord. Those three people were God's assignments for me.

As you spend time with Jesus and stay in fellowship with Him, you will grow stronger every day and it makes people take notice, without you even being aware of Jesus shining through you. He will lead you to your assignments; and if you are obedient, the angels will rejoice over sinners who repent.

The message for today: Let Jesus shine through you today. Hold out your candle to others.

Prayer: Dear Heavenly Father, Thank You for the provision that You have made for me to control my thoughts and actions. Help me to be an example to others today.

January 17 – My Wish for You

The grace of our Lord Jesus Christ be with you.
(1 Thess. 5:28)

I received a poem from a friend on the email recently. I wanted to share it with you and tell you that it is my prayer for you as you go about your day.

Today I wish for you…

> Confidence for when you doubt,
> Faith so that you can believe,
> Courage to know yourself,
> Patience to accept the truth
> And love to complete your life.

I asked the Lord to bless you as I prayed for you today, to guide you and protect you as you go along your way. His love is always with you; His promises are true. No matter what the tribulation, God will see you through.

So, when the road you're traveling on seems difficult at best, give your problems to the Lord, and God will do the rest.

The message for today: People are praying for you today.

Prayer: Dear Heavenly Father, Thank You that You are with me on the difficult days. Thank You that You are only a prayer away. Thank You for Jesus, my Lord and Savior. Help me to go to You every morning, at noon, and at night and know that You love me in a way that no human ever can. Help me to bless someone else today and not just think of myself alone.

✝
January 18 – God Can Use Me

And they went and came into a prostitute's house named Rahab and lodged there. (Joshua 2:1)

Rahab was a prostitute and tavern owner in the city of Jericho. She had heard about the true and living God and His great power from her customers' talk. God caused her to want to serve Him instead of worshiping idols.

Joshua, Israel's leader, sent out two spies to view the land and the city of Jericho. Rahab protected them from certain death, and because of this kindness, she and her family were saved when Jericho was destroyed. (Read Joshua 1 to 6.)

In Joshua 6:25 it says that Joshua was true to his word and saved Rahab, the harlot, alive, and her father's household, and she lived in Israel from then on. In Matthew 1:5 God's eternal purpose was revealed, "Salmon the father of Boaz, whose mother was Rahab; Boaz the father of Obed, whose mother was Ruth; Obed the father of Jesse, who was the father of David." On and on it goes until we read in Matthew 1:16 that Jacob begot Joseph, the husband of Mary, of whom Jesus was born.

God chose Rahab and included her in the genealogy of our Lord and Savior!

The message for today: God planned our lives before the foundation of the world, and that plan will come to pass!

Prayer: Dear Heavenly Father, Thank You for changing my life and turning me to You.

January 19 – Our Real Priority

Wherewithal shall a young man cleanse his way? By taking heed thereto according to thy word.
(Psalm 119:9)

The Bible needs to be our number one priority as Christians because we are like the soil. If we deplete the nutrients in the soil, nothing good can grow. If we do not read God's Word daily, we will not produce good fruit in our lives. We become dry in our spiritual walk.

When I was put in prison, I didn't have to worry anymore about the "big" sins. But I found myself sinning just as much by neglecting Jesus. He took second place until I finally made the necessary adjustments to give Him first place in my life. His Word became precious to my heart and life.

The Bible will change you if you spend time in it. If you read it daily, you will never have to worry about having something good to share with others. God will automatically give you opportunities to bless others by your words. "Out of the abundance of the heart, the mouth speaks" (Matt. 12:34); so what goes into our minds and hearts has everything to do with what we talk about.

Is God's Word part of your daily life?

The message for today: The Law of the Lord (the Bible) is perfect, converting the soul; the testimony of the Lord is sure, making wise the simple. (Psalm 19:7)

Prayer: Dear Heavenly Father, Please give me a hungering and a thirsting for Your wonderful Word, the Bible. Change me from inside.

January 20 – A Message from God

*Go now; leave your bonds and slavery. Put Babylon
behind you with everything it represents, for it is
unclean to you. You are the Lord's holy people. Purify
yourselves, you who carry home the vessels of the Lord.
You will not leave in a hurry, running for your lives for
the Lord will go ahead of you, and the God of Israel will
protect you from behind. (Isaiah 52:11, 12)*

I sent a visitation form to my friends who wanted to come and
see me in prison, and one of the statements caught my eye. It
said, "Explain how your relationship with the inmate would
assist in and contribute to this person's rehabilitation."

If I could send that form to God, He could answer the
question by using Isaiah 52:11, 12. His answer might go
something like this:

> *My relationship with Marcia (the inmate) assists in her
> rehabilitation because I help her to be holy and pure as
> she lives for me in prison. I'm going to make sure she is
> released in My timing. She will leave her bonds and
> slavery behind with everything they represent. When
> she is released, she will be prepared to meet society with
> success because she has been rehabilitated from within
> by My Spirit.*
>
> *—Almighty God*

The message for today: Purify yourself and carry home "the
vessels of the Lord" when you are released.

Prayer: Dear Heavenly Father, I put Babylon behind me with
everything it represents for I am Your holy vessel.

January 21 – God's Lessons

The Lord longs to be gracious to you. He rises to show you compassion. (Isaiah 30:18)

I've learned a lot about God in prison. If you have just come to jail or you are about to be released, here are a few lessons God wants to teach you. Let them sink deep into your heart.

1) You may have to experience the very worst before you are delivered, but you will be delivered! (Jeremiah 33:3 – Call unto me and I will answer you and show you great and mighty things, which you know not.)

2) God is never early, never late, but always on time to deliver you. (Hebrews 4:16 – He gives grace to help in time of need.)

3) God has a plan for your life and He's working it now. (Jeremiah 29:11 – For I know the plans that I have for you, says the Lord; plans of good and not of evil, to give you a future and a hope.)

4) You must do your part (trusting) and let God's part (working) up to Him. He has a thousand ways He could deliver you, no matter how desperate your situation is! (Psalm 34:19 – Many are the afflictions of the righteous, but the Lord delivers him out of them all.)

The message for today: Cancer is the same to God as a hangnail. Nothing is too hard for Him.

Prayer: Dear Heavenly Father, Teach me the lessons I need to learn in prison so that You will be glorified in my life.

January 22 – True Freedom

And He is before all things, and by Him all things consist and are held together. (Col. 1:17)

When I was incarcerated in a Georgia state prison, I began to pray for revelation knowledge from God. Being a Jamaican in a U.S. prison, people thought I was crazy for praying for God's will instead of my freedom.

Jesus has made me a new person in prison. I now get up each day with a song in my heart. It has made such a difference in my life since I have asked Jesus to be the LORD of my life — not just my escape from hell.

We have a faithful and loving Heavenly Father who knows how to get our attention. Colossians 1:21 reminds me that once I was alienated from Jesus; I was His enemy because of my wicked works; yet now He has reconciled me into the Body of Christ by His death, in order to present me holy and unblameable in His sight.

Whether you are physically in prison or imprisoned by your own confusion, Jesus Christ is the answer to all your problems. Why not ask Him to forgive your sins and come into your life? Ask him to straighten out your problems and become Lord of your life. He will do it, and you will sing a song of praise to Him every day as you continue to read His Word and pray.

The message for today: God, the Author of peace, is worth trusting.

Prayer: Dear Heavenly Father, Thank You for saving me and making me a new creation. Thank You for the freedom that only comes through Jesus Christ.

January 23 – What Mercy!

Look unto Me and be saved, all the ends of the earth, for
I am God and there is none else. (Isaiah 45:22)

Isaiah 45:5 tells me that God took care of my life, even when I didn't know Him or care about Him. It says, "I am the Lord, and there is none else; there is no God beside Me; I girded you, though you have not known me, that you may know from the rising of the sun that there is none beside Me."

We are to recognize God in everything, and we are to glorify Him in good or bad because He has done so much for us. Even the things that test our faith should cause us to thank Him, because He wants to make us holy. He doesn't just leave us out there on a limb to fend for ourselves. He works with us.

Look back over your entire life, and observe how merciful God has been to you. Just that fact that you can read this devotional proves that His mercy is still on you. He will never leave you or forsake you if you know Jesus as your Savior.

I will never know how many times God has pulled me out of harm's way, but I praise Him that I am still alive to show forth His praises!

The message for today: From the rising of the sun, there is none as awesome as God!

Prayer: Dear Heavenly Father, By Your mercies I am not consumed. Great is Your faithfulness!

January 24 – Our Life Preserver

For they have sown the wind, and they shall
reap the whirlwind... (Hosea 8:7)

The owner of the Titanic never thought of the huge ocean liner sinking. He thought that his large vessel could never sink.

We think many times that we can live the way we want because we are smart or independent, and we don't need God or anyone. Rich people often think that they don't need God because their money is enough.

The owner of the Titanic didn't make provision for disaster. There were not enough life boats or life preservers to accommodate its passengers. When it came time to grab a life preserver, there wasn't one available for many people, and they met a terrible death.

As we spend time in prison, we also need a life preserver. His name is Jesus, and He can keep us safe in any storm that life offers us. Grabbing hold of Him will enable us to stand when the sea billows roar and the winds of life get boisterous.

I know that God's presence in my life protects me from all kinds of dangers that I'm not even aware of. Let Him into your life as your Protector.

The message for today: Believe on the Lord Jesus Christ, and you will be saved. (Acts 16:31)

Prayer: Dear Heavenly Father, Thank You for Jesus, Who helps me stay afloat in all the storms of life.

January 25 – Who You Really Are

Just as a father has compassion on his children,
so the Lord has compassion on those who fear Him.
(Psalm 103:13, 14)

God does not forget His children, even when we get sent to jail. He loves us so much, no matter what we do. He loves us the same when we are being mean and sinful as He does when we are "good children". His love is unconditional, so we do not have to work to please Him. He looks at our hearts and our motives, not our works for Him.

A fellow inmate told me one day that she believed that God loved everyone else, but maybe she was just an "extra" – someone who didn't count in His kingdom. I assured her that God adores her, but she just needs to see it for herself.

As you read the Word daily, ask God to show you who you are in Christ Jesus. II Corinthians 5:21 is a good verse to repeat every day. It tells us that "we are the righteousness of God in Christ Jesus." God is called Jehovah-tsidkenu in the Old Testament. Since God never changes, we can still use that name today as we thank Him that He is our "righteousness". Jesus, who is perfect righteousness, died and became sin for us, so that we might be made the "righteousness of God in Him".

The message for today: Jesus took my sin, so that I might take His righteousness!

Prayer: Dear Heavenly Father, Thank You for sending Jesus Christ to die for me! Thank You that He is all I need to help me live this "exchanged life".

January 26 – Are You Healthy or Sick?

And he that takes not his cross and follows me is not worthy of me. (Matthew 10:38)

When the Corinthian believers were taking communion (the Lord's Supper), Paul had to tell them that there were many sickly people among them because they were allowing sin in their lives. He said something interesting in 1 Cor. 11:31, 32. Read it and meditate on it: "For if we would judge ourselves, we should not be judged. But when we are judged, we are chastened of the Lord that we should not be condemned with the world."

God, in His great love, tells us to humbly go before our Lord every day and ask Him to show us anything that is not in His will. When He shows us sin in our lives, He is doing us a great favor because He is keeping us from being condemned with the world (the sinners).

How we should praise our great Heavenly Father for loving us so much that He gives us chance after chance after chance to repent and judge ourselves!

The message for today: God cares about our spiritual health.

Prayer: Dear Heavenly Father, Thank You for Your patience with me. Help me to confess every sin in my life the moment I realize I have wronged You.

January 27 – Please Hush Up!

And now abideth faith, hope, and love, these three, but the greatest of these is love. (I Cor. 13:13)

In prison, there are many complainers who can't see any good in anything. If they have been brought up in homes of anger and fear, that's all they know, and they get that attitude from their parents.

I read a story about a sister and brother named Donna and Timothy. Before Timothy was born, it was just Donna and her parents, and that was nice. Donna got all the attention and love, and she was spoiled.

When Timothy, her little brother, was born, she was jealous and wouldn't show any love to him. As he grew up, he loved Donna more and more, but all she did was complain about him. She started saying that she wished he hadn't been born, even though she liked it that he helped her with all the household chores.

One day her parents took Timothy to a friend's house and had them watch him for a week. They assigned Donna all the chores around the house, and it wasn't long until she wanted Timothy back! When he finally came home, she was overjoyed and never treated him badly again.

The message for today: We all could have it much worse.

Prayer: Dear Heavenly Father, Help me to hear my own words and not speak negatively about the circumstances in my life.

January 28 – Looking Out for My Best

Then Peter said, "Silver and gold have I none, but such as I have, give I thee: in the name of Jesus Christ of Nazareth, rise up and walk." (Acts 3:6)

The crippled man in Acts 3 asked for money and got healing! When we pray, God takes it very seriously; and because He knows our life from beginning to end, He works the circumstances of our lives to turn out as HE wants.

My life was a mess, and I prayed to God and asked Him to deliver me from drugs, lying, and all the other sins I could think of at the time. I got desperate and asked Him to take me away from the things that were causing me temptation.

I was brought up to love Jesus and to obey Him, but my life didn't show anything that even resembled Jesus; so God got my attention and answered my prayers in a way that was surprising, to say the least. I was sent to prison.

I knew the Devil wanted to ruin my life, but God intervened and changed me dramatically. Had I not gone to prison, my life would have never changed. I shutter to think of what could have happened if God had not answered my prayer in the way HE wanted to. I praise him so much, because what the Devil meant for evil, God meant for good.

The message for today: Ask God to turn your life around today. He will do it.

Prayer: Dear Heavenly Father, I am so thankful that You know what is best for me. Please help me to trust You with every part of my life.

January 29 – Using Our Faith

Jesus said to them...for truly I say to you, if you have faith the size of a mustard seed, you will say to this mountain, "Move from here to there," and it will move; and nothing will be impossible to you. (Matthew 17:20)

People's unbelief made Jesus very sad. The Bible says that because of the unbelief of the people in Nazareth, He could do no great works there (Matt. 13:58). In Matthew 17:19 the disciples asked Jesus why they could not cast the demonic spirit out of the man, and He told them that they needed faith only the size of a mustard seed to cast a mountain into the sea! In other words, He was saying that their unbelief was so big that their faith didn't work.

What is your mountain? No matter what it is, it can be removed with faith that is used. Jesus said that we must speak to our mountain and tell it to go. We can't just wish for our problem to leave; we must take action against Satan and command our problem to leave in Jesus' Name.

Satan uses unbelief to make prisoners feel helpless and hopeless. He makes them think God doesn't love them or they wouldn't be in jail. Once unbelief kicks in, it is easy for him to command their thoughts.

The message for today: Don't limit God by believing the lies of the Devil.

Prayer: Dear Heavenly Father, Please forgive me for limiting Your power in my life through my unbelief. Lord, I believe. Help my unbelief.

✝

January 30 – I Can't See, Lord

*The Pharisees also with the Sadducees came, and
tempting desired him that he would show them
a sign from heaven. (Matthew 16:1)*

Sometimes we are like the religious people of Jesus' day. We want to see something happening in our lives. We have difficulty walking by faith.

In Matthew 16:8 Jesus had to teach the disciples again what to do in order to see something happening. The disciples had forgotten to bring food. They didn't have a clue as to where they would get something to eat. Jesus reminded them again about their unbelief. He said in Matthew 16:9, "Do you not yet understand, neither remember the five loaves of the five thousand, and how many baskets you took up, nor the seven loaves of the four thousand, and how many baskets you took up?" They said that they remembered, but somehow Jesus' great provision never entered their minds when another situation came up!

If God is being silent in your life today, and you do not see answers to prayer, just hold on. He sees what you are going through in jail, and He is so faithful to answer prayer when you have learned the lessons He wants you to learn. Sometimes, the very thing that is causing us pain is the thing that will give us a great testimony. That is what has happened to me. Had I not been sent to prison, I would not have learned how great God is.

The message for today: God sees exactly what you need and provides it.

Prayer: Dear Heavenly Father, Please help me to know that You love me, no matter what I am going through. Help me not to seek a sign from You but only trust Your love for me.

January 31 – Who are You Following?

And Elijah came unto all the people and said, "How long halt ye between two opinions? If the Lord be God, follow him, but if Baal, then follow him." (I Kings 18:21)

I met a wonderful Christian woman in prison. She told us about our spiritual mentality and how easy it is to allow worldly things to take control of our lives. Some of the women made excuses and said that they just couldn't help being lesbian, lying, stealing, and doing drugs.

Their words reminded me of the story in I Kings 18 where Elijah went up against the prophets of Baal. It was a match between the true and living God and the false god Baal. God took impossible circumstances and turned them around for His glory. The prophets of Baal tried so hard to get Baal to hear them, but their efforts proved futile because they were calling on an idol.

We are so blessed to serve the true and living God, who does hear us and knows each hurt in our heart. He longs to give us the desires of our hearts and prove He is there – even in prison.

The message for today: Since we reap what we sow, why not try sowing some good seed into your life and you will see good fruit coming to you in the harvest.

Prayer: Dear Heavenly Father, I thank You that You show Your children how to live according to God's Word, the Bible. Help me to learn Your ways and see my own life change for the better.

Notes

FEBRUARY

February 1 – You are Special!

But the Lord is faithful who shall establish you and keep you from evil. (II Thess. 3:3)

Did someone take you to Sunday school, church, or Vacation Bible School when you were young? So many times God provides a kind Christian neighbor or a dear grandparent to see that children get to church to learn about God.

I was reading Jeremiah 1:5 where God said to Jeremiah, "Before I formed you in the womb, I knew you; and before you were born, I sanctified and ordained you a prophet." I thought to myself how wonderful it would be if God loved me as much as He loved Jeremiah, because I am not a prophet who wrote a book of the Bible.

But then the Holy Spirit showed me that I am greatly loved by God, whether I am rich or poor, black or white, short or tall. He created me who I am to bring glory to Himself. In II Thessalonians 3:3 Paul says that the Lord is faithful. He will establish my life if I allow Him; He will teach me His word and sanctify me (set me apart for His special assignment that only I can fulfill on the earth).

You are special to Jesus! Take His yoke upon you today and learn of Him. He says that you will find rest unto your soul. (Matthew11:29)

The message for today: The Lord will perfect that which concerns me. (Psalm 138:8)

Prayer: Dear Heavenly Father, Thank You for thinking that I am special. Help me to please You in all I do, think, and say today.

February 2 – The Divine Connection

Then said Jonathan unto David, "Whatsoever thy soul desireth, I will even do it for thee." (I Samuel 20:4)

In the book of I Samuel we read about the relationship that Jonathan had with David. When David was anointed by Samuel to become king, he immediately made friends with King Saul's son, Jonathan. Their friendship was sincere and ordained by God.

Saul was jealous and started hating David because God had removed His hand from him. He tried to hurt David every chance he got.

During this time, Jonathan protected David. For over ten years David ran from Saul, even though he was anointed to be king. David knew that God was with him and would protect him no matter where he was. His faith was strong.

Each of us needs a "Jonathan connection" to teach and help us. God provides that person when we least expect it because He is God, and He knows how our life will turn out. While I was in the county jail, my Jonathan connection was a lady whom God sent to me. She became my spiritual mentor and counselor. When I was transferred to a state prison, we kept in contact. We will always be friends because God planned it all out before the foundation of the world.

Ask the Lord today to arrange a Jonathan Connection for you. I call them "divine connections" because only Jesus can arrange them.

The message for today: God has wonderful blessings in store for you. Ask Him to reveal His perfect will to you today.

Prayer: Dear Heavenly Father, I praise You for working in my life to give me divine connections. Please bring the right people into my life who will make an eternal difference to me.

February 3 – A Pleasing Vessel

...the vessel that he was making of clay was spoiled in the hand of the potter; so he remade it into another vessel, as it pleased the potter to make. (Jeremiah 18:4)

God specializes in broken vessels. In the book of Jeremiah God had a specific purpose in mind when He told him to go down to the potter's house and take a lesson from a broken piece of pottery. When Jeremiah got to the potter's house, he saw a marred clay pot on the potter's wheel. Since it had defects in it, the potter broke it and remade it into a new pot.

God spoke to Jeremiah and asked why He couldn't do the same with His people. He said that the clay in the potter's hand was just like God's people. When we are marred, He takes over and remakes us into vessels fit for His use. God cannot use dirty vessels, so He starts a "renovation project" on His children. He does this so He can use them for His honor and glory.

If you feel "marred" and useless in prison, just remember that you are being re-made by God's design. You will be beautiful when you are complete!

The message for today: Don't be sad when you are broken by the Lord. Allow Him to make you over so that you can be used for His honor and glory.

Prayer: Dear Heavenly Father, Thank You that You love me enough to work with me until I become a reflection of You. Help me not complain when I find myself whirling around on the Potter's wheel. It's only for my good. Thank You, Jesus.

February 4 – My Best Friend, Jesus

A man of too many friends comes to ruin, but there is a friend who sticks closer than a brother. (Proverbs 18:24)

"Who cares?" This is a question that people ask all the time. It is easy to wonder if anyone really cares whether I live or die. Prisoners ask this question because of all the times they have been betrayed. They wonder if they can trust anyone in the world. Sometimes it seems like the answer is no.

How did you come to know Jesus Christ as your personal Lord and Savior? Think back to the day you asked Jesus to come into your life. Was it when you were a child in Sunday School? Was it when you were a teenager in a church service or youth group? Where did you finally give in to God's will for your life? All these questions have a common denominator, i.e., someone cared enough about you to tell you of Jesus and His love.

Today, if you do not know Him and truly love Him, ask Jesus to be your personal Savior. This is the most important request you will ever make. Jesus will come in and have fellowship with you if you just ask Him (read Revelation 3:20). He will not come into your life if you do not ask Him.

The message for today: Jesus loved us so much that He laid down His life for each one of us. Now that is a friend!

Prayer: Dear Heavenly Father, I love You today, and I ask that You would show me Your great love for me. Help me to set my affections on things above and not just on things here on earth.

February 5 – A Personality Problem

And when Simon saw that through laying on of the apostles' hands the Holy Ghost was given, he offered them money, saying, "Give me also this power"…but Peter said, "Thy money perish with thee because thou has thought that the gift of God may be purchased with money." (Acts 8:18-20)

When Philip went to the city of Samaria to preach the Gospel, there were many Samaritans who took heed to the word of God. There was one man in particular named Simon, who was deceiving the people with sorcery. He said that he was great, and everyone believed that he had his great power from God. He did it so long that they became comfortable and actually believed that he had the power of God in him.

Have you ever met people in jail who talk louder than everyone else to show their power? Being loud and mean is only a cover-up for insecurity and fear. When we meet people like this, we need to pray for them and love them. We need to understand that there is an underlying reason for their need to "show out".

God changes people from the inside out – not the outside in. So many times we try to be "religious" and "do" what we need to do to get attention, but God is not pleased when our actions are only based on performance.

The message for today: Please God—not people.

Prayer: Dear Heavenly Father, I thank You that You love me, just as I am. I ask You to change me from the inside out and help my actions to show that Jesus is real and lives inside me.

February 6 – Go to the Word

Trust in the Lord will all your heart and do not lean on your own understanding; in all your ways acknowledge him, and he will direct your paths. (Proverbs 3:5, 6)

Can you think of an example of when you have trusted the Lord in prison? How did things turn out? God can be counted on in every situation, come what may.

When those hard times come, go to the Word of God. Isaiah 26:3 says that the Lord will keep us in perfect peace when our mind is concentrating on God. When we trust God, things turn out better.

I have found the best way to learn to trust God is through quoting the scriptures back to Him. I saw a wonderful truth in Psalm 119:49, 50 a few months ago. It says, "Remember the word to thy servant, upon which Thou hast caused me to hope. This is my comfort in my affliction for Thy word hath given me hope." If God tells us that we are more than conquerors in every trial, then we are more than conquerors! We need to quote those scriptures from Romans 8:35-39 to the devil and tell him that we are victorious over him because of the Word of God. He cannot fight that resource!

The message for today: Trust means to have faith, hope, and expectation for a good outcome. Why not trust Jesus today to keep His word to you?

Prayer: Dear Heavenly Father, I thank You that I can trust You in every circumstance. I give You my mind right now. I will concentrate on my Provision (Jesus) and not my problem today.

February 7 – Knowledge is Power

Wherefore, He is able to save them to the uttermost that come unto God by Him, seeing He ever liveth to make intercession for them. (Hebrews 7:25)

It has been said that knowledge is power, and I believe it. If knowledge is power, then lack of knowledge is weakness and failure. Hosea 4:6 says that God's people are destroyed because of lack of knowledge. What you don't know about God's Word, the Bible, can hurt you, but what you do know and practice brings blessings, answers to prayer, and growth in your Christian life.

Hebrews 8:6 says that Christ is the Mediator of a better covenant which was established upon better promises. The "better" promises of the New Covenant show me that my Christian life is based on Jesus' performance only – not mine.

When you are released from jail, your performance counts because of being on probation; but when Jesus saves you from your sins, He loves you just as you are without perfect performance. Remember that He ever lives to pray for your life and your future because He loves you so much. Start walking in the footsteps of Jesus today and reading His Word.

The message for today: If you start reading your Bible today, in five years your life will be completely turned around. It worked for me, and it can work for you.

Prayer: Dear Heavenly Father, Thank You for the Bible, the world's greatest book. Help me to look into its pages and learn daily from it. Please change my life through Your Word, Lord.

✝ February 8 – Listening to God

But thou, son of man, hear what I say to you. Be not thou rebellious like that rebellious house; open thy mouth and eat what I give thee. (Ezekiel 2:8)

Ezekiel was a prophet sent by God to the Israelites. He was a man who was honest and focused on God's plan for him. Ezekiel was with the Jews who were taken captive by the Babylonians about 600 years before Jesus was born.

God told Ezekiel in 2:8 to "hear" what He was saying to him. He told him not to be rebellious like the Israelites had been. That is why they were in Babylon instead of their own land. God had to do something to get their attention. God does the same thing to us. If we will not choose obedience to Him, He sometimes chooses incarceration for us in the hope that we will learn to love and obey Him. Many times it works. Many times it does not.

Today "open your mouth and eat what God gives you." That is not food; it comes from looking at your circumstances and examining how blessed you are to even be alive!

The message for today: God speaks through our circumstances, but it is always out of a heart of love – even in the bad times. If you can't see His hand, trust His heart.

Prayer: Dear Heavenly Father, Thank You that You know what is best for me, and You make Your will known through trials sometimes. Help me to trust You totally and know that Your plans are plans of good and not of evil, to give me a future and a hope. (Jeremiah 29:11)

February 9 – It's Time for Growing

*The Kingdom of God is like a man who casts seed upon
the ground and goes to bed at night and gets up by
day, and the seed sprouts up and grows – how,
he himself does not know. (Mark 4:26)*

Have you ever heard the word "abiding"? It is the secret to growing spiritually, and many people do not understand it at all. The parable in the Bible of the seed and the sower explains in a most unique way what abiding really means; but we have to put ourself in the seed's place to learn the true meaning of the word.

Think about that tiny seed planted in the ground. Let's say it is a kernel of corn. That little seed just lies in the soil and relaxes in the ground. Amazingly, it finds itself sprouting and growing; yet it does not know how it happened!

Day by day as we read God's Word, we grow in Christ, without even realizing that we are growing. That is the power of the Holy Spirit in our lives. He causes us to change, little by little, week by week until years have passed and we are truly changed. The Christian life is not a quick process; it is slow and takes many years to become what we need to become in Jesus; but oh, the joy of "becoming".

The message for today: Keep on growing in Christ.

Prayer: Dear Heavenly Father, Help me to grow in You every day until I produce good fruit for You.

✝ February 10 – The Real Thing

For God so loved...that He gave...His only Son. (John 3:16)

Jenny's mother bought her $1.95 strand of "beautiful" pearls. She wore them everywhere, even to bed. One night after her father read her a story, he asked Jenny to give him the pearls. She looked up and told her daddy that he could have her favorite doll but not those pearls.

A few nights later when her daddy came in, Jenny was sitting on her bed crying. "What's the matter, Jenny?" Without a word, the little girl placed her pearls into her daddy's hand. "Here, daddy, these are for you," she said.

Jenny's daddy reached out with one hand to take the dime-store necklace, and with the other hand he reached into his pocket and pulled out a blue velvet case with a strand of genuine pearls and gave them to Jenny. He had them all the time, just waiting for her to give up the dime-store pearls so he could give her the real thing.

Our Heavenly Father is also waiting for us to give up the cheap things in our lives so that He can give us His beautiful treasures. Are you holding on to things that God wants you to let go of? Are you holding on to relationships, habits and activities that you have become so attached to that it seems impossible to let go?

The message for today: God will never take away something without giving you something better in its place.

Prayer: Dear Heavenly Father, Thank You for the good things You have in store for me. Please help me to trust You enough to give up the bad things and know that You will replace them with the best things.

February 11 – You are Loved

I can do all things through Christ which
strengtheneth me. (Philippians 4:13)

In Lamentations 3:21-23 there are some wonderful thoughts. The writer says, "This I recall to my mind; therefore I have hope. It is of the Lord's mercies that we are not consumed, because His compassions fail not. They are new every morning; great is thy faithfulness."

He goes on to say that "The LORD is my portion, saith my soul; therefore will I hope in Him. The LORD is good unto them that wait for Him, to the soul that seeketh Him."

When Paul said in Philippians 4:13 that he could do all things through Christ who strengthened him, he was pondering how much he had learned about God's faithfulness. It was only by God's mercy that he was "not consumed". His faith grew daily as he watched the Lord do awesome things in his life.

Satan likes to make prisoners feel as if God is not even listening to their prayers. He attacks their thought life and tells them that God just doesn't care about them. He tells them that they have no power. If they listen to him, he wins. If they listen to the Word of God and trust it totally, God wins the battle for them. So, the next time you doubt that God is hearing your prayers or that He doesn't care, just stop and quote Philippians 4:13, "I can do all things through Christ who strengthens me!"

The message for today: Turn your problems over to the Lord and watch Him work.

Prayer: Dear Heavenly Father, Thank You for Your mercies which are new every morning. Thank You for protecting me last night as I slept. You are an awesome God!

February 12 – Don't Limit God

God is able to make all grace (every favor and earthly blessing) come to you in abundance so that you may always and under all circumstances..., be self-sufficient (and furnished in abundance for every good work and charitable donation). (II Corinthians 9:8)

I have heard many people say that they have tithed for years, and they are still in debt. They just seem to have financial problems all their life, no matter what they do. What is the problem?

Psalm 78:41 says about the Israelites in the wilderness, "Yea, they turned back and tempted God, and limited the Holy One of Israel." They did not believe God would provide!

A dear old lady was left all alone when her husband died, and her son was worried about her because she had no money. He was amazed when he watched what she did the day after the funeral as she held her Bible up to God and said, "Lord, I believe Your Word when it says that You will provide my every need according to Your riches in glory by Christ Jesus. You have never lied, so I am calling down Your mighty power to provide for me now and in the future." The man reported that, sure enough, God provided her every need until her death many years later.

What was her secret? She believed God. She did not doubt or complain because she was in such a state. She just quoted God's Word back to Him and reminded Him of His promises.

The message for today: God's promises are His performances. Believe it!

Prayer: Dear Heavenly Father, Please help me to quote Your Word daily and live by Your promises to me and see financial blessings come my way.

February 13 – Praise the Lord Anyway

Then you will say on that day, "I will give thanks to You, O Lord; for although You were angry with me, Your anger is turned away, and You comfort me." (Isaiah 12:1)

Incarceration can be very lonely and sad, but you can decide to praise the Lord and trust Him.

Praising God, even when you are sad, makes Him happy. He inhabits the praises of His people. God has provided salvation for us through His Son, Jesus Christ. What better reason to rejoice? Your name is written in the Lamb's Book of Life!

Many times in the Psalms, David said, "I will praise the Lord." It wasn't a matter of feeling like praising God everyday; it was a matter of the will. If something is settled in your will, your mouth, body, and attitude will follow. In 21 days you can make something a habit. If you decided to praise God every single day (no matter what you are going through), and you do that for 21 days, the habit will be formed, and your attitude will change your life. Try it. It works.

The message for today: Bless the Lord, O my soul, and forget not all his benefits, who forgives all your iniquities and heals all your diseases, who redeems your life from destruction and crowns you with loving kindness and tender mercies. (Psalm 103:2-4)

Prayer: Dear Heavenly Father, I bless Your name, and I praise You for forgiving my sins and redeeming my life from destruction. How wonderful You are!

✝ February 14 – God Hears You

My little children, let us not love in word, neither in tongue, but in deed and truth. (I John 3:18)

The advertising world has made Valentine's Day a very special day of candy and cards. Have you ever received a special Valentine greeting? When I was in second grade, I was so happy to receive a little card from my "boyfriend", who was 8, and I liked him so much. My heart fluttered, even at that age, that "someone" cared enough to send me a card.

God has sent us a love letter, the Bible. In it we read about all different kinds of people, their problems, their sins, and their forgiveness.

In Numbers 14:11-20 Moses begs God to pardon the Israelites who have complained against Him. God is "fed up" and says that He will destroy this people, but Moses intervenes and reminds God that His name and His reputation are at stake. In Numbers 14:20 God says, "I have pardoned according to thy word." Isn't that wonderful? Moses had an influence in God's decision! We can influence God, too. It's just that we don't ask the right questions many times.

God says that we need to ask in faith, nothing wavering, in our prayers. When we ask for wisdom and help, God sees our faith and answers our prayers according to His perfect will.

The message for today: Today, love God in everything you do and say, and fulfill I John 3:18.

Prayer: Dear Heavenly Father, Thank You that my prayers make a difference to You.

February 15 – A Changed Life (Part 1)

For a brief moment I forsook you, but with great compassion I will gather you. (Isaiah 54:7)

Isaiah 54 tells about Israel, God's chosen people, and His dealings with her. The unique thing about the Bible is that the Gentiles are greatly loved of God also.

Paul, the apostle to the Gentiles, was as Jewish as a person could get. He had all the necessary requirements and was a Jew in good standing, but God chose him before the foundation of the world to be an apostle to the Gentiles.

The day Paul (formerly Saul of Tarsus) was apprehended by Jesus probably started out like every other day for him. He planned to kill a few Christians and enjoy his day, but God interrupted his plans and showed up on the road to Damascus where He stopped him. He asked him why he resisted His plans for him. He blinded his eyes and left him blind for three days. Then He asked a Christian, Ananias, to go and touch Saul's blinded eyes, lay hands on him, and thrust him into the ministry of Jesus Christ. Ananias was very fearful, but he obeyed God; and Saul's life changed forever (Read Acts 9:10-19). He became Paul the Apostle, who wrote 2/3 of the New Testament!

The message for today: God loves us – every one.

Prayer: Dear Heavenly Father, Thank You that You are no respecter of persons. You love each one of us as if there were only one of us.

February 16 – A Changed Life (Part 2)

For a brief moment I forsook you, but with great compassion I will gather you. (Isaiah 54:7)

We are like Paul in many ways. God has to apprehend us in the midst of our mess because He has a plan for our lives. He has to get our attention, and He knows just how to do it because He created us. How has God apprehended you? Has He taken your children away? Has He imprisoned you? Has He taken a loved one who meant the world to you?

When we accept Jesus Christ into our lives, the Holy Spirit of God comes to live inside us by a supernatural power (the same power that raised Jesus from the dead!). Our lives are never the same. However, sometimes we think we can get away from the Lord, so we go our own way, which is a big mistake. That is when the Lord steps in and chastens (child trains) us in the form of a punishment to get our attention. If we listen, we grow and change. We get better instead of bitter. If we don't, God keeps at it until He does get our attention.

The message for today: God doesn't give up on His chosen children, but His child training is always out of a heart of love.

Prayer: Dear Heavenly Father, Thank You for loving me from before the foundation of the world. I don't understand Your great love, but I accept it and give You my entire life to do with as You please.

February 17 – An Awesome Change

And as he journeyed, he came near Damascus, and sud-
denly there shined round about him a light from heaven;
and he fell to the earth and heard a voice saying unto
him, "Saul, Saul, why persecutest thou me?" (Acts 9:3, 4)

In Acts 9:1 we read that a man named Saul went to the high priest and asked for letters telling the leaders of the Damascus synagogues that he had permission to kill people who acknowledged that they followed "The Way". He had no idea that he was living his last day as a murderer.

As he journeyed, he came near to Damascus, when all at once, he was knocked down by Jesus Himself. As he looked up, he asked, "Who are you, Lord?" What a question for one who hated "The Way"! Jesus answered him by telling him that He was the very One whom he was persecuting. Jesus told him that his killing days were over and that he might as well turn himself over to God because there was such a great call on his life.

The story goes on to say that Saul started preaching Christ everywhere he went after being saved. People could hardly believe that this murderer had changed so much, but soon it was evident that a major change had taken place in Saul's life.

Has Jesus made a major change in your life? It can happen, even in prison.

The message for today: When God calls you to serve Him, you might as well give in.

Prayer: Dear Heavenly Father, How I praise You that You loved me enough to get my attention! Help me to live for You alone and show the world what a great God I serve.

February 18 – Singing at Midnight (Part 1)

And at midnight Paul and Silas prayed and sang praises unto God; and the prisoners heard them. (Acts 16:25)

Many people today are in prison for crimes they did not commit. It causes us to wonder why bad things happen to people every day. They are in the wrong place at the wrong time, and life deals them a very bad hand of cards. I have learned, though, that God is in control of everything, and He allows many people to go to jail in order to quiet them and reveal Himself to them through incarceration. I have heard over and over that "God put me here, and I asked Jesus Christ into my heart because of this time in prison."

Paul and Silas had a different story. They were revolutionaries in the infant Church that Jesus had died for, and they found themselves in prison because the religious leaders did not like anyone to "rock the boat". Satan controlled the leaders; he was their father, and he certainly did not want this "Jesus" to come on the scene; but they could not control God, so problems broke out.

Paul and Silas decided at midnight to SING in prison. Just picture the scene. It was pitch dark and filthy. The place was not fit for humans to be in, but they sang!

The message for today: God helped Paul and Silas in prison, and He will do the same for you. He never changes.

Prayer: Dear Heavenly Father, Help me to have the faith "of the Son of God" and to know that You are with me, wherever I am. You will never leave me or forsake me.

February 19 – Singing at Midnight (Part 2)

And at midnight Paul and Silas prayed and sang praises unto God; and the prisoners heard them. (Acts 16:25)

We might look at that situation and ask what could ever make a suffering person sing at midnight; but we have to look at what was on the inside of Paul and Silas. They were predestined to serve a mighty God named Jesus. They were driven to trust Him, come what may. And "trust" they did!

What about you? Can you sing when things keep going wrong? Can you quote scriptures that promise that God is with you wherever you go? Can you trust God to bring you through? Most of us cannot, unless we have had a true experience with the Jesus Christ of the Bible, like Paul and Silas did.

Numbers 23:19 says, "God is not a man that He should lie, neither the Son of man that He should change His mind. Hath He said, and shall He not do it, or hath He spoken, and shall He not make it good?" Hebrews 13:5 says that Jesus will never leave us or forsake us, and He means it. He does not lie.

The message for today: Only God can make us rejoice in bad times.

Prayer: Dear Heavenly Father, Help me to have the faith "of the Son of God" and to know that You are with me, wherever I am. You will never leave me or forsake me. Thank You!

February 20 – Don't Lose Your Birthright

And Jacob said to Esau, "Sell me this day your birthright." (Genesis 25:31)

In Genesis 25-27 we see Esau selling his birthright to Jacob for a dish of stew (Gen. 25:27-34)! In Bible days, a person's birthright was the most important thing he could possess. It carried honor and prestige to be the first-born in a family.

Jacob tricked his father, Isaac, into blessing him instead of Esau. Esau lost everything for a bowl of soup!

We, too, can lose our blessings if we are not careful. We each have a God-given inheritance from Jesus Christ. In fact, we are called "joint heirs with Christ" in Romans 8:17. Everything that is His, is ours! And yet, we do not act like fellow-heirs most of the time. We find ourselves listening to the devil as he comes to steal, kill, and destroy our walk with God.

People will try to steal your inherited birthright, too. Do not be deceived by smooth talkers who will try to sway you toward sin. If you do not know God's Word, you will listen to them and make wrong decisions that can ruin your life.

Our birthright comes from the precious blood of Jesus Christ, our Savior, and it is eternal.

The message for today: Press toward the mark for the prize of the high calling of God in Christ Jesus (Philippians 3:14). It's worth it.

Prayer: Dear Heavenly Father, Please help me to know You so well that Satan cannot succeed in stealing my birthright.

February 21 – Angels Around Us

For I was hungry and you gave me food; I was thirsty, and you gave me drink; I was a stranger, and you took me in; naked, and you clothed me; I was sick, and you visited me; I was in prison, and you came unto me.
(Matthew 25:35, 36)

The future is nearer than we think. Daily we prepare for the future, even if we aren't aware we are doing so. Is your life filled with good deeds, or are you just drifting along in the stream of life with no goals? Many of us are doing just that.

Every day we sow seeds of goodness or meanness in preparation of our future. When we talk kindly to a stranger, Jesus says that He is watching. Hebrews 13:2 tells us to be kind to strangers because some of them might just be angels, of whom we are unaware!

The "angel" could be someone in prison with you. The "angel" could be the girl that you gave $1.00 to as she begged on the street corner. The "angel" could be the stranger in the hospital that you prayed with.

The message for today: Maybe you have entertained an angel today.

Prayer: Dear Heavenly Father, You said that if I love my neighbor like I love myself that You are pleased. Help me to love sincerely and be found faithful by You when Jesus returns to receive me unto Himself.

February 22 – Going Forth (Part 1)

"...this one thing I do, forgetting those things which are behind and reaching forth unto those things which are before." (Philippians 3:13)

Genesis 19 tells a story about the city of Sodom and the sin that was in it. There was a man named Lot, who lived in Sodom, with his wife and two daughters. Sodom was a city filled with homosexual activity and depravity, and Lot lived right in the middle of it. But the Bible says that Lot was "righteous" in II Peter 2:8.

Read Genesis 19 and II Peter 2:6-8, and compare them. As the story unfolds, we see that God wanted to rescue Lot and his family before He totally destroyed the city. The two angels who came to rescue Lot and his family out of Sodom almost had to force them to leave.

Lot's wife made a huge mistake. God had told them to flee the city and not look back, but we read in Genesis 19:26 that "his wife looked back from behind him, and she became a pillar of salt." She had really become conditioned to the sin, and she did not want to leave.

As Christians in prison, we need to love the Lord our God so much that we will turn our backs on the sin we used to commit and not look back.

The message for today: The only time we should look back is to praise God that we are not where we used to be.

Prayer: Dear Heavenly Father, Thank You for loving me so much. Help me to fight Satan with the blood of the Lamb and the word of my testimony (Rev. 12:11) and not look back.

February 23 – Going Forth (Part 2)

"...this one thing I do, forgetting those things which are behind and reaching forth unto those things which are before." (Philippians 3:13)

We listen to swearing, bad TV programs, and bad music and wonder why we do not have power with the Lord Jesus. We want to "flirt" with sin and not have any punishment. True, we will not turn into a pillar of salt like Lot's wife; but our hearts become de-sensitized and before we know it, we are trapped by Satan into accepting sin as "normal".

Paul had been a murderer, but he understood who he was in Christ Jesus. He knew that since he had asked Jesus Christ to be his Savior, all his past sins were "under the blood of Jesus". He was no longer, "Paul the murderer". He was now "Paul, the born-again Apostle of Jesus", and he was as pure as could be!

Our verse for today is good advice for all of us. Every time Satan comes to us and says that we are rotten sinners, we need to say, "Oh, no, Satan! I am the righteousness of God in Christ, according to II Corinthians 5:21. God has forgotten all my past sins, and so do I; so be gone in Jesus' Name!"

The message for today: The only time we should look back is to praise God that we are not where we used to be.

Prayer: Dear Heavenly Father, Thank You for loving me so much. Help me to fight Satan with the blood of the Lamb and the word of my testimony (Rev. 12:11). Help me to fight him with scripture, and I know I'll be "more than a conqueror".

February 24 – Be Persistent

And without faith it is impossible to please Him, for he who comes to God must believe that He is, and that He is a rewarder of those who diligently seek Him.
(Hebrews 11:6)

Luke 18:1-7 talks about a mean judge who did not love God. There was a widow in the same city who went to the judge constantly, asking him to do something about her enemy, and he would not; but the widow was so persistent that she kept going back to him. She decided that she was not going to stop until he did something for her. The widow was so persistent, and she would not give up. She finally touched the judge's heart and wearied him with her constant petitions, so he ruled on her behalf and avenged her of her enemy.

Persistence does pay off in everything. Sometimes in jail we want to give up; but if we don't, we are blessed mightily. How often we ask God for something and become weary because we do not see results.

Matthew 7:7 says, "Ask, and it shall be given you; seek you and shall find; knock and it shall be opened unto you." This means that every time we pray, our prayer is answered in Heaven immediately. However, the answer may not be manifested until months or years later. It all depends on God's perfect timing and not ours.

The message for today: Ask God for whatever you want, and leave the results with Him.

Prayer: Dear Heavenly Father, Thank You for giving us all things that pertain to our life and godliness. Help us to grow daily in You and have faith that pleases You.

February 25 – It's Time for Church

Not forsaking the assembling of ourselves together, as the manner of some is... (Hebrews 10:25)

Thousands of Christians have become disillusioned with organized religion and never darken the door of a church. They say that the church does not meet their needs, so why go? In many of the churches today, I agree with them.

There is a story in Ezekiel 10 about the glory of God moving around the temple until it finally left because the people's hearts were so hardened to God. One of the saddest verses in the Bible is Ezekiel 10:18, "Then the glory of the Lord departed from the threshold of the temple..."

In I Samuel 4:22, after Eli the priest and his son Phinehas died, Phinehas's wife gave birth to a child, and she named him Ichabod, which means "the glory has departed". It was a sad, sad day when the Philistines took the Ark of the Covenant away from Israel, but the lesson is clear. When God's Name is not reverenced, His glory departs.

The Lord tells us that we should not forsake the assembling of ourselves together with other believers (as the manner of some is). He tells us to go to church and love each other. He advises us that as His coming draws nearer and nearer, we ought to attend God's house more.

The message for today: Ask the Lord to give you the desire to attend jail church services. Why not start going and let the Holy Spirit show you what a wonderful experience it can be?

Prayer: Dear Heavenly Father, You created the church for Your purpose to bless believers. Thank You that You loved us enough to give us a reason to attend church   Jesus.

✝

February 26 – Coincidence?

And we know that God causes all things to work together for good to those who love God, to those who are called according to HIS purpose. (Romans 8:28)

Romans 8:28 reminds me of a story about a woman named Anna who decided to go on one last missionary trip before retiring. She had all her materials ready for British Honduras. The medical staff decided at the last moment to take some intravenous needles (IV's), although they never took them before.

They arrived at their hotel and went out to dinner. After dinner Anna became violently ill with food poisoning, which dangerously dehydrated her body. The nurses took her to her room. They immediately knew why God had prompted them to take the IV's, but now they needed an IV stand, from which to hang the IV. They looked up, and there was a tiny nail in the wall above the bed. This was the only room in the hotel with a nail above the bed, and they used it for the IV.

God had prepared everything perfectly to save Anna's life. Only He could have placed Anna in that very hotel room and a medical staff to give her an IV to save her life! Have you had things like this happen to you? Have you wondered if they were just "coincidence"? Someone has said that "coincidence is God's way of remaining anonymous," and I believe it.

The message for today: God makes even bad things turn out for our benefit.

Prayer: Dear Heavenly Father, Thank You for caring about every detail of my life. Help me to trust You when I can't see ahead.

February 27 – Free Indeed!

"...how blessed are the people whose God is the LORD."
(Psalm 144:15)

Every day is special, but the most special and important day of my life was the day I gave my life to Jesus Christ. Even though I was in jail, preparing to go to prison, I'll never forget that day.

I had known for some time that my life of sin was wrong. I just could not stop sinning; try as I might to be "good". On that day I remember bowing my head and asking Jesus to come into my life and save me. I just could not handle life any more by myself, so I gave up. At that moment, I got "freedom" for the first time in my life, and it was marvelous!

I went to prison and spent much time there, but in my spirit I was free. I started an every-day process of becoming like Jesus by reading my Bible and spending time with the One who had made me free. He became my best Friend in the entire world because of how He changed my life. My mind eventually started to get re-programmed to think the best instead of the worst. I memorized Scripture after Scripture, which gave me something to say to Satan when he approached me with the thought that God did not love me. In fact, I have never felt such love as my Heavenly Father gives me.

The message for Today: Believe on Jesus and you will be free!

Prayer: Dear Heavenly Father, Thank You for loving me enough to stop me in my tracks. I give my life to You. Come into my heart and forgive my sins. Help me to live a holy life for You.

February 28 – The Best Decision

"...how blessed are the people whose God is the LORD."
(Psalm 144:15)

If you have never really done business with God, here is how to accept Jesus into your life by faith.

1) Read Romans 3:23; 6:23; 5:8; 10:9, 10; 10:13
2) Say a prayer something like this:

> *"Dear Heavenly Father, I ask You to forgive me of every sin I have ever committed. I believe that Jesus died on the cross to save me from my sins, and I ask You, Jesus, to come into my heart and save my soul. I give my life to You for whatever purpose You have for me. Thank you for saving me today, _____, and helping me to live a life worthy of Your acceptance. In Jesus' Name, Amen."*

3) Turn to Hebrews 13:5 and say these words: "He will never leave me." Say this every day of your life until you believe it.
4) If you sin (which you will), quote I John 1:9, "If we confess our sins, He is faithful and just to forgive us our sins and cleanse us from ALL unrighteousness."
5) Tell someone what you have done and ask God for a Bible study partner. You need to be reading the Word of God daily and talking to other Christians.

The message for Today: Believe on the Lord Jesus and you will be saved.

Prayer: Dear Heavenly Father, Thank You for saving me. Help me to have a walk that matches my talk.

MARCH

March 1 – God's Perfect Plan (Part 1)

"With men this is impossible; but with God all things are possible." (Matthew 19:26)

Have you ever had a problem or crisis in your life; and try as you might, you could not find an answer? You reasoned. You prayed. You hoped. You cried. You tried to figure it out – all to no avail. It was just impossible!

We all have had those times when we "reasoned" something to death and still were no further along than when we started.

Abraham had the same problem, but he handled it God's way. Romans 4:20, 21 says, "He staggered not at the promise of God through unbelief, but was strong in faith, giving glory to God; and being fully persuaded that what He had promised He was able also to perform." Read that verse over and over and memorize it. I did, and it has come in so handy through my years in prison.

I saw God do the impossible for me when I first went to prison. I was charged with four of the worst charges anyone could get. During that time, I got saved. I kept praying that God would reduce those charges and give me something I could see an end to. I was not asking to be completely free, because I knew I was guilty by association, and then something wonderful happened.

The message for today: God will perfect that which concerns me. (Psalm 138:8)

Prayer: Dear Heavenly Father, I praise You for loving me and helping me when I cry unto You.

✝ March 2 – God's Perfect Plan (Part 2)

But Jesus beheld them and said unto them, "With men this is impossible; but with God all things are possible." (Matthew 19:26)

Yes, something wonderful happened regarding my sentence in prison.

One day before I went to court, I was on my knees praying, and I heard God speak to me directly for the first time in my life. He told me that my charge was going to be changed to a lesser charge. At that moment the district attorney and my attorney came to my cell and told me the exact same message! I then knew that God cared for me, and He specializes in the impossible. I still got prison time, but I was very content and had perfect peace because I knew that He was involved in my life. How precious that memory is to me.

Whatever you are going through right now has not caught God by surprise. He knew all your circumstances before the foundation of the world; and He is right there with you to go through your problems with you. Do not stagger at the promises of God through unbelief, but be strong in the faith, giving glory to God. Ask God for a special Bible verse for you, and He will give it to you. Hang on to that verse and quote it over and over, even when you are in your worst doubt.

The message for today: God will perfect that which concerns me. (Psalm 138:8)

Prayer: Dear Heavenly Father, I praise You for loving me and helping me when I cry unto You. You are great and greatly to be praised. I will not doubt that You love me ever again.

✝ March 3 – Knowing God

For just as the body without the spirit is dead, so also faith without works is dead. (James 2:26)

What do you do every time something goes wrong in your life? If you live by weak faith, you go to pieces and get upset. But if your faith is accompanied by works, you might cry, but you know to trust God's promises and you quietly do just that. You quote Scripture; you praise Jesus for your blessings, and you rest in God's promises in the Bible. Now you are operating in faith because faith with works is a living, overcoming faith – not a dead faith that gets no results from God.

I must remain stable and fixed in all situations, and it can be done if I trust God's character and not what I see with my eyes. Since life is made up of circumstances, God allows difficulties to mold us and shape us after His will. The way we handle difficulties determines our maturity in our Christian lives and how well we really know our God.

Daniel 11:32 says that "the people who know their God shall be strong and do exploits." If you really know your God, you will display strength and take action and not allow the situation to hurt you. However, if you look at the opposite meaning of this verse, you could say that "the people who don't know their God shall be weak and doubt His promises." It all comes down to choice.

The message for today: What a mighty God we serve! Get to know Him better.

Prayer: Dear Heavenly Father, I pray that I might know You and the power of Your resurrection. Help me to grow daily in the grace and knowledge of my Savior, Jesus Christ.

✝ March 4 – Good or Bad Fruit?

But this one thing I do: forgetting those things that lie behind and reaching forward to what lies ahead...
(Philippians 3:13, 14)

In prison it is difficult to forget past failures because we are reminded daily of them.

Paul said that, in spite of all his past failures, he forgot those things and was only interested in reaching forth to what lay ahead of him. He said that daily he pressed toward the mark for the prize of the high calling of God. What a wonderful prize awaits us – heaven and all its glory. But life here on earth can be peaceful or terrible, depending on how we deal with anger and past hurts.

When a person is consumed with old anger and hurts, it colors every part of their life. It's like a tree that looks healthy and green, but all the fruit that is produced from it has a big black spot in it because the root is poisoned. That is how unresolved conflict and anger work. We can look good on the outside, but we process every thing in our life by that old hurt and anger. We are like a bomb ready to explode on anyone or anything that gives us the chance.

How do we get rid of unresolved anger and hurt? We take it to the Cross of Jesus and bury it there. We stop denying that we are hurt and angry. We humble ourselves under the mighty hand of God and let Him take it and resolve it.

The message for today: This one thing I do – forgetting those things which are behind.

Prayer: Dear Heavenly Father, Thank You for forgiving me of all my sins. Help me forgive others just as You have forgiven me.

March 5 – Good Health (Part 1)

"...the Lord be magnified, who delights in the prosperity of His servant." (Psalm 35:27)

So many people believe God's Word until it comes to their health. I have heard many well-meaning Christians say, "If it's God's will, I will be healed."

Isaiah 53:5 says, "But he was wounded for our transgressions; he was bruised for our iniquities: the chastisement of our peace was upon him, and with his stripes we are healed." Many good Bible scholars say that this means salvation and salvation alone, but let's look more closely at it. Jesus refers to this very verse in Matthew 8:17, "They brought to Him many who were demon-possessed; and he cast out the spirits with a word and healed all who were ill. This was to fulfill what was spoken through Isaiah the prophet: *'He Himself took our infirmities and carried away our diseases'.*" This is talking about physical healing, not salvation only.

Jesus took our weaknesses and our diseases in His own body on the Cross. He died to give us salvation; but within that salvation, there are four distinct parts:

1. Salvation (saving our souls)
2. Healing (diseases, headaches, bad backs, etc.)
3. Deliverance from bondages (mental illnesses, demonic possession, anger, etc.)
4. Prosperity (providing everything we physically need)

The message for today: My health was part of the Atonement!

Prayer: Dear Heavenly Father, I praise You for Jesus' death on the Cross for my salvation, healing, deliverance, and prosperity.

March 6 – Good Health (Part 2)

"...the Lord be magnified, who delights in the prosperity of His servant." (Psalm 35:27)

I am so glad that we have a God who knew that we would get sick and need His help.

Look at I Peter 2:24 (and compare it with Isaiah 53: 4, 5 and Matthew 8:17). It says, "Who his own self bore our sins in his own body on the tree that we, being dead to sins, should live unto righteousness: by whose stripes you were healed."

Ask the Lord to open your mind to the truth that Jesus Christ died on the Cross for your salvation and your abundant, healthy, prosperous life. It will change the way you pray and believe. We do not have to be sick or poor. That is just Satan's trick to make us doubt God's love for us.

Every time I get a headache or illness, I quote Colossians 2:15 and I say to Satan, "You were defeated on the Cross by the Lord Jesus because He spoiled your principalities and powers, making a show of them openly, triumphing over them in His cross. Now headache, I speak to you in Jesus' Name – Be Gone!" I quote scriptures like I John 5:14, 15 and I watch for the headache to disappear. Our God loves to heal us as we "take back what the devil has stolen from us."

The message for today: God is the health of my countenance! (Psalm 42:11)

Prayer: Dear Heavenly Father, Thank You that I have all I need in You for my salvation, healing, deliverance and prosperity!

March 7 – The Secret to Success (Part 1)

But in all these things we overwhelmingly conquer through Him who loved us. (Romans 8:37)

I used to be sad and discouraged all the time. It seemed that everything I tried ended up badly. Everyone I loved seemed to leave me. I couldn't find happiness in anything I did; but one day that all changed.

I read my Bible every day and memorized scriptures that meant a lot to me. After doing that for 365 days, things started to happen. God knew I was serious about this Christian life.

A few of the scriptures I memorized are below. I guarantee (100%) that your life will change as the Word of God gets inside your heart and your head. It's a great weapon to fight Satan with!

Rev. 12:11 – And they overcame him (Satan) by the Blood of the Lamb (Jesus) and the WORD of their testimony.

II Cor. 10:4, 5 – For the weapons of our warfare are not fleshly but mighty through God to the pulling down of strongholds. Casting down imaginations and every high thing that exalts itself above the knowledge of God, and bringing into captivity every thought to the obedience of Christ.

The message for today: The armor of God includes using the Sword of the Spirit, the Bible.

Prayer: Dear Heavenly Father, Please help me to learn to take control of my thoughts instead of letting Satan control my mind.

March 8 – The Secret to Success (Part 2)

*Put on the whole armor of God that you may be able to
stand against the wiles of the devil. (Ephesians 6:11)*

It took me a long time to understand why I needed to protect my
mind against my negative thoughts in jail until one day God
showed me about the armor of God in Ephesians 6:11-18. I started consciously putting on the armor by quoting these verses.

I put on the whole armor, not just part of it. The armor
consists of the Belt of Truth, the Breastplate of Righteousness,
the Gospel Sandals of Peace, the Shield of Faith, the Helmet of
Salvation, and the Sword of the Spirit (the Bible). With these
on, Satan doesn't have a chance because we are in control of
our hearts, minds, and actions. Praise the Lord!

Try this test. Every time you think a negative thought like,
"I'm lonely", replace it with a verse from the Bible. Learn about
15 scriptures, and watch your thoughts change. When I'm
lonely and want to pity myself, I say, "Thank you, Jesus that You
are with me always, even unto the end of the age."

Learn scriptures that deal with self-pity, loneliness, anger,
forgiveness, victory and peace. Every time you can't sleep or
you are worried, quote your scriptures from the Lord. Watch
your insomnia and worry leave!

The message for today: The human mind can only hold one
thought at a time. If it is worry, anger, fear, etc., we have no
victory. If we consciously replace the bad thoughts with
scripture, we win the battle for our mind! It's our choice.

Prayer: Dear Heavenly Father, Please help me to learn to
substitute Scripture for worry and fear.

March 9 – Our Only Hope

Out of the depths have I cried unto thee, O Lord. Lord, hear my voice: let thine ears be attentive to the voice of my supplications. (Psalm 130:1, 2)

What do you want today? Do you want a court date, a letter from home, or a friend?

We all have needs – some greater than others. We all pray and ask God to help us with those needs. The Psalmist was under severe trials, but he knew where to look and that was up. I can picture him as he took his quill and began to write after months of prayer, "Out of the depths have I cried unto you, O Lord."

God was his only hope. Something in him knew that Jehovah-God was listening to his prayer. The writer of this psalm knew that he was only human and thus sinful. He called upon God's great mercy when he said, "If you Lord, should write down sins and look at us humans, who would be left? Not one of us…" (Psalm 130:3).

In Psalm 130:4 the psalmist uses the word "but". That means that what comes after that word is opposite to how he was feeling at the time when he said, "…but there is forgiveness with you."

Meditate today on Psalm 130. Put your name and your feelings and fears into that psalm. Then do what the writer did, i.e. hope in the Lord. That's the secret. Just believe that God is no respecter of persons, and He loves you.

The message for today: Hope in God's Word, and wait for the morning. (Psalm 130:5, 6)

Prayer: Dear Heavenly Father, Help me to quiet myself and just hope in You and Your Word.

March 10 – Why Wait?

I wait for the Lord; my soul waits, and in His Word do I hope. (Psalm 130:5)

God makes us wait for answers to our prayers, and He lovingly molds our character while we wait.

I read a poem in prison when I was at the lowest point in my life. It comforted me because it showed God's awesome control of my situation.

"So He waited there with a watchful eye, with a love that was strong and sure; and His gold did not suffer a bit more heat than was needed to make it pure." This is an excerpt from The Refiner's Fire that had to be written by a great saint of God.

Since God is in control of our lives, He can "turn up the heat" and give Satan permission to place us in terrible situations for awhile until He sees that we are yielding to His *"heat"*. We say we cannot stand much more, but only He knows how to purify us, His *"gold"*.

God wants us to be pure and holy before Him. What joy we miss, what blessings we miss by trying to do instead of wait.

The psalmist in Psalm 130 knew so much about God's sovereignty. He prayed, he waited, he hoped, and he trusted God's Word, mercy, and forgiveness.

The message for today: If you know Jesus as your personal Savior, believe that He knows what He is doing in your life.

Prayer: Dear Heavenly Father, Help me to pray, wait, read Your Word, and trust You to bring me out of my trials.

March 11 – Growing Up

But grow in grace, and in the knowledge of our Lord and Savior Jesus Christ. (II Peter 3:18)

Everyone thinks that babies are beautiful. They are helpless and tiny; and as they are cared for, they grow up to be healthy and happy adults. At least that is the way it should be. But if a baby never grows, there is something very wrong.

This is how it sometimes is when we accept Jesus Christ as our Savior. Everything is wonderful for the first few months; but if we do not mature, things go very wrong. You may ask, "Well, how do I grow in the knowledge of the Lord?"

We grow by reading God's Word, the Bible, every day and by seeking God in prayer. It is a long process but oh so worth the effort. "If it's going to be, it's up to me." That is how the Christian life works. Paul said that he "pressed toward the mark for the prize of the high calling of God in Christ Jesus." He had to press; he did not ask Silas or Barnabas to do it for him.

Ask yourself how your life is changing in jail. Do you feel guilty when you sin? Do you want to be with Christians and not with sinners all the time? Do you desire to be pure before the Lord? If your answer is yes, you are on your way to "growing" in Christ.

The message for today: Growing is easy when we eat the right food.

Prayer: Dear Heavenly Father, Please help me to grow in Your grace and knowledge by meditating daily on Your wonderful, inspired Word.

March 12 – Call On God

For He will give His angels charge concerning you, to guard you in all your ways. They will bear you up in their hands, that you do not strike your foot against a stone. (Psalm 91:11, 12)

Psalm 91 is one of my favorite portions of scripture because it shows us the security that comes when we put our trust in the Lord. It tells us that we will be blessed if we "dwell" in the secret place of the Most High God. It does not say that we will be blessed if we "visit" the secret place and only talk to God in a crisis. We need to dwell daily in His wonderful presence and get to know Him. Then and only then will we learn what God means when He says to "rest" in Him.

Mediate today on Psalm 91, and think about it all day. I did this, and I found out that the promises in that Psalm are so precious! God wrote the Bible through men who were inspired by His Holy Spirit, and His words are life because they change us if we let them. As I read Psalm 91:15 and 16, I rejoiced because it says that I can call on Him and He will answer me! He will be with me in trouble; He will rescue me and honor me. He will satisfy me with long life and let me see His salvation!

God is with you in jail. You can develop an awesome relationship with Him by learning to love and appreciate His Word.

The message for today: Let God's Word be your delight today.

Prayer: Dear Heavenly Father, Thank You for being so concerned about me and all that concerns me.

March 13 – Planning Ahead

The kingdom of heaven will be comparable to
ten virgins, who took their lamps and went out to
meet the bridegroom. Five of them were foolish,
and five were wise. (Matthew 25:1, 2)

Incarceration can be a time of simply existing or a time of planning ahead for your release. God sees right where you are and wants to teach you to live for Him in preparation for your future.

In Matthew 25:1-13 we read Jesus' story about the ten virgins who took their lamps and went out to meet the bridegroom. Five were wise and five were foolish. The five foolish ones did not plan ahead and take enough oil for their lamps. When they ran out of oil, they had to replenish their lamps, so off they went to buy more. While they were gone, the bridegroom came and they missed him!

This is a story about people who claim they know Jesus but will not make it into heaven when He comes back for His true followers. One would think they are prepared because they probably go to church and do good deeds, but they have never really been saved. Jesus said in Matthew 25:13, "Be on the alert then, for you do not know the day nor the hour."

The message for today: Don't be like the five foolish young women who never planned ahead and were left behind.

Prayer: Dear Heavenly Father, Thank You for helping me to prepare for Jesus' coming.

March 14 – Thinking About What Matters

But it is good for me to draw near to God; I have
put my trust in the Lord God, that I may
declare all thy works. (Psalm 73:28)

Consequences from sin cause new thought patterns. It is not until the consequences come that we realize that we reap what we have sown, either good or bad.

Today I send you a very special, timely message: Focus on Jesus Christ and His love for you. Focus on Him — not your circumstances or the consequences of your actions. He loves you dearly.

I was in prison with a lady who lived every day to gamble, curse, lie, and basically do her own thing. She thought it was all about her. She was so consumed with her needs that no one else mattered...until the September 11, 2001, attack on the World Trade Center. All at once she stopped thinking about herself and started praying for her family to be safe! She finally realized that only God could protect the people she loved.

Draw near to God today and put your trust in Him. He will never fail you.

The message for today: Seek first God's kingdom and His righteousness, and all His provisions will be added unto you. (Matthew 6:33)

Prayer: Dear Heavenly Father, Thank You for keeping me until this very moment in Your kind and loving care. Help me to live for You and others — not just for me.

March 15 – Waiting for Answers

Trust in the Lord with all your heart, and do not lean on your own understanding. In all your ways acknowledge Him, and He will make your paths straight. (Proverbs 3:5, 6)

In I Samuel 1:1-15 we read that Hannah and Peninnah were the wives of Elkanah. Peninnah had children, but Hannah did not. Peninnah was always criticizing Hannah and putting her down because she was childless. Hannah was so sad; no matter how hard she prayed, she could not conceive a child, but God had a good plan, and it all started unfolding when Hannah told the Lord that she would offer her child to Him for service as soon as it was weaned.

God gave her a child the next year, and Samuel was used mightily as a prophet. She prayed according to God's perfect will, and things started happening.

If you have been spending much time in prayer, asking God for something that means a lot to you, do not give up. God will answer your prayer in His time and His way, just like He answered Hannah's prayer. Just trust Him because He loves you.

The message for today: "And this is the confidence that we have in Him, that, if we ask anything according to His will, He hears us; and if we know that He hears us, whatsoever we ask, we know that we have the petitions that we desired of Him." (I John 5:14, 15)

Prayer: Dear Heavenly Father, Help me to trust in You 100%. When I doubt, help me to quote Your word and stand on it.

March 16 — Diligence

Give all diligence to add to your faith virtue, and to your virtue, knowledge, and to knowledge, self-control, and to self-control, patience, and to patience, godliness, and to godliness, brotherly kindness, and to brotherly kindness, love. (I Peter 1:5-7)

Have you ever realized, as you looked back over your life, that God played a great part in it? Even if you were sent to prison, God went with you, and He knew what it would teach you.

Peter was especially chosen by Jesus. The Lord knew that he would mess up in his life; but Jesus could see all of Peter's life. Peter denied Jesus three times before His crucifixion. He failed God, but God knew the end from the beginning.

Something marvelous happened to Peter after Jesus was crucified. The Holy Spirit came into his life and empowered him to live victoriously. As a result, he did great things for God. He was sold out and began to "live Christ" – not just "live". He went on to write two books of the Bible, I and II Peter.

The scripture for today gives a progression of how we grow in Christ. First, we have faith in Him. Next, we need to develop godly characteristics in our life. Read the list in today's scripture and see where you are on the progression.

Peter says that "if these things be in you and abound, they make you that you should neither be barren or unfruitful in the knowledge of our Lord Jesus Christ." (I Peter 1:8)

The message for today: Ask God to help you live I Peter 1:1-13.

Prayer: Dear Heavenly Father, I pray that I will grow in the knowledge of You.

✝ March 17 – Chill Out

*And the servant of the Lord must not strive but be gentle
unto all men, apt to teach, patient, in meekness,
instructing those that oppose themselves; if God perhaps
will give them repentance to the acknowledging of the
truth, and that they may recover themselves out of the
snare of the devil, who are taken captive by
him at his will. (II Timothy 2:24-26)*

Paul had some good advice for Timothy, God's servant, in our
verses for today. He told him to stop striving (worrying) and
just "chill out". Next he said, "In meekness instructing those
who oppose themselves…". I wondered what "opposing
myself" was and the Lord showed me that if all I do is worry
and get upset all the time, I'm not acting like a victorious
Christian should act and I'm actually opposing myself
(fighting against my victory in Christ).

In II Timothy 2:26 we read, "And that they may recover
themselves out of the snare of the devil, *who are taken captive
by him at his will.*"

Did you get that? We have to recover ourselves out of the
emotional and mental snare that Satan has placed for us and
stop letting him control our thought life. The only way to do this
is to substitute scripture for worry and crying.

The message for today: I can recover myself out of the devil's
trap and not be taken captive by him.

Prayer: Dear Heavenly Father, Help me to realize that Satan is
a defeated enemy and I can fight him with my "two-edged
sword", the Bible. Teach me to use it effectively and get victory
over every circumstance in my life.

✝
March 18 – Wait Diligently

*And without faith it is impossible to please Him,
for he who comes to God must believe that He is, and
that He is a rewarder of those who diligently seek Him.
(Hebrews 11:6)*

If you are in God's waiting room while in jail, just keep trusting. The answer is coming. Psalm 46:5 says that God will help us and that "right early". That means that He is on our side, and He will help us. We must keep persevering.

I recently read II Peter 1:3-11 where Peter is telling the saints that God has given unto us *all* things that pertain to life and godliness through the precious promises in His Word and His mighty power. He goes on to say that we should continually be maturing. He says, "Add to your faith, virtue; and to your virtue, knowledge; and to your knowledge, self-control; and to your self-control, patience…"

I was especially impressed with those verses since I have very little self-control in eating. As I was praying about this, God showed me that I have to add patience to my self-control. I cannot just expect to have self-control "all at once". It takes months and even years for God to mature us as He wants, so I have settled down to "one day at a time". One day, two days, three days: on and on it will go until I see some results in my weight and in my Christian life.

The message for today: Ask God for whatever you want, and leave the results with Him.

Prayer: Dear Heavenly Father, Thank you for giving us all things that pertain to our life and godliness. Help us to grow daily in You and have faith that pleases You.

March 19 – Turning from Sin

He is holy and true and has the key of David;
he opens and no one will shut, and shuts
and no one will open... (Rev. 3:7)

Most prisoners feel as if their life is so messed up that there is no hope. However, Jesus doesn't see it that way.

There are several things we can do when we have made wrong choices and end up failing. God wants us to be victorious, and He has made every provision for our victory. We must claim it, though. Next time you are faced with a major temptation to do wrong, think about these things.

1. It is *not* wrong to be tempted because it gives us a choice of choosing God's way. Victory over temptation develops character.
2. Satan's job is to tempt us to sin; if we listen to him, we will end up thinking about the sin and actually committing it. It is our choice.
3. When we fail to read the Word and pray and seek God's face and *turn* from our wicked ways, He can't work because we are choosing sin.
4. Failure isn't permanent. *If* we confess our sins, He is faithful and just to forgive our sins and cleanse us from all unrighteousness.

The message for today: *Choose* you this day whom you will serve.

Prayer: Dear Heavenly Father, Help me to choose to serve You and You only from now on. I love You and ask You to help me to be so close to You that I will make the right choices. I praise You for the Holy Spirit's presence to help me to do right.

March 20 – A Good Mentor

The servant of the Lord must not strive but be gentle
unto all men, apt to teach, patient...
(II Timothy 2:24-26)

Paul loved his spiritual son, Timothy. He took him under his wing, mentored him, and groomed him to be a great man of God. Timothy needed a lot of teaching, and Paul was the man God chose to teach him. Can you imagine being mentored by the Apostle Paul? What a blessing!

I can almost picture Paul sitting patiently and writing to his beloved Timothy. Read both I and II Timothy at one setting, and ask the Lord to enlighten your mind with wisdom as you read. Count how many things Paul tells Timothy to do. These books are truly inspired by the Holy Spirit because they contain such practical advice, which we need so desperately today.

Prisoners have a precious gift of time. Using it wisely to read God's Word and pray brings great rewards. We learn to *fellowship* with Jesus. Fellowship means going below the "How are ya?" level and really learning to know Jesus as our best friend. That takes time. How many friends do you have who really know your deepest fears, your happiest memories, and your biggest hurts? I can guess that you could count them on one hand. I know I could.

The message for today: Be an example of those who believe — in speech, conduct, love, faith and purity. (I Timothy 4:12)

Prayer: Dear Heavenly Father, Only by Your Holy Spirit can I become an example to others.

March 21 – Forgiveness

*Be kind to one another, tender-hearted, forgiving each
other, just as God in Christ also has forgiven you.
(Ephesians 4:32)*

It has been said that when we refuse to forgive someone, it
is like pouring acid on ourselves and expecting it to hurt
someone else.

If there is someone in your life whom you haven't forgiven,
here are some suggestions on how to begin: Start by asking
their forgiveness to take them off the defensive. Although that
sounds exactly the opposite of what we *want* to do, we need to
do it. If your offender is not alive, take a chair, place it across
from you, and talk to the person as if they were there.

My friend said that she did this with her deceased parents, and
before she was done, she was crying and telling them how they
failed her as she was growing up. After twenty minutes, she
stopped and asked *their* forgiveness for her attitude toward them
for 30 years! She was immediately released and has been free ever
since, with no anger toward her parents. If you ever have an experience like this, you will see that forgiveness really does work.

Unforgiveness, on the other hand, hinders your fellowship
with God and prevents answers to prayer. David said that if he
regarded sin (unforgiveness) in his heart, the Lord would not
hear him (Psalm 66:18-20). Right now forgive those people
who have caused you so much hurt. God will then hear you
and be free to answer your prayers.

The message for today: Forgive others because you have been
forgiven of so much.

Prayer: Dear Heavenly Father, Thank You for Jesus dying on
the cross to secure my forgiveness eternally!

March 22 – Trusting Jesus

There truly is a reward for those who live for God;
surely there is a God who judges justly here on earth.
(Psalm 58:11)

When we find ourselves caught in the legal system, we go before a judge who decides our fate. Many times he judges wrongly; sometimes his judgments are right.

Do you have a court date coming up? Have you prayed for the judge deciding your case? The Bible tells us that the Lord will guide us as we ask Him. In Deuteronomy 31:8 we read that it is the Lord who has gone before us; He will be with us; He will not forsake us. Therefore, we should not fear or look anxiously around. God has every situation in our lives under control, but He cannot do much if we do not trust Him. His hands are tied by our doubts.

Even in jail you can live for God and see His hand working on your behalf. Even if no one else loves you, Jesus *does.* Even if no one else helps you, Jesus *will.* You are special to Him, and that is why He has allowed Satan to put you in jail to quiet you and get your attention. He alone knows your future, and it can be a great one if you only allow Him into your life.

God loves each of us – no matter what we have done or where we have been. Our part is to *trust.* His part is to *work.* Today, ask Him to judge your case and help you. You could not be in better hands!

The message for today: Get right with God, and *everything else* will fall into place. (Mt. 6:33)

Prayer: Dear Heavenly Father, Please help me to trust You with my future.

March 23 – Walking with Jesus

Ah Lord, God...nothing is too difficult for You.
(Jeremiah 32:17)

No one is exempt from troubled times. God said in Isaiah 43:2, "*When* you pass through the waters, I will be with you...*when* you walk through the fire, you will not be scorched."

The question isn't if you will have difficult times, just *when*. Even Jesus, who lived a perfect and sinless life, suffered great physical and spiritual pain while on the earth.

If you are going through a difficult time in jail, you may be asking if God could have stopped this from happening. The answer is "Yes. God can do anything." If He *can*, then why doesn't He stop us from being hurt?

God is more interested in our spiritual growth and well-being than our temporary comfort. It is not something we want to hear when we are going through difficult times, but we grow and are strengthened during trouble in our lives.

Have you ever stood by the coffin of a loved one feeling hopeless and sad, and all at once you looked up and there was a special friend? Your pain was still there, but knowing a beloved friend had come to walk beside you made the tragedy easier to endure.

That's how it is with Jesus. He comes alongside and walks with you during painful times.

The message for today: God is with us in our darkest hours.

Prayer: Dear Heavenly Father, Please help me to remember that You are with me.

✝

March 24 – These Things!

But none of these things move me… (Acts 20:24)

Have you ever noticed how many times Paul used the words "these things"? He went through so many trials and tribulations in his life that he could have been complaining about everything, but he refused to murmur.

Paul said that he had learned to be content in whatever circumstances he found himself. He said that in every circumstance he had learned the secret of being filled and going hungry, both of having abundance and suffering need. (Philippians 4:11, 12)

That is a lot of learning. In Philippians 4:13 Paul said, "I can do *all* things through Christ who strengthens me." Let's look at a few verses that deal with "these things", as Paul puts it.

Romans 8:35-39 – What shall separate us from the love of Christ? Shall tribulation, or distress, or persecution, or famine, or nakedness, or peril, or sword?...In all *these things* we are more than conquerors through Him who loved us.

Acts 20:24 – But none of *these things* move me; neither do I count my life dear to me, so that I might finish my course with joy…

The message for today: Next time I feel low, I need to think about Paul and *his* sufferings, but also his great peace.

Prayer: Dear Heavenly Father, Thank You for teaching me to trust *You* in all circumstances.

March 25 – I Need Wings

*And the God of peace shall bruise Satan under
your feet shortly. (Romans 16:20)*

Nothing can come into our lives until it gets God's permission to do so. We read in Romans 8:28 that all things work together for our ultimate good if we love God. We see the words on the page, but do we really believe those words?

Did you know that your problems actually give you "wings"? David cried out to God when he was depressed and sad. He said, "Oh, that I had wings like a dove! Then I would fly away and be at rest" (Psalm 55:6). Little did David realize that his wish could come true.

Psalm 55:18 says that "He hath delivered my soul in peace from the battle that was against me…" I am so thankful that we have a God of peace. His name is Jehovah-Shalom, the God of Peace. David settled down and meditated on the Lord, and we hear him give some great advice in Psalm 55:22, "Cast your burden on the Lord, and He will sustain you; He will never allow the righteous to be moved."

The word "burden" means "what Jehovah God has given you". Troubles make us wait upon the Lord. When we wait and pray, we realize that our burdens are gifts from God to mold us into the saints He wants us to become.

The message for today: Whatever your burden today, wait upon the Lord for your deliverance. It will come.

Prayer: Dear Heavenly Father, I praise You for helping me to wait on You until this storm passes by. Help me not to tell You how big my storm is, but to tell my storm how big my You are!

✝
March 26 – You're God's Kid

Sanctify them through thy truth: thy word is truth.
(John 17:17)

Jesus prayed a "High Priestly Prayer" in John 17. His prayer was for those of us who would accept Him into our lives and want to live godly lives for Him. He asked the Father to "sanctify" us. What does that mean?

To be sanctified means to be set apart for holiness. The utensils in the wilderness tabernacle were "set apart" to be used only by the priests for their holy rituals to Jehovah God (see Exodus 25:29). If they would have been used in any other way, God would have been displeased.

When we go our own way after we have asked Jesus Christ to be our Savior, He "child trains" us. The Bible calls this training "chastening". Hebrews 12:5 says, "My son, do not regard lightly the discipline of the Lord, nor faint when you are reproved by Him, for those whom the Lord loves He disciplines (child trains), and He scourges every son whom He receives."

The Bible goes on to say in Hebrews 12:8 that if we are without discipline from the Lord, then we are illegitimate children and not true children of God. That verse gives me hope because I have been disciplined by the Lord because He loves me so much that He cannot bear to let me remain "marred" and "dirty". He wants me to be useable and clean (set apart and sanctified) so that when people see me, they see the reflection of Jesus in me.

The message for today: If you have been disciplined by the Lord, rejoice that you are truly one of His own beautiful children.

Prayer: Dear Heavenly Father, Thank You for loving me enough to discipline me when I do wrong.

March 27 – When You Are Sad

It is good for me that I have been afflicted that I might learn thy statutes. The Law of your mouth is better to me than thousands of gold and silver. (Psalm 119:72, 73)

I came across this verse one day in my prison cell, and it changed my life. I did not know that it was "good" for me to have trials! The writer said that it was good for him to have problems so that he could learn God's answers through the Bible.

Psalm 116 shows a writer who was in the depths of depression, but he knew that his help came totally from the Lord. As I read this Psalm, I pictured him saying that he loved the Lord because He knew that God cared about his situation.

This writer was sad! He said in Psalm 116:3, "The sorrows of death compassed me, and the pains of hell got hold upon me: I found trouble and sorrow." Have you ever been there? We find ourselves in trouble and sorrow many times, and those are the times when we can do what verse 4 says, i.e. call upon the name of the Lord and beg Him to deliver us from the problems.

God is so gracious, righteous, and merciful. He loves us when we don't know what to do, and He is there for us – no matter what we are going through.

The message for today: God is as near as a prayer.

Prayer: Dear Heavenly Father, Thank You for Your Word which says that You hear my voice when I call on You.

March 28 – The Defeated Enemy

"...he spoiled principalities and powers, making a show
of them openly, triumphing over them in it (His Cross)."
(Colossians 2:15)

In ancient days when a king was conquered, the victorious king would strip him of his kingly garments, cut off both thumbs and both big toes and would parade him through the town for everyone to see. This showed the people that the king could never hold a sword again to hurt them and that he could not run to kill them.

Jesus Christ, our Lord, has stripped Satan of his power and openly shown the world that he can't hurt us. The only thing he can do is to *deceive us.* He does it so well that if we don't know the Word of God, we will let him do it. We need to come against him with the Word of God in power!

Picture yourself back in school when you made a display of dead insects by sticking pins through them and attaching them to a board for the class to see. Those insects could not bite or sting you ever again because you took away their power to hurt you. Colossians 2:15 says that Jesus removed Satan's power over us through His cross!

The message for today: Memorize Colossians 2:15 and quote it to Satan every time he comes to you and puts doubts in your mind about anything.

Prayer: Dear Heavenly Father, Help me to realize that because of *Jesus'* victory on the Cross, I too have the victory over Satan!

March 29 – Speak Up

For truly I say unto you, that whosoever shall say to this mountain, be thou removed and be cast into the sea, and shall not doubt in his heart, but shall believe that those things which he says shall come to pass; he shall have whatsoever he says." (Mark 11:23)

Did you know that we must speak to our problems — not just pray to God about them? I was so impressed with this teaching that I have actually started talking to pain in my body, the money in my checkbook, and my fears!

In the Old Testament, only God could rebuke Satan, but in the New Testament, believers can take authority over the wicked one because of Jesus' sacrifice for us.

Why not try *speaking* to your depression and problems and command them to leave in Jesus' Name? Then, as you concentrate on God's mighty Word, He will start doing something awesome, and you will see that *speaking* the Word to your problems really works.

Satan has assigned demonic powers to each one of us who belongs to Christ. The closer you get to Jesus, the more he attacks you *until* he finds out that you know the Word of God and you are willing to use it! Satan can stand our prayers and our threats, but he is no match for God's mighty Word, the Bible.

The message for today: Speak God's Word to your problems.

Prayer: Dear Heavenly Father, Thank You for giving me authority over the enemy of my soul.

✝

March 30 – God Heard You

Therefore I say unto you, "Whatsoever things ye desire when ye pray, believe that ye receive them, and ye shall have them." (Mark 11:24)

The Bible says that our prayers are answered in heaven the moment we pray them; but because we don't see the manifestation (answer) to our prayers, we *assume* that God isn't answering. Daniel said that God answered his prayer in about *three minutes* in Daniel 9:20, 21; but in Daniel 10:12, 13, it took *three weeks* because a wicked demonic spirit hindered the angel of the Lord from getting the answer through to Daniel.

In Daniel 10:12, 13 the angel of God says, "Fear not, Daniel; for from the *first day* that you did set your heart to understand and to chasten yourself before your God, your words were heard, and I am come for your words. But the Prince of the Kingdom of Persia withstood me 21 days; but lo, Michael, one of the chief princes came to help me, and I remained there with the Kings of Persia. Now I am come..."

If you are praying about something today, God has already heard your heart cry, and He is answering. Keep on praying and persevering for the visible answer. It will come.

The message for today: Blessed is the one who perseveres (James 1:12). Hang in there!

Prayer: Dear Heavenly Father, Help me to know that You are my Helper, and I should not doubt when I don't see Your answers right away.

March 31 – It's Your Choice

I have given you the choice between life and death...
oh that you would choose life! Choose to love the Lord
your God and to obey him and commit yourself to
him, for he is your life. (Deuteronomy 30:19)

Every day we make choices that affect us in some way. It has been said that prisoners make about 600 choices a day, while those who are not incarcerated make about 1,400. Those choices might include scratching your arm, standing up, sitting down, etc. – on and on it goes – but the fact still remains that we all make choices daily.

I was put in jail because of my bad life choices. I thought I could "beat the system", but I soon found out that the system had beaten me!

All through the Bible we read about choices that people made, which affected the future of nations, the birth of Jesus, and our salvation. If Joseph had not *chosen* his reaction to the prison officials, he would have never found favor with Pharaoh and saved a nation. If Mary had not *chosen* to suffer the embarrassment of being pregnant and misunderstood, God would have blessed someone else in being the Mother of God. If our Lord Jesus would not have made the choice to remain on the Cross of Calvary, we could never be saved from our sins.

The message for today: Today, choose life in Christ. It will be the best choice you ever made!

Prayer: Dear Heavenly Father, Help me to choose obedience and blessings from today on.

Notes

APRIL.

April 1 – Settle Down

But the God of all grace…after that you have suffered a while, make you perfect, establish, strengthen, and settle you. (I Peter 5:10)

We have a mighty God who keeps track of everything we do and controls every situation in our life. He is the "God of all grace". He helps us to be at peace inside, even when our whole world seems to be falling apart outside.

One day I asked God to guide my paths and settle me. He showed me I Peter 5:6, 7.

1) Humble yourself under the mighty hand of God (I Peter 5:6)

2) Cast all your worries and cares on Him, because He cares for you (I Peter 5:7)

The only way we can have peace in our souls is to humble ourselves before the Lord, give the situation to Him in prayer, and stop worrying. If that sounds difficult, that's because it is!

How do you stop worrying? Every time a negative, unsettling thought comes into your mind, quote scripture – any scripture that gives you peace. It could be Proverbs 3:5, 6 or Romans 15:13, or a hundred other verses on peace and trust.

The message for today: Don't worry about anything, but pray about everything, and the God of peace will keep your heart and mind stable.

Prayer: Dear Heavenly Father, Help me to know You and the power of Your resurrection.

✝ April 2 – He Leads Me

The Lord is my shepherd; I shall not want.
He makes me to lie down in green pastures;
He leads me beside the still waters. (Psalm 23:1, 2)

When you can take time to mediate on Psalm 23, stop and examine each verse and see what a wonderful Savior we have! I was thinking about the green pastures, and God showed me something so precious.

Most living, healthy plants are green. Green grass is cool and refreshing when we lie down on it. I remember as a child just lying down on the grass on a hot summer day and looking at the clouds. I can still feel the cool refreshment it offered.

Jesus Christ is our Shepherd. We are His sheep, and we are not very smart at times; but He still leads and guides us through our whole lives. If we obey Him and His Word, He is in a position to meet our every need. If we go astray, He lovingly brings us back if we are one of His own.

The Psalm ends with an awesome promise: "Surely goodness and mercy shall follow me all the days of my life." Think of the goodness and mercy of God actively pursuing you all the days of your life! I am sure my life has been spared many times when I didn't even have a clue that God's goodness and mercy were on my life!

The message for today: Learn to relax in the "green pastures" of God's protection.

Prayer: Dear Heavenly Father, Thank You for loving me so much and watching over me every moment of every day.

April 3 – We Can Run, but We Can't Hide

The sacrifices of God are a broken spirit.
A broken and a contrite heart, O God,
You will not despise. (Psalm 51:17)

Have you ever done something and been so conscious of it that it always seems as if someone is watching you? At times you find yourself running, and there is no one chasing you – at least no human is chasing you.

Sometimes we run from our past and its sin. We run from the things we did that give us a guilty conscience. All that running makes no difference to God. He has already found us out because He sees and knows all things.

One day I asked a friend what to do about all my running and she gave me an honest answer. She said, "Stop running and face the consequences of your actions. Work it out with your Master and be free from the fear of exposure." It wasn't easy, but I took her advice. I confessed my sin to Jesus and took necessary steps to make things right with the others I had hurt.

We try to hide our sin in many ways. Adam used fig leaves when he sinned and the Lord made him aware that he was naked. People use many "masks" to hide their sin, but those masks come off when they stand quietly before a holy God who loves them.

The message for today: Only one sacrifice can wash away our sins, and that is the blood of Jesus Christ. Get things right with Him today.

Prayer: Dear Heavenly Father, Thank You for saving my soul and forgiving my sin – past, present, and future. Thank You for covering me with Your righteousness.

April 4 – Looking Unto Jesus

My help comes from the Lord, who made heaven and earth. (Psalm 121:1, 2)

David was a great leader who was zealous for God; but even though he was God's chosen king, he wasn't perfect. He had won many battles because he sought the Lord before he went out to fight; but the next Spring at the time when kings went out to battle, David stayed behind in Jerusalem and sent Joab. There is no mention of his asking God's advice about doing this.

One evening he went up on the roof to relax, and the temptation was waiting for him. As he walked around on the roof, he saw a beautiful woman bathing. He sent messengers and took Bathsheba; and when she came to him, he slept with her, and she became pregnant with his child. Satan had won a very important victory by making David yield to temptation.

God sends each of His children to do a job for him. Satan knows this and lies in wait with the very temptation that will make them fall. The temptation always comes where we are the weakest.

As I talk to prisoners, I see David's story replayed over and over. They tell me that they believed in Jesus, but the temptation to sin became so great that they yielded to it, with prison as one of the consequences.

Learning from David's experience, we know we have to keep our eyes on God. The moment we look at other things, the enemy enters and tries to trick us.

The message for today: Keep looking unto Jesus, the Author and Finisher of your faith.

Prayer: Dear Heavenly Father, Help me to seek You first and keep my eyes fixed on You – not what this world offers.

April 5 – What a Conversation!

And He had to pass through Samaria. (John 4:4)

Jesus had a very important appointment in Samaria, which He had to keep. No one understood why He would purposely pass through a city that the Jews hated, but Jesus had eternal reasons that only He could see.

Jesus sat down at Jacob's well about 6:00 in the evening because He was tired from His long day's journey from Judea. A Samaritan woman came to the well at that time because she had a bad reputation and could only draw water after the "decent" women left.

He engaged her in a conversation that would change her life. He asked her for a drink, and the woman asked, "How is it that You, being a Jew, ask me for a drink since I am a Samaritan woman?" Jesus told her that He could give her "living water" that would cause her never to thirst again, but she didn't understand.

Jesus talked to her for a while and then asked her to go and get her husband. She told him that she had no husband, and He amazed her by His answer in John 4:17, 18. He told her she answered correctly because she had had five husbands, and the man she was living with was not her husband. Only God could have known that, and she was impressed! She immediately went into the city and started telling people about this man who told her all that she ever did! She got saved, and many more people came to know Jesus as Messiah because of her testimony.

The message for today: After a true encounter with Jesus, there's no keeping you quiet!

Prayer: Dear Heavenly Father, Please lead me by the Holy Spirit's power to tell others about Jesus.

April 6 – Show Me and Tell Me

My little children, let us not love in word, neither in tongue; but in deed and in truth. (I John 3:18)

The apostle John gave some excellent advice to people who truly love God. He told us to not just *talk* love but to show love. In the "old days", a person's word and handshake were all that was required to make sure that something got done. We have lost that today. It is so rare to find someone who will say, "Yes, I'll take care of that," and it actually gets done!

We Christians need to be in regular, close fellowship with other believers to develop the skill of loving. Love cannot be learned in isolation. Even in the Garden of Eden, God said, "It is not good for man to be alone" (Genesis 2:18). We have to be around all kinds of people, even the irritating and the difficult ones.

Have you ever noticed that all 10 Commandments deal with relationships? Four deal with our relationship with God, and 6 deal with our relationship with people (see Exodus 20). Relationships matter the most in life.

Jesus said to love God and love others in Matthew 22:37-40. Rick Warren says in his book, *The Purpose Driven Life,* that "Life minus love equals zero" (Zondervan, Grand Rapids, MI, 2002, p.125). That about sums it up. A life without love is really worthless because love will last forever.

I Corinthians 13:13 says, "These three abide, faith, hope, and love; the greatest of these is love."

The message for today: He who would be a friend *must show himself friendly.*

Prayer: Dear Heavenly Father, Thank You for people to love. Bring those people into my life whom You would have me love.

April 7 – God is Calling You

Amend your ways and your doings, and I will cause you to dwell in this place. (Jeremiah 7:3)

Our destiny was determined before the foundation of the world. Psalm 139 says so beautifully that God's eyes saw our unformed substance, and in His book were written *all the days that were ordained for us* when as yet there were none of them (Psalm 139:16)! God knows what we will do at 10:16 a.m. He knows what will happen tonight at 7:04 because He is God!

Jeremiah was chosen by God to be a prophet to the people of Israel before the foundation of the world. His message in Jeremiah 7 took real courage to deliver to the people, but someone had to do it.

Has anyone ever asked you to change the direction your life is taking? If they have, you are most blessed because that is God speaking through them. Do you want blessed in your life? God's message through Jeremiah is for all of us when He says, "For if you *thoroughly* amend your ways and your doings…neither walk after other gods to your *hurt*, then will I cause you to dwell in this place (of blessing) (Jeremiah 7:5-7).

Look back over your life. If you are in prison, God could have allowed it so He could get you to choose *Him* instead of sin. He has a plan that could only have come to pass by your incarceration.

The message for today: Let God work His plan in your life.

Prayer: Dear Heavenly Father, Help me to live according to Jeremiah 7 and choose to turn my life around. Thank You for Your mighty hand giving me strength to seek You first.

April 8 – The Best Weapon in the World

Then Jesus said to the devil, Get thee behind me, Satan, for it is written... (Matthew 4:10)

Matthew 4 makes us realize that the devil chooses specific times, weaknesses, and thoughts to use his strategy of deception on us. Satan knew that Jesus had just been baptized and commissioned to start His public three-year ministry on earth, so he came to Jesus after He had fasted for 40 days! (I can't imagine what I would be like if Satan did the same thing to me!) Jesus was hungry and weak and Satan chose the "appropriate" temptation by asking Him to turn the stones to bread because that would instantly satisfy His flesh.

Satan has a strategy of defeat arranged for you. That is why he has been permitted by God to put you in jail. He thinks he has won the victory but you can turn his "so-called" victory to defeat by learning scripture, which defeats him.

Satan will always be Satan, and his only trick is *deception*. He's a liar and the father of lies, and the only thing that defeats him is God's powerful Word. Hebrews 4:12 says that the Word of God is living and active and sharper than any two-edged sword. That is a power that all the devils in hell cannot fight!

The message for today: Use "it is written" on Satan today, and watch him flee with his tail between his legs!

Prayer: Dear Heavenly Father, Thank You for the written Word of God, the Bible. Help me to wield my "Sword" well today.

✝

April 9 – Forgiven!

To the Lord our God belong mercies and forgiveness,
though we have rebelled against him. (Daniel 9:9)

It is a fact that Christians sin. As long as we are in this world, our flesh will fight against God and His laws; but His forgiveness is just a prayer away.

Daniel 9:3 contains good advice for Christian prisoners. It says, "And I set my face unto the Lord God, to *seek* by prayer and supplications, with fasting, and sackcloth, and ashes; and I prayed unto the Lord my God, and *made my confession*...Oh, Lord, we have sinned and committed iniquity, and have done wickedly and have rebelled by departing from Your word."

God hears our prayers of confession, too. I John 1:8-10 is written to Christians and it says, "If we say that we have no sin, we deceive *ourselves*, and the truth is not in us. *If* we confess our sins, He is faithful and just to forgive us our sins, and to cleanse us from all unrighteousness. If we say that we have not sinned, we make Him a liar, and His word is not in us."

We are not perfect. As long as we live on this earth, we will sin in some way, but Jesus died to forgive every sin we could ever commit. Confession means "saying the same thing as God says." Admit your failings to God without mixing words, and forgiveness will be yours.

The message for today: He who conceals his transgressions will not prosper, but he who *confesses* and *forsakes* them will find compassion. (Proverbs 28:13)

Prayer: Dear Heavenly Father, Thank You for Jesus who was made unto me "wisdom, and righteousness, and sanctification, and redemption"!

April 10 – Where am I on the "Humility Scale"?

For everyone who exalts himself will be humbled, and he who humbles himself will be exalted. (Luke 14:11)

In James 2, the Bible gives us some great advice on how to treat people. James says that we become judges with evil motives when we treat rich people one way and poor people another way. He asks us to picture how we would act if a rich person came to church in beautiful clothes and we asked him to sit in a place of honor, and a poor person came in and we asked him to sit in the back and keep quiet.

God says in Proverbs 6:16 that He hates pride and its results.

There are two sides to pride, which Satan makes so deceptive, but they both hurt people badly – pride and shame. Pride says, "I'm wonderful"; but the other side of pride is shame, which says, "How could you do that to us? You've ruined our family's reputation!" Both of these come from our insecurities and fears. Since Satan is the author of fear, guess where pride and shame come from?

When we humble ourselves under God's mighty hand and give Him all our worries and troubles, He grants us peace, the wonderful by-product of humility and trust! Prisoner, wouldn't you like some peace today? (See I Peter 5:6, 7).

The message for today: Jesus must increase in my life, and I must *decrease.* (John 3:30)

Prayer: Dear Heavenly Father, Please forgive my pride which tries to figure things out myself. Help me to rely on You alone.

April 11 – The Power of Love

For it is better, if the will of God be so, that you suffer for well doing, than for evil doing. (I Peter 3:17)

I once heard a story about Derrick, who had been brought up in a broken home with much verbal and physical abuse. Since he never had anyone who showed him love, he grew up very bitter and hateful. When he was a teen-ager, he started to get involved with the law and was soon sentenced to do time in prison.

After a few weeks of being in jail, some volunteers came by his cell to tell him about Jesus and His love. Of course, he refused to listen to them and told them to go away, but one young man named Jim kept coming back, month after month.

One day Jim visited Derrick again; but as he saw him coming to his cell, he yelled out, "No one could love a sinner like me, so go away!" Not willing to just leave, Jim tried to hand him a tract; but when he stuck his hand in between the bars of the cell, Derrick broke his wrist. Jim went away in a lot of pain that day, but the next week he came back to Derrick's cell.

"Jesus loves you, Derrick," Jim said, "and if it would make you love Him and get out of the devil's grip, I would let you break my other wrist!" That day, Derrick prayed to accept Jesus.

The message for today: God's love is the strongest power on earth!

Prayer: Dear Heavenly Father, Help me to love others the way You loved me when You sent Jesus to die for me.

April 12 – God's Perfect Sacrifice

Forasmuch as you know that you were not redeemed with corruptible things, as silver and gold, from your vain manner of life received by tradition from your fathers, but with the precious blood of Christ, as of a lamb without blemish and without spot. (I Peter 1:18, 19)

I have always read in the Old Testament about the sacrificial animals being perfect. God refers to it many times that the lamb must not be crippled or sick in any way. It must be the person's best lamb, without any physical defects. I realized after reading the entire Bible that God deserves our *best* sacrifices – not what is left over.

In the Old Testament, when someone sinned, they had to go to the priest and offer a sacrificial animal for that sin. The priest offered it, and their sin was atoned for. It went on that way for thousands of years until the New Testament. God had a better plan, which did away with the actual sacrificing of animals when Jesus Christ came to be our "once-and-for-all" sacrifice – the perfect Lamb of God with no blemish at all, thus satisfying God.

We cannot please God by offering our "good works" to Him. He was *totally* satisfied with Jesus' death on the cross and His blood shed "once for all". Salvation is all about Jesus and *His* work – not about us and *our* works.

The message for today: Not by works of righteousness which we have done, but according to *His mercy* He saved us. (Titus 3:5)

Prayer: Dear Heavenly Father, Thank You for Jesus and His atoning work for me on Calvary.

April 13 – Listening to God's Voice

I was not disobedient to the heavenly vision...
(Acts 26:19, 20)

Mrs. Riggins went to a yard sale with the intention of purchasing some things for her mission trip to Africa. On her way out, she saw three soccer balls on a table. She glanced over at them and she heard a voice telling her to buy them. She wondered why she would ever need soccer balls in Africa, but she obeyed the voice.

When she left for her mission trip, the same voice spoke to her again and told her to pack the balls, too. She obeyed again.

She arrived in Africa and had a wonderful time telling the people about Jesus and His love. On the day she left, she decided to have lunch with one of the missionaries before she started for the airport. While she was at lunch, a man walked up to her and introduced himself. He asked if she could please ask the people of her church to help with some equipment needs for their new soccer team. He said that they needed uniforms and three soccer balls!

She asked him to come with her, and she presented him with the three balls the small voice had told her to bring. The coach was elated, and so was Mrs. Riggins! She knew that God always does things that look as if they don't make sense at the time; but if we obey that "still, small voice", God will show us His marvelous plan to bless someone.

The message for today: Listen for God's voice today and ask Him to use you to bless other prisoners who need encouragement.

Prayer: Dear Heavenly Father, I pray I will listen more so I can hear the voice of the Holy Spirit.

✝
April 14 – Lift Jesus Higher

And I, if I be lifted up from the earth,
will draw all men unto me. (John 12:32)

Many things in today's world originate from the Bible. Have you ever seen a picture in a hospital or doctor's office of two snakes on a pole? That insignia is taken directly from the story of the bronze serpent in Numbers 21:6-9 where God punished the Israelites for complaining against Him.

In Numbers 21 they had just come from a great victory over the Canaanites, but they started complaining that they hated this wilderness God had put them in. Because of their murmuring, God sent snakes among them that bit them and killed many of them. They immediately ran to Moses and said, "We have sinned because we have spoken against the Lord. Do something, Moses!"

God told Moses to make a serpent and put it up on a pole. Everyone who had been bitten could then look at the serpent on the pole and be healed.

Jesus said in John 12:32 that if He were lifted up from the earth (on a cross), He would draw all men to Himself. When they looked to the Cross of Calvary, they could be healed of the sin "sickness" that we all suffer from. He was referring to Numbers 21.

We need to lift Jesus Christ up in our daily lives, too. People should be able to look at us and see "something different", i.e. Jesus in our lives. His sweet presence in us will draw people to know Him as their Savior.

The message for today: I am the Lord, who heals you. (Exodus 15:26)

Prayer: Dear Heavenly Father, Help me to lift You up daily and draw many people to You.

April 15 – Hi, Neighbor!

Bless those who curse you, and pray for those who despitefully use you. (Luke 6:28)

The moment you prayed and asked Jesus Christ to be your Savior, the Holy Spirit of God entered your entire being. You might not have felt differently; but if you truly asked Jesus to be your Savior, you started acting differently.

Because of the Holy Spirit's presence, you have a super-natural ability to love, which differs greatly from your natural ability. The Bible says that the Holy Spirit of God comes "alongside" to change your way of thinking and acting for the rest of your life here on earth. He is a constant companion.

Jesus told His disciples that He was going to leave them, but He would send a "Comforter" to be with them. That Comforter is the Holy Spirit of God.

Jesus told us to love God and love others. It's that simple. He said that the second greatest commandment was for us to love our neighbor as ourselves. In I Peter 3:8, 9 it says, "Finally, all of you, be of one mind, having compassion for one another. Love as brothers; be tenderhearted and courteous, not returning evil for evil or reviling for reviling, but on the contrary, blessing, knowing that you were called to this, that you may inherit a blessing."

Who is causing you trouble today? Breathe that person's name to God and obey His command to love. Ask God to mightily bless them. As you continue to pray for them, watch what supernaturally happens. I have done it and it works!

The message for today: My neighbor is everyone I meet.

Prayer: Dear Heavenly Father, I can't love_____
_____(person's name) as I should, but would You please love them through me?

✝

April 16 – It Takes Time

Men ought always to pray and not to faint. (Luke 18:1)

I used to pray "grocery list" prayers. You know the type, "Dear God, help me to get out of this situation today. Help Mom to have the money to come and see me." One day God actually let me hear myself praying, and I was ashamed. It sounded like, "OK, God, here's the deal. Here's what I need. Got it? Good."

Sometimes we don't pray every day because we don't need anything that day. We think of God as our Heavenly Butler, who jumps when we call. What a wrong perception of God that is, and we wonder why He doesn't answer our prayers!

Psalm 100:4 tells us to enter His gates with thanksgiving, and come into His courts with praise. Be thankful unto Him and bless His name. Why? Because Jesus Christ has given His life for you and me, and He is praying for us. That's why. If you know Jesus as your Lord and Savior today, there are not enough words with which to praise Him!

Why not start a prayer list? Divide it into Monday, Tuesday, etc. On Mondays, have 10 people to pray for. On Tuesdays, do the same. You will find that your prayer time will last almost one hour as you take time to read your Bible, read your daily devotional, and pray to our loving Heavenly Father. I think He really would like that!

The message for today: Take time to be holy. Speak often with your Lord.

Prayer: Dear Heavenly Father, You are not in a hurry. Help me not to be either. Calm my spirit and help me set a regular time of communion with You, my Best Friend.

April 17 – Top Priorities

What good thing shall I do that I may have eternal life?
(Matthew 19:16)

Probably, all his life, the rich young ruler was very spoiled and got everything he wanted. In Matthew 19:16-22 he came to Jesus and asked what good thing he could "do" to inherit eternal life. Jesus led him into a short discussion, which showed the young man who he really was.

Jesus started out by telling him that he had to keep the 10 Commandments. "Which ones?" he asked. Jesus said that he should not murder, commit adultery, steal, or lie. Then He told him to honor his father and mother and love his neighbor as himself. The rich young ruler told Him that he had kept all the commandments all his life, and then he asked what he lacked since he had done all these things.

We don't want to know who we really are, but it is God's business to expose us to ourselves. Jesus had to show the young ruler where his priorities really were, so He targeted on his riches. He told the young ruler to sell everything he had and give it to the poor! Ouch! The young man went away sad because he had great wealth. What would you do if you worshiped your money, and someone said to give it all away?

If he would have obeyed Jesus, probably he would have been blessed with double riches, but he just couldn't let go of the love of his money. His pride got the better of him.

The message for today: Be careful what you worship. Jesus might ask you to give it up.

Prayer: Dear Heavenly Father, I humble myself before You and ask You to help me obey You in everything I do.

April 18 – Can You Sing?

For I have learned, in whatsoever state I am, therewith to be content. (Philippians 4:11)

Paul spent a great deal of his adult life in prison. In Acts 9:15, 16 we can get a good perspec tive of God's plans for Paul. It says, "…he is a chosen vessel unto me… for I will show him how great things he must suffer for my name's sake."

Have you suffered for the name of the Lord? I don't think many of us can answer yes to that question; but if we had to suffer, I would hope that God would be proud of us and our testimonies for Jesus.

If you have been incarcerated, you know that it is not an easy life. Sometimes you just want to give up, but God tells us to persevere – no matter what – in James 1:12. James says, "Blessed is a man who persev ercs under trial…" In other words, "Hang in there, beloved one."

As you read this poem, think of your own attitude. Can you sing?

> *He placed me in a little cage, away from gardens fair,*
> *But I must sing the sweetest songs, because He placed me there.*
> *Not beat my wings against the cage, if it's my Maker's will,*
> *But raise my voice to heaven's gate, and sing the louder still.*

The message for today: Your "atti tu de" determines your "altitude" spiritually.

Prayer: Dear Heavenly Fathe r, Help me to run my race and finish it successfully for You, no matter what hu rdles I may have to jump.

April 19 – A Faith like David's

But as for me, I will hope continually and will praise You yet more and more. (Psalm 71:14)

Have you been to the doctor recently and been told that you have a chronic illness, cancer, or aids? It seems as if there are no words for the fear and sadness that come over us when we are given a bad report; but according to God's Word, we have a choice to make regarding bad reports.

We can be discouraged and give into the sickness, or we can claim the promises of the Bible and come out victoriously. It is our choice. We can walk by faith or walk by sight, but not both of them.

The name and the power of Jesus are greater than any sickness or disease. David said that he would trust in the Lord and praise Him at "all times". That takes faith, but David had it. He said in Psalm 34:8, "Oh, taste and see that the Lord is good; blessed is the man who trusts in Him!" He goes on to say that those who seek the Lord shall not lack any good thing. Now that's a good report!

After receiving a bad report and turning to these words, there is nothing you can do but trust in Jesus, just like David did. Jesus is our healer, provider, doctor, judge, protector, and lawyer. We can't lose with Him on our side!

The message for today: Bad reports are just smoke screens from Satan.

Prayer: Dear Heavenly Father, I praise You that You are greater than anything that can come into my life. Help me to trust You more.

April 20 – God Said It and That Settles It!

He is not here, for He has risen, just as He said.
(Matthew 28:6)

It used to be that when someone gave you their word, it was as good as done. A firm handshake of agreement was all it took to bind someone to keep his word. But all that has changed and it is difficult to get anyone to keep their word – ever!

The Bible is full of promises from a God who keeps His word all the time. Jesus said in Matthew 5:18, "For truly I say to you, until heaven and earth pass away, not the smallest letter or stroke shall pass from the Law until all is accomplished."

Have you ever heard the word "covenant"? It is like a contract between two people. God made a covenant with Abraham in Genesis 15:18 that will someday be fulfilled – no matter what. He told Abraham that the land from the river of Egypt to the Euphrates River would belong to the Israelites, and it will someday. His covenant cannot be broken by anyone.

When a man and woman marry, they enter into a covenant with each other and God. Jesus said that what "God hath joined together, let no man put asunder" (separate). What unhappiness we could avoid if we only kept our covenant with God and man!

The angel announced to the women at Jesus' tomb that He had risen, just as He said. He kept covenant with His Father and kept His word to the disciples and future generations. He died and rose again that we might live!

The message for today: God's promises are His performances! (Romans 4:21)

Prayer: Dear Heavenly Father, Thank You for keeping Your word to us at all times.

April 21 – Keep Asking

...You have not because you ask not. (James 4:2)

A kindergarten teacher wanted to do an object lesson about what God means when He tells us to ask Him for what we want, so he sat down in a chair and asked the class to move him out of it. One child pulled on his arm. Another pulled his shirt. Another tried to push him out, but nothing worked.

Finally, one child looked at another one and said, "Why don't we just ask him to get out of the chair?" When they asked, he got up.

Having made his point, the teacher told the children that God just wants us to ask Him for what we need, and He will move on our request, according to His will.

Are you praying for something and nothing is happening? Are you manipulating circumstances and "pulling strings" to get your own way? Have you stopped asking God for something because it seems He is not answering?

A story is told of a lady who prayed for 25 years for her sinful son to love Jesus. As her casket was lowered into the grave, he fell on his knees and in tears asked Jesus Christ to be his Savior. That dear mother's prayers were answered, even though she never saw them answered in her lifetime.

I John 5:14, 15 tell us that if we ask anything according to His will, He hears us; and if we know that He hears us, we know we have the petitions that we desire of Him.

The message for today: Keep on asking. Your prayers will be answered in God's time.

Prayer: Dear Heavenly Father, My main prayer request today is: _____. Thank You for answering it in Your perfect time.

April 22 – Don't Miss Your Blessings

Not forsaking the assembling of ourselves together, as
the manner of some is... (Hebrews 10:25)

What do you miss when you don't go to jail church services? I was thinking a lot about this, and the Lord showed me one main thing. You miss many blessings. We don't need to go to church to gain entrance to Heaven, but there's something about belonging to a group of believers that gives us a corporate blessing as we go about our daily lives. It is like being under an umbrella of protection.

Lydia would never have been saved from her sins, had she not assembled with a group of ladies one Sabbath day. Read what Luke says in Acts 16:13 about her, "And on the Sabbath day we went outside the gate to a riverside, where we were supposing that there would be a place of prayer, and we sat down and began speaking to the women who had assembled. A woman named Lydia, from the city of Thyatira, a seller of purple fabrics, a worshiper of God, was listening; and the Lord opened her heart to respond to the things spoken by Paul." Lydia was called a worshiper, but she wasn't saved. God placed her with a group of women that day because of a hungering in her heart. He then placed Paul there, too, and a miracle happened. This story would never have been written if the ladies had not assembled together. Lydia and her whole household accepted Jesus and were baptized that day! What a miracle!

The message for today: No man is an island. We need other believers.

Prayer: Dear Heavenly Father, Help me to start attending church services and worship You in spirit and in truth.

April 23 – What Are Your Plans?

I take joy in doing your will, my God, for your law is written on my heart. (Psalm 40:8)

Statistics show that most people do not enjoy their jobs. Sometimes in life we prepare for years to do something that does not fulfill us at all, and we end up frustrated and sad.

In life we think we know what is best for us. We struggle and claw at life, trying to make things happen, only to find out that we are miserable with the life choices we have made. I have been there and done that.

The Bible offers a better solution when it advises us to "seek first the Kingdom of God and His righteousness, and all these things will be added unto you" (Matthew 6:33). God has an abundant life for us if we will only seek Him and His purposes, instead of our own.

"For I know the plans I have for you," declares the Lord, "plans to prosper you and not to harm you, plans to give you a hope and a future" (Jeremiah 29:11). When the Lord declares something, it carries with it the meaning that He is positively and emphatically showing and revealing to us that we can find peace that passes understanding and strength through His wonderful power.

God knew before I knew what was going to happen in my life and made the promise to me that it was to prosper and not to harm me. His plans were to give me a future and a hope, and there I can rest. He has it all under control – even the trials and tribulations.

The message for today: Don't worry about tomorrow. God is already there.

Prayer: Dear Heavenly Father, I praise You that I am special to You.

April 24 – Running the Race

*Do you not know that those who run in a race all run,
but only one receives the prize? (I Corinthians 9:24)*

It has been said that life is like a race, and at the end the one "with the most toys" wins. You have heard the saying that "Nice guys finish last" and "You only go around once". Well, all those sayings are wrong, according to God's Word, the Bible.

Indeed, life is like a race, and there are many runners. Sometimes we need to be reminded that the point of the race is not the race itself. It is so easy to focus totally on the race that all we do is Bible studies, fellowship groups, support groups, church activities, and on and on it goes.

In I Corinthians 9 Paul tells us to stop thinking so much about the race and start thinking more about the prize. We are running for a heavenly prize, Jesus. The whole point of life is to "prize" (honor) our Savior.

What is your prize? Is it money, prestige, looking good? Your prize is what you focus on. Paul didn't want to be disqualified from winning the race; but he wanted to hear Jesus say at the end, "Well done, thou good and faithful servant."

The message for today: Get refocused today and let the race be about Jesus.

Prayer: Dear Heavenly Father, Help me to be still before You, spend time with You, and know that You are God. Please get my focus on Jesus Christ and His righteousness.

April 25 – Addictions

Let your moderation be known to all men. (Philippians 4:5)

The word addiction comes from the original word "addictus", which means "to surrender". When a person is addicted to something, he has literally surrendered to its power.

Addictions come from Satan. He lures people with a little bait and then reels in the line tighter and tighter until they are held captive and have "surrendered" to their addiction. The addicted person lives an out-of-balance life. We can get addicted to substance abuse such as drugs and alcohol, or the addiction can be more subtle. It can be anything from chewing gum, to overeating, to watching TV.

How do we stop addictive behavior? Here are some suggestions:

1. Admit to yourself that you have a problem with

   _____.

2. Tell someone close to you about your problem. You will be amazed how this helps!

3. Be accountable to a close friend. Report once a week to the person and tell them how things are going.

4. Keep a journal of your successes and failures. Sometimes you will fail, but more times than not, you will succeed if you know you will have to write it down.

The message for today: Jesus comes alongside with strength, grace, and power to help you overcome any addiction that is holding you captive.

Prayer: Dear Heavenly Father, Please deliver me from my addiction to_____. Help me to help myself by Your grace.

April 26 – One Way or the Other

Do you not know that friendship with the world is hostility toward God? Therefore, whoever wishes to be a friend of the world makes himself an enemy of God. (James 4:4)

"You can't have your cake and eat it, too." Have you ever heard someone say that when they wished they could have things both ways? Sometimes that is how we want our lives to be in serving Jesus – a little bit good and a little bit bad.

In prison, I have watched my own reactions when I am with ungodly inmates. If I am not careful, I start acting like they do in my attitudes and words. Paul said that "bad company corrupts good morals" in I Corinthians 15:33.

If you are sold out to Jesus Christ, and your life is free from habitual (continual) sin, you will be miserable in the company of the unsaved. It's like oil and water, and the two don't mix. God told us that we should not be "unequally yoked with unbelievers". It is like putting a mule and a cow together and plowing a field. It would not be easy, to say the least, because they are not the same species.

As born-again, blood-bought Christians, we are citizens of heaven, and we just don't fit in here on earth with the ungodly. Give in to the Holy Spirit's gentle nudges and surrender yourself totally to Jesus and His will for your life.

The message for today: We can't have it both ways.

Prayer: Dear Heavenly Father, I surrender all I am to You today. Bring fellow believers into my life, and help me to not to love the world more than my Lord.

April 27 – Metamorphosis!

*But we had to celebrate and rejoice, for this brother
of yours was dead and has begun to live, and was
lost and has been found. (Luke 15:32)*

Joe had two daughters. The older was obedient and very humble, and the younger was rude, disobedient and disrespectful to everyone. As time went by, the humble daughter finished school and became a teacher. The younger daughter got caught up in drugs and prostitution and was sent to prison for several years.

She started attending church services in prison and learned that Jesus Christ loved her and gave His life for her. Soon she accepted Jesus into her life, and a transformation took place. She became kind and respectful. She attended Bible studies regularly and started learning how to deal with life and difficult situations.

When she was released and went home, her whole family saw the change, and they were astonished. They told her they were so glad that she had been "rehabilitated". She told them that the "system" couldn't rehabilitate her, but Jesus could and did!

It was as if her life had been in a cocoon; but when Jesus was ready, spiritual metamorphosis took place and He transformed her and gave her a new reason to live!

Whether we are in or out of prison, we need a transformation from Jesus.

The message for today: True salvation results in transformation.

Prayer: Dear Heavenly Father, Today I praise You that You loved me enough to send Jesus to die for my sins.

✝ April 28 – Plan Ahead

Seven years of great abundance are coming in all the land of Egypt, and after them seven years of famine will come... (Genesis 41:29, 30)

Joseph's life had a lot of ups and downs, to say the least. His jealous brothers hated him and sold him to the Ishmaelites, who took him to Egypt when he was only 17. He was framed by Potipher's wife and accused of raping her and thrown into prison.

Joseph found exceptional favor with the prison rulers and the Egyptian Pharaoh, but he still went to prison for over seven years because God was preparing everything that concerned his life and the economy of Egypt. God was going to use Joseph to deliver a nation!

Never once does the Bible mention that Joseph complained or got depressed. He interpreted Pharaoh's dream one day, that there would be seven years of plenty and then seven terrible years of famine in the land.

Joseph told Pharaoh that someone had to be in charge who was a good planner, because the seven years of famine would kill everyone if there were no reserves in the storehouses of Egypt. Here is the good part. Pharaoh set him over the whole land of Egypt! (Genesis 41:41)

The way we act now definitely determines our future.

The message for today: A journey of a million miles begins with the first step.

Prayer: Dear Heavenly Father, Help me to start acting differently so that my future will be happy and bright.

April 29 – God Doesn't Make Mistakes

Those who compare themselves among themselves are not wise. (II Corinthians 10:12)

What happens when we compare ourselves to other people? We do two things:

1) We look at their strengths and our weaknesses.
2) We blame God for not doing a better job on our appearance, talents, or intellect.

We set ourselves up to believe Satan's lie that we are inferior; and when we feel inferior, we act inferior.

Ephesians 2:10 says that "we are His workmanship (poetry), created in Christ Jesus for good works, which God prepared beforehand so that we would walk in them" (Ephesians 2:10). I never knew I was God's special poem that the entire world could read! Isaiah 64:8 says, "But now, O Lord, thou art our father; we are the clay, and thou our potter, and we all are the work of thy hand."

Isaiah 45:8 catches us up short when we complain about the way God made us when it says, "Shall the clay say to Him that fashioned it, 'Why did you make me this way?'"

If you have been told all your life that you are no good, ugly, or dumb, don't believe it! Start quoting Ephesians 2:10 at least ten times a day until you do believe it.

The message for today: I am special to God (John 3:16 – For God so loved me......)

Prayer: Dear Heavenly Father, Help me to praise You more for who I am instead of complaining about who I am not.

April 30 – T.G.I.F.

Seek first the kingdom of God and His righteousness...
(Matthew 6:33)

Have you ever said, "Thank God it's Friday!" – T.G.I.F.?

There is another TGIF that I like better now. It says, "Today God Is First", and that is a good word. Today, if God is first in my life, things will go better and turn out better.

How can we put God first in our lives? Glad you asked because there are several ways.

1. Spend the first part of every day with your Bible in your lap, reading His living Word, if only for 15 minutes.

2. Spend time in prayer and tell Him that you are available for anything or anyone He wants to put in your path. I have a little prayer that goes something like this, "Father, today bring the people into my life that You want in my life, and take the people out of my life who are not supposed to be there. Bless everyone I talk to today and bless everyone who talks to me." You would be surprised how seriously God takes my prayer. Some days He surprises me with wonderful conversations where I can point someone to Jesus or get some great advice.

3. Do things that count for eternity every day. We all can be busy and wonder where the time went during the day because there is absolutely nothing that we accomplished for Jesus. We are all given the same 24 hours, but how we use them affects our spiritual lives a great deal.

The message for today: Only one life, 'twill soon be past. Only what's done for Christ will last.

Prayer: Dear Heavenly Father, I'm available to You today. Use me in your eternal kingdom.

MAY

May 1 – In God's Waiting Room

Trust in the Lord with all your heart, and do not lean on your own understanding. (Proverbs 3:5)

We cannot see the big picture that God has for our lives. I once read a story about a man stuck in a traffic jam. He kept beeping his horn and yelling at everyone to move, all to no avail. There was another man in a sky scraper, looking down on the whole mess. He saw a wrecked car up ahead of the angry man. Finally, the accident was cleared and everyone started moving again.

Just like the man in the sky scraper, God looks down and sees the whole mess we are in. He knows how it could be fixed, but many times He purposely waits…and waits…and waits until we learn what we are supposed to know about Him and His character.

When you are waiting and you don't understand God's purpose for the delay, remember this verse from Isaiah 30:18, "And therefore will the Lord wait, they He may be gracious unto you, and therefore will He be exalted, that He may have mercy upon you…blessed are all they that wait for Him".

Are you waiting right now? Don't faint. Just believe in God's love for you.

The message for today: Wait on God. He's always on time.

Prayer: Dear Heavenly Father, I will trust You in my situation, and I will wait patiently until You reveal Your perfect will to me.

✝

May 2 – Look Who's Coming!

John saw Jesus coming and said, "Behold, the Lamb of God, who takes away the sin of the world!" (John 1:29)

When Jesus Christ came on the scene in the New Testament, He was a type of the perfect lamb offered in the Old Testament days under the old covenant of The Ten Commandments (the Law). When John saw Him, he could only exclaim, "Look, everyone, it's the Lamb of God (Jesus) who takes away the sins of the whole world!"

Today Jesus is being introduced to thousands of people and giving them the opportunity to accept Him as their perfect blood sacrifice. They no longer have to work at their salvation and be uncertain of their sins being forgiven.

I can picture what happened in heaven after Jesus arose from the dead at Easter. He went up to heaven and showed God the Father His blood which had been shed on Calvary. He probably said something like, "Father, I present to You My blood sacrifice on behalf of everyone who will ever be born. Never again will You need to see the blood of animals because My blood covers all sins. I have done the work of redemption, once and for all." With that statement, Jesus sat down at the right hand of the Father because His work was done!

Have you accepted the blood sacrificed for you on that old rugged cross? If not, why not do it now?

The message for today: Your salvation has already been paid for.

Prayer: Dear Heavenly Father, Thank You for Jesus taking my sins on Himself on the cross. Thank You that all I have to do is accept the free gift He offers.

May 3 – Real Living

Why seek ye the living among the dead? (Luke 24:5)

The morning that Jesus was raised from the dead was a morning unlike any other. The women came to His tomb and found that the massive stone had been mysteriously rolled away from the entrance. They went into the tomb and saw that there was no body! What had happened? Where was their beloved Messiah? Two angels asked them why they sought the living Christ among the dead things of the world.

So many times people seek life in this dead carnal world. They live in the world and take no thought that there might be a different, better life.

I know a man who thought that no one could have a good time without drinking and doing drugs. He had never known anything else, so he thought that his lifestyle was "normal". But one day he met a Christian woman who told him about Jesus Christ. He listened for the first time in his life to a story about a different life – an abundant life – with a happy ending in heaven.

That man soon surrendered his life to Jesus Christ. He told me that he had been like the maniac of Gadara, who lived in a cave and was possessed by demons. When the Savior came along, He reached out to the man and cast the demons out of him. He took him out of the cave; and when the town's people found him, he was clothed and in his right mind for the first time in his life.

The message for today: Only Jesus can make your life really come alive.

Prayer: Dear Heavenly Father, Help me to seek spiritual things and not just those things that are earthly.

May 4 – Deliverance from Bondage
(Verna Bradley's story)

But now we have been released from the Law, having died to that by which we were bound... (Romans 7:6)

I read a book by Verna Bradl ey *(Looking Ba ck betwe en the Cracks, 2001),* who said that if she had not been sent to jail for the third time, the dru gs would have taken her life. The "highs" were obsessing her; but every time she got high, she had to sit down or she would faint. Her eyes were so swollen that she could not see. She didn't bathe or brush her teeth for days at a time. She was out of con trol. But God...intervened. As she was praying one night, G od spoke direct ly to her and said, "I didn't tell you to buy any rock. I didn't tell you to sell any rock. I told you that 'on THIS ROCK, Je sus Christ, I would build My Church'. Now accept Me into your life and tu rn from these drugs!"

That night in a jail cell, alone and broken, she asked Jesus into her life, and her life turned completely around. She knew she had to return to a crack house, but God said that He would go before her. She prayed her way through every temptation and she was victorious through Jesus!

Today she has a full-time job in her church. She owns her own car and lives in a Habitat for Humanity home! How about that for God's grace? She has her children back, and she is at peace for the first time in many years!

The message for today: And we know that God works all things together for good. (Romans 8:28)

Prayer: Dear Heavenly Father, Please rescue me from myself. Change me from the inside out.

May 5 – Do Your Homework

*May the Lord reward your work, and your wages
be full from the Lord... (Ruth 2:12)*

It's been said that every cloud has a silver lining. What could be the silver lining (blessing) in being sent to jail?

As I thought about this, God showed me some blessings that many of us could only get in jail, e.g., an education.

Can you imagine how I felt when I was offered a chance to get my G.E.D. while in prison? I decided that whatever it took, I was going to study and study and see my educational dream become a reality. Today I am working steadily toward that goal, and it is happening – one day at a time.

I was told that I could be anything I wanted to be if I would only spend time in preparation. I heard a speaker say that "when preparation meets opportunity, success results." Nothing can take the place of preparation.

God prepares us to be used in the most unique ways. David was a shepherd, who killed a lion and then a giant! Then he became a king! Moses couldn't speak without stuttering and became the deliverer of an entire nation! Paul went to prison and wrote 2/3 of the New Testament, which encourages us every time we read it!

Can you imagine where you could be in five years if you used your time in jail getting your G.E.D. or bachelor's degree? It can be done with God's help and your persistence.

The message for today: Keep your hand to the plough and keep going forward. It pays rich rewards.

Prayer: Dear Heavenly Father, Help me to start using my time instead of spending it doing nothing.

May 6 – Getting the Victory

They overcame him by the blood of the Lamb and the
word of their testimony. (Rev. 12:11)

Give yourself a test regarding your thoughts. Do you think mostly about freedom, betrayal, or your childhood?

Our thought life affects everything we do. If you were brought up being told that you were stupid, the natural thing to think when a challenge or a good job comes up is, "I am stupid. I can't do this." That is exactly how Satan wants you to think, but you can fight him and conquer your thoughts.

Satan is the accuser of the brethren. Just as Jesus lives day by day to pray for Christians, Satan lives to accuse them to God. In the Garden of Eden, he asked Eve, "Hath God said…?"

Satan also uses our past life as a stronghold. We filter everything we think, say and do through our experiences. If you were abandoned when you were a child, your thought life will filter everything through abandonment. You will be insecure about people, and relationships will never work out because you will always believe they will abandon you.

There is a remedy for wrong thoughts. You must fight fire with fire and use the Sword of the Spirit, the Word of God, as a substitute for unfruitful thoughts. As you substitute scripture each time a condemning thought comes to your mind, the strongholds that Satan has held you under for years will begin to disappear, one by one.

The message for today: Take authority over your thought life. Listen to the Word – not Satan's lies.

Prayer: Dear Heavenly Father, Thank You for Your Word. Help me to realize its power over the Devil and wield my Sword of the Spirit with excellence against him.

May 7 – Becoming Bitter or Better

Choose you this day whom you will serve...
I will serve the Lord. (Joshua 24:15)

Viktor Frankl, a famous psychiatrist, who lived through the Nazi concentration camps, wrote the book, "Man's Search for Meaning" in which he said,

"We who lived in the concentration camps can remember the men who walked through the huts comforting others, giving away their last piece of bread. They may have been few in number, but they offer sufficient proof that everything can be taken from a man but one thing: the last of the human freedoms – to choose one's attitude in any given set of circumstances, to choose one's own way.

And there were always choices to make. Every day, every hour, offered the opportunity to make a decision, a decision which determined whether you would submit to those powers which threatened to rob you of your very self, your inner freedom; which determined whether or not you would become the plaything of circumstance, renouncing freedom and dignity to become molded into the form of the typical inmate."

If you are incarcerated today, you can make a very wise decision to seek the Lord and find meaning for your life.

The message for today: Good life choices bring great rewards.

Prayer: Dear Heavenly Father, Help me to start honoring You by my choices.

✝ May 8 – Don't Settle

They chose that in which I delighted not. (Isaiah 66:4)

Why do some Christian prisoners settle for a lifestyle that doesn't come up to the Lord's standards?

God gives every one of us all the tools of life needed for holiness. He supplies the Bible to teach us, the Holy Spirit to guide us, and the ability to make good decisions.

I used to ask God why He didn't make me like a robot that could just "be good". I did not want to take responsibility for all the mistakes I had made over the years; and try as I would, I still made bad decisions until one day the light bulb came on in my "lightening fast mind," and I realized it was time to choose my destiny more carefully.

I read the following poem, which changed my life. It was from a little book called *Think and Grow Rich* by Napoleon Hill that talked about success or failure coming from the way we think. See if it speaks to you as you read it several times:

> I bargained with Life for a penny, and Life would pay no more
> However I begged at evening when I counted my scanty store.
> For Life is a just employer; he gives you what you ask;
> But once you have set the wages, you must bear the task.
> I worked for a menial's hire, only to learn dismayed
> That any wage I had asked of Life
> Life would have willingly paid!

The message for today: Have you settled for "pennies" when God wants you to have "riches"?

Prayer: Dear Heavenly Father, Your Word says that Jesus came to give me an abundant life, and I haven't seen that yet. Help me to live under Your anointing from this day forward.

May 9 – Be Ready

The Lord Himself shall descend from heaven with a shout... (I Thessalonians 4:16)

Sean and Julie knew that God wanted them to marry, so they went out and bought everything they needed. Julie bought the wedding dress of her dreams, and it seemed as if they were all set until Sean was suddenly called to the military.

Before Sean left, he promised Julie that they would marry when he returned. He told her to be ready and waiting for that wonderful day. They wrote back and forth, but Sean's letters stopped coming. Julie finally heard that Sean was missing in action.

Julie read and re-read Sean's letters. She asked the Lord to protect him. She was worried and sad. Several months later, she told her mother she was going to her room and she didn't want to be disturbed. Julie put on her wedding dress and stood in front of the mirror, looking beautiful. Would it ever take place? Was Sean dead?

Just then, a knock came at the bedroom door. When Julie said, "Come in," there was Sean! With tears of gratitude and love, they embraced. Sean just looked at her and said, "I've kept my promise. I'm here to get married, my love. I'm glad you're dressed and ready!"

This story reminds me of us Christians. We read and re-read God's love letter, the Bible, and sometimes we fear that Jesus won't be back as He promised. But we have to "be dressed and ready", because He will be back when we least expect Him!

The message for today: In the twinkling of an eye, the last trump will sound!

Prayer: Dear Heavenly Father, Help me to live in expectancy of Your Son's return.

✝

May 10 – A Good Mother

A virtuous woman, who can find her? Her price
is far above rubies. (Proverbs 31:10)

Each year America celebrates Mother's Day, but many people don't realize what a good mother is. I thought I was the best mother in the world when my children were growing up. I went to the extreme to give them their hearts' desires. I made sure they went to school and had clean clothes. I kept a clean home for them and fed them well, but one thing was missing out of our lives.

After I became a Christian in prison, I knew that Jesus was the puzzle piece that was missing from our lives all those years. I portrayed most of the characteristics of a good mother in Proverbs 31:10-31, but I left Jesus Christ out – a big mistake! If I had lived my life with God being number one, things would have been different.

In prison, I worried over my children's lives every day, but one day I gave them over to the Lord and continued to pray fervently for them. I just received a letter from my youngest son, and my heart rejoiced as I read his words of hope for our family.

In spite of my time in prison, my three children now arise and call me "blessed" because they see my faith in a mighty God who is working in my life, in spite of our separation.

The message for today: Turn your life over to Jesus today and leave your legacy of faith to your kids.

Prayer: Dear Heavenly Father, Help me to be the best mother I can be – no matter what the circumstances. Help me to point my children to Jesus Christ.

May 11 – A Heavy Load

Cast thy burden on the Lord, and he shall sustain thee.
(Psalm 55:22)

I heard a story about Ann, a woman who begged God to let her die in her sleep one night as she went to bed. She couldn't stand the weight of her burdens; but the Lord appeared to her and asked her a question.

"My child, haven't I told you to cast all of your burdens upon Me, because I care for you? My burden is light. If you would like, I could give you another set of burdens."

"Yes, Lord, I would like that," she said as she looked at several burdens lying at His feet, so she picked one that belonged to Kim. As God placed Kim's burden on her back, she screamed, "Take it off. It's too heavy, Lord." Kim's burden was a daughter who had just had brain surgery to remove cancer, but it hadn't worked. Kim also had a brother on drugs who had killed a police officer. Ann thought, 'How could Kim seem so peaceful and loving?'

After trying two more burdens, Ann picked her own up again and decided that it wasn't that heavy after all. Jesus had lightened the load that she carried with His grace and love. She looked up to Him and saw His nail-scarred hands. He took her burden from her back and threw it into the pool of blood at the foot of His cross. He said, "You may leave it here if you wish. You don't need it."

The message for today: Whatever your burden, whatever your pain, God always sends rainbows after the rain.

Prayer: Dear Heavenly Father, I bring my burden of
_____ to You, and I leave it at the cross.

May 12 – The Odds Are Against You

He that believes on the Son has everlasting life,
but he that believes not the Son shall not see life,
but the wrath of God abides on him. (John 3:36)

The rich man in Luke 16:19-31 thought the odds were in his favor all during his life. He had everything money could buy – except for salvation. Lazarus, the poor beggar, suffered all his earthly life and had nothing – except for salvation.

When both men died, Lazarus went to Abraham's Bosom, and the rich man went to Hell. Then and only then did he acknowledge the poor beggar, but it was too late. When he saw Lazarus in heaven, he begged Abraham to send him with a drop of water on his finger to cool his tongue because he was tormented in the flames of Hell.

If we die without having asked Jesus into our life, it will be too late. No one can ever rescue us from Hell and its torment once we die, but there is hope. We can have the "living water" here on earth if we ask Jesus Christ to be our Savior and never have to suffer in an eternity without Him.

The message for today: The odds are against us if we insist on sinning all of our life without repenting and turning to Jesus Christ for salvation. Life is short and eternity is l – o – n – g.

Prayer: Dear Heavenly Father, I know I am a sinner and I need Jesus Christ in my life. Please forgive me of every sin and come into my life, Lord Jesus. Thank You for writing my name in the Lamb's Book of Life and saving me today, _____.

May 13 – I Surrender All

If you are without chastisement…then are you
illegitimate children and not sons. (Hebrews 12:8)

For several years a friend of mine lived in rebellion to God. She was called of God to serve Him, but she strayed away.

God knows exactly what it takes to make us surrender to His will, and my friend was no exception. Her children were taken away from her. She went to God in tears and begged Him for her children back. She prayed for eight years for her children to be returned to her – all to no avail. During those terrible years, God got her attention. She started reading the Bible and spending time before the Lord, and He started working in her life.

Because she was truly born of the Holy Spirit of God, He would not let her out of His grip. God is a good parent, and He chastens those He loves. Hebrews 12:6-10 says "whom the Lord loves, He chastens (child trains) every child He receives." It goes on to say that, if we are without God's chastening, we are illegitimate children and not truly born again. Hebrews 12:10 gives the reason why truly born-again Christians are child trained by our Heavenly Father. He really cares about us and this verse proves it. God chastens us for our profit that we might be partakers of His holiness!

Today my friend is actively serving Jesus in prison ministry, and she never forgets that God loved her enough to chasten her. She remembers with great thankfulness how He pursued her until she surrendered her whole life to Jesus.

The message for today: God gives teaching which instructs and punishment which reminds His children.

Prayer: Dear Heavenly Father, Thank You for loving me enough to correct me.

May 14 – Someone's Watching You

…in speech, conduct, love, faith and purity, show yourself an example of those who believe. (I Timothy 4:12)

John grew up in a lukewarm Christian home. As he grew up, he witnessed his father's abuse of his mother and his sinful lifestyle. John thought that this was the mark of a real man, so he started acting like his dad as he grew up.

His dad's bad example caused him to live the same way. For a while he tried to be what he thought was a tough guy, a real man. When he married, he found out that his wife was a Christian; but her life was far different from what he knew as "Christian".

John started going to church after he was married, and soon he knew that he was not a true believer, so he went to the altar and gave his entire life to the Lord Jesus. Suddenly he realized that looking at his sex magazines, drinking, smoking, and hanging out with bad companions didn't please God, so he stopped it. He asked his pastor one day if he was still a real man by not doing all the things he saw his father doing as he grew up.

His pastor explained to him that he had "caught" the things his father did and adopted them as a lifestyle, without even knowing that they were wrong; but God uses men with wisdom and integrity to be leaders in their homes and churches — not lukewarm, carnal men. John finally understood and became a "real man" for Jesus.

The message for today: More things are "caught" than "taught" in our families.

Prayer: Dear Heavenly Father, Help me to be an example of Jesus in all I do.

May 15 – Jesus Loves Me, This I Know

They cried to the Lord in their trouble, and
He brought them out of their distresses.
(Psalm 107:28, 29)

The Canaanite woman in Matthew 15:23-28 was a cast-out. She was poor with no influence. In fact, the disciples asked Jesus to send her away because of her loud conduct; but He saw something of worth in her and wanted to help her.

That's how it is with us. Jesus sees something in us worth saving! Let's look at the rest of the story and learn from it.

The woman did several things that got her honorable mention in the annals of history because of her faith.

1. She cried out to Jesus and recognized Him as "Lord."
2. She knew He could heal her demon-possessed daughter.
3. She knew that He loves everyone, not just a select few.
4. She worshiped Him and fell down before Him and begged for help.
5. She was persistent in her request to Jesus.
6. She got Jesus' attention, and He told her that her faith was great and her daughter was healed at once!

Is God done with you yet? Put your hand on your heart. If it is still beating, God is not done with you yet.

The message for today: Don't give up on the Lord. He will be found if you seek Him with all your heart.

Prayer: Dear Heavenly Father, Thank You for caring about me and all that concerns me.

May 16 – No Longer Bound

Lo, I see four men loose, walking in the midst of the fire, and they have no hurt, and the form of the fourth is like the Son of God. (Daniel 3:25)

Nebuchadnezzar could not believe his eyes when he looked into the furnace and saw that the men were not even getting burnt by the intense flames! He had tied their hands behind their backs and had his servants throw them into the flames, but to his amazement he saw them walking around loose – with no bonds. Then, as he looked, he saw a fourth person in the fire with them. This was Jesus Christ appearing to him! Jesus was not scheduled to be born for hundreds of years, but there He was in the fire with them!

The King saw a miracle happen that day, so he decreed in Daniel 3:28, "Blessed be the God of Shadrach, Meshach and Abednego, who hath sent his angel, and delivered his servants that trusted in him, and have changed the king's word, and yielded their bodies, that they might not serve nor worship any god, except their own God."

Are you in a fiery trial today? Our faithful God can break any bondage in your life and bring you out victoriously!

The message for today: God is a very present help in trouble. (Psalm 46:1)

Prayer: Dear Heavenly Father, Help me to stand up for my faith – no matter what!

May 17 – Book Ends

The fruit of the Spirit is love, joy, peace, patience, kindness, goodness, faithfulness, gentleness and self-control. (Galatians 5:22)

In order to produce fruit, a tree must have sunshine and rain. With no rain, the tree would die. Many people think that they can achieve any goal they want with self-control and discipline, but they leave God out of their goals.

The Holy Spirit, the third member of the Trinity, is responsible for producing "fruit" in our Christian lives. He ever lives to honor Jesus Christ; and when God's children are loving, joyful, peaceful, patient, kind, and good, etc., Jesus is honored.

When a person is living for the Lord Jesus, their life shows it. It's been said that if you are in fellowship with the Lord, you want to be helpful and kind to others, and you are not even aware of it. It just comes "super" naturally.

If you notice, love is at the one end of the fruit of the Spirit and self-control is at the other end. It makes me think that these two qualities are like book ends which hold up the others.

It is God who fills us with the fruit of the Spirit. Romans 15:13 says, "May the God of hope fill you with all joy and peace in believing that you may abound in hope by the power of the Holy Spirit." The only way we can remain peaceful in stressful situations is to be in God's Word daily and soak it up daily. He can then fill us with hope, joy, and peace.

The message for today: What a mighty God we serve!

Prayer: Dear Heavenly Father, I know my life is not lived by might or power but by Your Holy Spirit. Thank You.

✝

May 18 – The Great Exchange

He hath sent me to bind up the brokenhearted, to pro-
claim liberty to the captives, and the opening of the
prison to them that are bound...to comfort all that
mourn, to give unto them beauty for ashes, the oil of joy
for mourning, the garment of praise for the spirit of
heaviness... (Isaiah 61:1-3). (Also see Luke 4:18, 19.)

It was not an accident when Isaiah wrote that he had been anointed to help people. I can almost feel his heart cry as he wrote that he wanted people trade their "ashes" for "beauty", their "mourning" for the "oil of joy", and their "spirit of heaviness" for the "garment of praise". What a wonderful exchange!

Prisoner, God wants to open your heart and free you from every bondage that Satan has kept you under all your life. He can do it, but you must be willing. You must be willing to sit in God's presence daily and get His thoughts – not just the thoughts of others. You must be willing to grow up and feed yourself instead of having someone else feed you. Spoon feeding is for babies.

Jesus used Isaiah 61:1, 2 when He spoke in the synagogue after having been tempted in the wilderness for 40 days (Luke 4:18, 19). The people were so impressed with His wisdom, and He told them that they had just heard God speak, because He was God!

The message for today: Hearing God speak takes time, but it's worth it.

Prayer: Dear Heavenly Father, I'm tired of my ashes, mourning, and sadness. Please help me to spend enough time with You to exchange them for happiness, peace, and joy.

May 19 – Lord, I'm Listening

But God led the people about, through the way of the wilderness…and the Lord went before them …
to lead them in the way. (Exodus 13:18, 21)

I received a note from a friend last week, and I wanted to share it with you. She wrote:

"I just wanted to share something with you. I know God is using Bill's time in jail to speak to his heart. He had to get Bill alone so that HE could have his undivided attention without any distractions from the outside world. Last night when he called me, the first thing he told me was that he was able to get a Bible from the jail chaplain. I was so excited because I shared the verses from last night's Bible study at church with him. It was about God's will and Bill wrote them all down. We had a great conversation, and I told him that whatever happened before he went to jail (and that's between him and God) is in the past and just as God has forgiven him already, so do I."

God tells us in Isaiah 55:8, "For my thoughts are not your thoughts; neither are your ways my ways." He also tells us in Jeremiah 29:11, "For I know the thoughts that I think toward you, saith the Lord, thoughts of peace, and not of evil, to give you an expected end."

Let God get your undivided attention today. He has good things in store for those who seek Him with all their heart.

The message for today: God, our Heavenly Father, knows best.

Prayer: Dear Heavenly Father, Thank You for getting my undivided attention. Speak, Lord, for Your servant is listening.

May 20 – Down, but Not Out!

We are troubled on every side, yet not distressed; we are perplexed, but not in despair; persecuted, but not forsaken; cast down, but not destroyed. (II Corinthians 4:7)

If we could follow II Corinthians 4, we would be the most victorious Christians around! Paul's faith in Jesus carried him through any trial Satan could bring to him.

In 4:1 he said that he could not give up (faint) because he was commissioned by God to lead people to Jesus, his Savior.

In 4:2 he said that he had renounced the "hidden things of dishonesty". He didn't lie any more.

In 4:3, 4 he said that Satan, "the god of this world," tries to keep people in darkness, but the glorious gospel shines through.

In 4:5 he said that he didn't preach himself, but Christ Jesus.

In 4:6, 7 he said that God's light has shown into our hearts through Jesus Christ; and because of that, we have the Holy Spirit in our lives. II Corinthians 4:7 goes on to say that the Holy Spirit is our "treasure in earthen vessels," so that the excellency of the power may be of God and not of us. If we listen to the Holy Spirit in every decision, we will never make bad decisions!

After telling us all the good things, Paul tells us that he has trouble and confusion; but through it all, he remembers that the Holy Spirit of God is in control. He says he might be cast down, but he's still alive. What an optimist!

The message for today: Whatever is true, honest, just, pure, and lovely – think on these things.

Prayer: Dear Heavenly Father, Help me to learn from the Apostle Paul to always look to Jesus in every trial.

May 21 – I'm Telling!!!

Let us therefore come boldly unto the throne of grace that we may obtain mercy and find grace to help in time of need. (Hebrews 4:16)

"I'm telling!" Veronica said as she stomped off the playground heading for her mother who was sitting on a bench enjoying a book. "What happened?" asked mom as she wiped her tears. "Jimmy pushed me off the swing and look; my shirt got torn, and I skinned my knee!" she said sobbing. Mom quickly opened her purse, took out a tissue and a package of band-aides and began cleaning Veronica's knee. Then she walked over to the car and brought back a clean shirt and an icy-pop out of the cooler. "Here. That should make you feel better. Now you sit here and enjoy your icy-pop while I go deal with Jimmy."

As I watched I thought: 'That's just like God'. He always cares for His children. He comforts, heals, restores, takes revenge for us, and disciplines. While meditating on what I had just witnessed, I realized that Veronica did not go to tell her playmates all about what Jimmy had done. She went straight for mom because she knew that mom would comfort, heal, restore and then deal with Jimmy.

The Bible teaches us to pray for each other, to carry each other's burdens, cry with those who cry, rejoice with those who rejoice; but ultimately, the solution to any situation is to "Take it to the Lord in prayer."

The message for today: Let God solve every problem you have today. He's waiting on you to come to Him first.

Prayer: Dear Heavenly Father, I'm glad I can trust You to keep my secrets and solve my problems. No one else can do that for me.

May 22—Religion or Relationship?

Submit yourselves to God…draw near to God, and He will draw near to you. (James 4:7, 8)

Have you noticed how everyone has a perception of God? Some people think He is a mean judge sitting up in Heaven just waiting for us to mess up so He can punish us. Some think that He has a big book of "Good Deeds and Bad Deeds" that He marks daily. Very few people really know the true and living God.

It has been said that religion is people reaching up to God (working their way to heaven), but relationship is God reaching down to us through Jesus Christ and His death on the Cross for us sinners.

In II Chronicles 20 Jehoshaphat, King of Judah, shows us a picture of what true relationship with God means. The enemy was coming against him; and he was afraid so he "set himself to seek the Lord". He went to God and just worshiped Him by telling Him how great He was. Then he told God something we should say every day, "O our God…we are powerless before this great multitude who are coming against us; nor do we know what to do, but our eyes are on You."

God answered the king by telling him to go to battle against the enemy because the battle wasn't his; it was God's. II Chronicles 20:15-17 says, "You need not fight in this battle; take your position (of worship); stand and see the deliverance of the Lord. Don't be afraid – the Lord is with you."

The message for today: Work at your relationship with God, not your religion.

Prayer: Dear Heavenly Father, I am powerless and I don't know what to do, but my eyes are upon You.

May 23 – Don't Give Up!

...the race is not to the swift nor the battle to the strong..., but time and chance happen to everyone. (Ecclesiastes 9:11)

God created us all with a specific plan in mind. He knew before the foundation of the world that you would be reading this devotional today. He knows you are in prison today; but I have found that, even though God is in total control, He never forces us to do right. He allows us to go our own way and do our own thing until He is ready to stop us through circumstances.

I needed to accept God's plan for my life by faith and obey His every command, but I messed up by not trusting Him with every part of my life. I thought I could handle it all, but He showed me that I could not. I needed to rely on Him and Him alone.

God has given each of us gifts, which He wants us to develop as we grow in the faith. The problem is that Satan sees our progress and tries to stop it. He chokes the seed of righteousness planted in our hearts (Read Mark 4:14-20) and wants us to stay in the congregation of the wicked.

The only way we can go forward with the Lord is to let the seed of the Word of God grow in us on a day-to-day basis. We must maintain our walk with God.

The message for today: Just "keep on keeping on." (Ecclesiastes 9:11)

Prayer: Dear Heavenly Father, I know it is only by Your grace that I have strength to run every day in the race of life. Help me to win the race and be with You for eternity.

✝
May 24 – I'm Blessed

O taste and see that the Lord is good! Blessed (happy, fortunate, to be envied) is the man who trusts and takes refuge in Him. (Psalm 34:8)

When I first got locked up, I was in deep despair. My mother, children, and relatives were out of state. My husband and I were separated, and the few friends I had suddenly "disappeared".

I had tried everything I could think of to be happy, but I was still a defeated person. In desperation, I tried calling on Jesus for help. I begged Him to get me out of prison.

I started to pray and read the Bible every day. I was told to thank Him – no matter what – every day. I started to praise and worship God; and as time went by, my mind rose higher and higher in the things of God. I stopped thinking about prison so much and started thinking about Jesus. He had answered my prayer, at least spiritually. I was truly "out of prison" in my spirit, even though I was still incarcerated physically!

The more I learned of the Bible, the more peace came upon me. I just wanted to learn about the Lord in a way that I can't explain. He had put His Holy Spirit in me, and now I was free!

Psalm 34:8 tells us to taste and see how sweet the Lord is. I have tasted of this Christian life, and I don't ever want to return to my old ways.

The message for today: O magnify the Lord with me, and let us exalt His name together. (Psalm 34:3)

Prayer: Dear Heavenly Father, Thank You for freeing me from myself and my surroundings. Thank You for supernatural peace.

May 25 – Dream Makers

Now Joseph had a dream and he told it to his brothers,
and they hated him still more. (Genesis 37:5)

Joseph had a dream which the devil tried to cancel; but he
couldn't, because what the devil meant for evil, God worked
out for good. Joseph was sold into slavery and went to prison,
but God still fulfilled his dream.

Do you have a dream that never came to pass? Has God
given you a "Rhema" word that someday you would do
something for Him, but nothing ever happens? Well, take
heart. God can bring your dream to reality.

I have a former schoolmate who was born with an illness
that left him with only 20% use of his right arm and leg. People
told him that he wasn't going to amount to anything. After all
the negative comments, he developed low self-esteem; but he
still did his best at everything he tried. He graduated from high
school and put himself through college. He learned to play
guitar, golf, and pilot a plane.

All the negativity did not stop him. I think it made him
stronger, and he fulfilled every dream he had during those sad
childhood years.

The message for today: Tell God your secret dream and ask
Him to bring it to pass.

Prayer: Dear Heavenly Father, Thank You for loving me
enough to give me hope. Help me to love You enough to trust
You to fulfill my dreams.

✝

May 26 – Hidden Treasure

For I know the thoughts and plans that I have for you, says the Lord…for welfare and peace and not for evil, to give you hope in your final outcome. (Jeremiah 29:11)

One day as I was reading Exodus 2, God showed me that Moses was a "hidden treasure". He had to be hidden by his mother for three months after he was born in order not to be killed by the Pharaoh, who had ordered all Jewish baby boys to be murdered since the Israelites were increasing by alarming numbers.

Because of the plans of God, Moses was rescued by Pharaoh's daughter who raised him as her own son. He learned how to act in the palaces of Egypt. He learned the language and the customs of Egypt (knowledge he would need in order to go up against Pharaoh).

As he was growing up, being cared for by his real Jewish mother, he was taught the ways of Jehovah, the true and living God. Even though his mother had to hide her feelings and true identity, she taught him who he really was.

One day he saw one of his Hebrew people being beaten, so he killed the Egyptian who was beating him. When he was discovered, he ran to the wilderness, right into God's plan for his life.

Maybe that is where you are today – in the wilderness, right in the middle of God's plan to get your attention. Our Heavenly Father sees the hidden treasure in your life and wants you to discover it, too.

The message for today: God will have His will in our lives, regardless.

Prayer: Dear Heavenly Father, Please instruct me and teach me in the way I should go to fulfill Your plans.

May 27 – Don't Be a Stranger

*They said, "An Egyptian delivered us from
the shepherds; also, he drew water for us and
watered the flock." (Exodus 2:19)*

Moses was a stranger in a strange land after fleeing from the wicked Pharaoh of Egypt, but at least he was alive. He soon became acquainted with the people of Midian, got married, and had a child in that desert land.

Moses had murdered a man, but God was still willing to use him, because He saw the bigger picture of the Israelites.

God sees the bigger picture of our lives, too. He is still the same God whom Moses served, and He works all things together for good to those of us who love Him and are the called, according to His purpose for our lives.

Being a prisoner, I am a stranger in a strange land, too. A Jamaican in the United States doesn't have it easy – no matter where she is placed; but God wanted to use me, just like He wanted to use Moses. He inspired me to write this message to you to let you know that you can be used as a servant of the Most High God, even if you are in a strange and scary land.

Being out of our "element" and comfortable surroundings can actually be an asset to show God's sovereignty to others.

The message for today: Jehovah-shammah, my Lord, is with me everywhere I go.

Prayer: Dear Heavenly Father, Thank You that You will never leave me or forsake me.

May 28 — Are You Faithful?

Moreover, it is required of stewards
that a man should be found faithful (proving
himself worthy of trust). (II Corinthians 4:2)

God is looking for faithfulness in His children. It doesn't matter who you are or where you have come from, God still looks for your personal faithfulness to Him.

A young man was interviewed for a management job by a pastor for a position in a store that sold Christian materials. The pastor told him that he was not experienced enough and thus not qualified for the job.

A few days later, the pastor went to a church where he would be preaching the following Sunday, and to his surprise, there was the young man who had interviewed for the job. It was late Saturday night, and he was there working faithfully to get everything ready for the crusade, with no one watching but the Lord.

The pastor went up to him and told him that he had reconsidered. "How about coming in on Monday morning for a second interview?" he asked the young man. He saw faithfulness, which spoke more loudly than any words ever could.

How about you? Can God count on you to be faithful in the little things of life? He tells us in His Word that if we are faithful in the little things, He will reward us and give us more because He sees our heart motives.

The message for today: "Well done, thou good and faithful servant." That's what I want to hear as Jesus welcomes me to heaven.

Prayer: Dear Heavenly Father, Thank You for the Holy Spirit who helps me to be faithful to my Savior, Jesus.

May 29 – Going Around in Circles

Be sure your sin will find you out... (Numbers 32:23)

Consequences come from disobedient acts. Many times prisoners think they can get away with sin, but natural laws and God's laws won't allow that to happen.

No matter who we are or how important we are, wrong actions cause problems. I was one of those people who thought she could make bad choices and still not get caught. How wrong I was! I ended up in prison. Thankfully, I have found Jesus as my personal Savior, and I am making right choices now. When I am released, I will still serve Him forever. Wrong life choices are no longer an option for me.

The children of Israel (the Jews) were disobedient and rebellious to the Lord. Their main form of rebellion was grumbling and complaining, but it had enormous consequences. The journey to the Promised Land normally would take 11 days, but it took the Israelites 40 years! They just kept going around in circles. Every time God tried to teach them something, they limited His power by doubting and complaining. He tried for 40 years, and finally had to kill a whole generation of people before allowing them to go into the land of Canaan.

The Bible can teach us so much about life and how to make good decisions which will have good results. Start your journey with God today and enter His promise land.

The message for today: Read the Word of God daily, and it will keep you from sin.

Prayer: Dear Heavenly Father, Please help me to make choices in life and be pleasing to You.

May 30 – You're Important

God has established strength because of His foes, that He might silence the enemy and the avenger. (Psalm 8:2)

In prison, it is very easy to be discouraged. Walking by faith is a difficult task, because all one can see is confinement and rules.

One day as I started to write yet another devotional, I was very sad because my fellow prisoners said some discouraging words the night before. One part of me asked, "What's the use of all this, Lord?" How can I make a difference in anyone's life in here? God's Spirit spoke to me and told me to keep going – no matter what.

I thought of Psalm 8:2 where the Psalmist says that God has given strength to us to silence our enemies. The writer went on to encourage my heart when he asked the same question I have asked over and over to the Lord, "What is man that You are mindful of him and You care for him?" Even though I am one person in prison, I am still a puzzle piece of God's plan that only I can fulfill in His great scheme of things. That is exciting!

You are also important to God. So many prisoners say that they believe that everyone else is important to God, but not them. I share with them that God loved them so much He gave His one and only Son to die for them. If no one else had ever been born but them, Jesus would still have come to earth to give His life's blood to save their souls.

The message for today: Silence Satan by believing God's Word.

Prayer: Dear Heavenly Father, Please prepare, strengthen, and direct my heart, and hear my cry to never quit. (Psalm 10:18)

May 31 – Following God's Ways

Hear, my son, and accept my sayings, and the years of your life will be many. (Proverbs 4:10)

Have you ever asked why God allows children to die? I have, and there is no answer, except to say that He is sovereign and knows the beginning from the end. We cannot second-guess our Heavenly Father, who always acts in love.

Psalm 115:3 says that our "God is in the heavens, and He does whatever He pleases." God has a plan, and no one can change it. He chooses to take some people when they are young, and others are allowed to live long lives. Why?

The Word of God says that "it is appointed unto man once to die..." (Hebrews 9:27). God knows the exact moment of our death because He has appointed it. However, the Bible says that we can extend our lives by obeying a simple commandment, "Honor your father and your mother that your days may be prolonged..." (Exodus 20:12).

Psalm 34:12 asks, "Who is the man who desires life and loves length of days that he may see good?" Then the writer gives the answer when he says that we should do four things in order to prolong our days on the earth:

1) Keep our tongues from speaking evil
2) Depart from evil
3) Do good
4) Seek peace and pursue it

The message for today: Following God's ways has great rewards!

Prayer: Dear Heavenly Father, Only You know what lies ahead in my life, but I know You are leading me, so I will rest in You.

Notes

JUNE

June 1 – Use the Right Door

Jesus said, "I am the Door; anyone who enters in through me will be saved". (John 10:9)

Jesus told people that He was the living water and that they would never thirst again once they truly asked Him into their lives. He said that He was the bread of life, and anyone who tasted this bread would never be hungry again (John 6:35). He told people that He was the only door to heaven.

Satan wants us to believe that "religion" can save us, so he has cleverly devised a plan that tells us that, if our good works outweigh our bad works, we can expect to go to heaven. People work so hard, trying to make sure that they have done enough. I know people from a large religion who go to church every morning of their lives, hoping that they will be good enough to get to the first level of heaven.

Other religions teach that, once you say a salvation prayer, no matter how you live, you are going to go to heaven. That doctrine is sending many thousands of people to hell.

Jesus Christ offered Himself once for our sins, and He desires that we will accept Him into our hearts and have relationship with Him – not religion. Jesus did all the work of salvation. It is our part to believe that He is the only way to heaven, to spend time with Him, and to put Him first in our lives.

The message for today: Religion says, "Do". Jesus says, "Done". Accept Him today.

Prayer: Dear Heavenly Father, Help me to know the real Jesus who is the only way to heaven.

June 2 – Forever Changed

But know that the Lord hath set apart him who is godly
for Himself; the Lord will hear when I call unto Him.
(Psalm 4:3)

After five long and lonely years, Kelley walked out of prison, a free woman. Her story is unlike the typical inmate's story because she was incarcerated and held without trial for five years.

When I read Psalm 4:3, the Lord showed me that He sets the godly apart for His purposes, and all that happens to them has eternal significance. So it was with my friend Kelley. Little did she know that ending up in prison would forever change her life.

She accepted Jesus Christ into her life in 1998 in a church service at the jail, and soon it was evident that God was changing her from the inside out. She desired God and His Word. She studied everything she could get her hands on.

Many people came in and out of her life – some good, some bad, but Kelley held on to God and His promises and lived victoriously most of the time. She started crying unto God for release and trusting His promise to hear her prayers a few years ago.

Through circumstances engineered by God, she walked to freedom after learning the lessons necessary for her to remain true and faithful to her Lord.

Through loving Christian friends and family, she is getting her life back, but the lessons learned at Jesus' feet in prison will anchor her life forever.

The message for today: God's preparation for our service comes in ways that only He can engineer.

Prayer: Dear Heavenly Father, Please help me to see that You have a good plan for my life. Show me Yourself in everyday life.

June 3 – Friends

Julius gave Paul liberty to go unto his friends and refresh himself. (Acts 27:3)

You are an answer to someone's prayer for a friend. Your influence will go far to be a comfort, a counselor, and a sweet incense to a hurting soul.

The Bible says, "He who would be a friend must show himself friendly" (Proverbs 18:24). Ask the Lord to make you a friendly person. Ask Him to get you out of your own little world and take you where He wants you to go. You will be surprised at the opportunities He will give you to be there for some hurting person.

Jesus is our greatest example of a true friend:

- He does not judge you, but He listens quietly while you pour out your heart to Him.
- He does not monopolize your time, but He lets you have your space when you need it.
- He is not possessive and insecure when you have other friends.
- He is always there with a kind word and a loving nature.
- He never brings up your past failures or makes fun of you.

The message for today: Jesus is the best Friend anyone could have.

Prayer: Dear Heavenly Father, Please use me to show people how kind and thoughtful You really are.

June 4 – What Fragrance are You Wearing?

For we are the sweet fragrance of Christ unto God, among those who are being saved and among those who are perishing... (II Corinthians 2:15)

While I was incarcerated, I used to identify the staff members by the perfume they wore at night. When I was locked down in my cell, I could tell which staff member was walking by, just by the scent of her cologne.

Every Christian should also be recognized for wearing a perfume, the fragrance of Jesus, the fragrance that emits love in their life. That aroma should be noticeable in all their actions. This fragrance of Christ cannot be bought at any cosmetic counter; it cannot be bottled or sold. This particular perfume is imported by the Holy Spirit and is worth so much!

We are to waft a subtle yet noticeable influence toward others by the very nature of God within us. No matter where we go, people should know that we are Christians because of the word of our testimony and the impartation of our Christ-like attitude.

A tree is known by its fruit. Apple trees produce apples. The Holy Spirit in us produces the fruit of the Spirit (Galatians 5:22, 23). Do you have this fruit? It is evidenced by love, joy, peace, longsuffering, gentleness, goodness, faith, meekness, and self-control. Just try to fight with someone who is walking in the fruit of the Spirit. You will have a tough time fighting against the sweet fragrance of the Holy Spirit in a person's life.

The message for today: We are God's workmanship, created in Christ Jesus for good works. (Ephesians 2:10)

Prayer: Dear Heavenly Father, Help my witness for Jesus Christ to be sweet and fragrant, no matter what I am going through. Use me right where I am.

June 5 – Check Yourself

Let a man thoroughly examine himself, and only
when he has done that, should he eat of the bread and
drink of the cup. (II Corinthians 11:28)

Jesus told the disciples that in taking Communion, they remembered His death until He would come back. (I Cor. 11:26)

Most people take The Lord's Supper as a ritual, with no confession or remorse for their sins. I heard a pastor tell his congregation the following: "If you are not a believer in Jesus Christ, go ahead and take Communion. It won't hurt you, but it won't help you either. However, if you are born of the Spirit of God and you take Communion with known sin in your life, you are opening yourself to God's judgment. Let's quiet our hearts right now and confess to our Father any sin in our lives so that we will not partake unworthily."

I am active in church and love to serve the Lord. I am an usher and a member of the worship team. One Sunday morning I went to church and it was Communion Sunday. I reached out to take the bread and instantly remembered a disagreement I had the week before with another sister, to whom I had not apologized. I could not take Communion because I would have brought God's judgment on myself.

I Corinthians 11:28 tells us to thoroughly examine ourselves before we partake of The Lord's Supper. If we don't, I Corinthians 11:30 comes into play, "That careless and unworthy participation is the reason many of you are weak and sickly…"

The message for today: If we judge ourselves, God doesn't have to.

Prayer: Dear Heavenly Father, Please help me to live a pure life before You and keep short accounts with You.

June 6 – The Choice is Mine

Do not be deceived…whatever a man sows, that only is what he will reap. (Galatians 6:7)

Before I actually was sentenced to go to prison, I prayed fervently to God and asked that I would go free. I thought God was such a loving God that maybe He would not let me go to prison, even though I had committed sin.

I knew I deserved prison time; but once again I tried to convince myself that, since I was not the prime suspect, I would go free. What a lie from Satan!

After my sentencing, I asked God why I had to go to prison. It was so unmerciful of Him! God immediately showed me Galatians 6:7, which told me that I had been paid, according to my works. I was sad and discouraged, but I started seeking God in a way I had never sought Him before. To my surprise, He showed up in my cell and started ministering to me by His precious Holy Spirit. Soon I began to get peace as I read Psalm 91 over and over again.

He showed me how much He loved me and that He was the God of the second chance. My life started changing. God truly had shown me His salvation! It was a great relief to know that although I will pay for what I have done, He will satisfy my life and be with me forever.

The message for today: Submit yourself to God; resist the devil and he will flee from you; draw near to God, and He will draw near to you. Cleanse your hands, you sinners, and purify your hearts, you double-minded. (James 4:7, 8)

Prayer: Dear Heavenly Father, I praise You for Your presence in my life!

June 7 – Peace from Above (Part 1)

Jesus said, "I am leaving you with a gift – peace of mind and heart. And the peace I give isn't like the peace the world gives. So don't be troubled or afraid." (John 14:27)

Worry, confusion, and agitation are all around us. Prisoners get used to confusion and chaos. They are with people daily who have never been around peace. They have grown up with hurt and sin, so they don't know how to be at peace.

In prison, when I asked Jesus to forgive my sin and come into my heart, the Holy Spirit came into my very being and infused it with peace and rest. I could actually feel myself resting in what the Bible said about this supernatural peace, in spite of all that was trying to steal that perfect peace.

Jesus was talking to His disciples in John 16:33, and He told them that major life crises would come, but then He added, "I have told you these things, so that in Me you may have perfect peace and confidence. In the world you will have tribulation and trials and distress and frustration; but be of good cheer (take courage; be confident, certain, undaunted)! For I have overcome the world. (I have deprived it of power to harm you and have conquered it for you.)"

The message for today: It's time for God's peace to rule your heart, mind, and body.

Prayer: Dear Heavenly Father, Peace, peace, wonderful peace, coming down from the Father above. Sweep over my spirit, Oh Savior I pray, in fathomless billows of love!

June 8 – Peace from Above (Part 2)

Jesus said, "I am leaving you with a gift – peace of mind and heart." (John 14:27)

After learning that the Holy Spirit was my Source of Peace with God in prison, things didn't worry me as much. Once I finally realized that Satan's main goal is to cause me to doubt, that is to lose my peace, I started talking and acting differently. I took control over him by deliberately seeking peace and pursuing it through reading the Word daily. The Bible comforts when no person can. The Bible gives hope.

Jesus is the Source of Peace. All He needed to do in Mark 4:39 was to speak to the wind and the sea, and immediately the storm ceased. We need to speak to our storm with Jesus' authority and command peace to come into the situation.

Our Heavenly Father is the Source of Peace. Jeremiah 29:7 gives direction as to how I should pray for the prison I am in. God our Father tells us that we are to "seek the peace and welfare of the 'city' to which He has caused us to be carried away captive; and pray to the Lord for it, for in the welfare of the city in which you live you will have welfare."

Even in prison, God can make the chaos cease, both externally and internally, as we trust His power over every situation.

The message for today: Start taking control over the devil by countering every negative, doubtful thought with this verse: "May the God of hope fill me with joy and peace in believing that I may abound in hope through the power of the Holy Spirit." (Romans 15:13)

Prayer: Dear Heavenly Father, I praise You for Your peace that is available to me!

✝
June 9 – Fulfillment

For a branch cannot produce fruit if it is severed
from the vine, and you cannot be fruitful apart
from me – Jesus. (John 15:4)

Someone has said that you are as close to God as you want to be. For years I made excuses that I never got anything from reading the Bible and praying.

What a revelation came to my heart when I got to know the "real Jesus". I had known a religious icon that I prayed to when I was in big trouble, but I never bothered with Him when things were fine.

Since God had a higher plan for my life, He allowed me to go to prison. God knows how to touch each of us when He wants to get His point across. I begged Him to teach me about His nature and character, and teach me He did!

As I grew, I desired to read my Bible daily. I desired to pray for people, instead of things. Something was stirring me to tell others about my Lord. One day a lady told me that she wanted to be like me because she saw Jesus in me!

It all started to make sense. We ask Jesus into our life. He causes us to desire Him; and when we do, we start changing our actions and attitudes. When our attitudes start changing, our actions follow. Soon we say with Paul, "For to me to live is Christ." We bear fruit for the eternal Kingdom of God! What a perfect cycle!

The message for today: Healthy plants produce sweet, delicious fruit.

Prayer: Dear Heavenly Father, Thank You for pruning my life so I would bear more fruit for Your Kingdom.

✝
June 10 – Good King Gone Bad

The Lord is able to give you much more than this!
(II Chronicles 25:9)

Amaziah was a good king over the land of Judah with God's favor on him, but disobedience caused him to end up badly. The king decided to raid several cities and take their wooden idols home with him. Then he made a second bad decision and worshiped those idols! He knew better than to sin against the Living God, but he chose to disobey the first Commandment, "Thou shalt have no other gods before Me." (Exodus 20:3)

The Lord was angry with this disobedience and sent a prophet to talk to Amaziah; but the king rudely interrupted the prophet and asked, "Since when have I asked your advice? Be quiet now before I have you killed!"

The prophet told him that God was going to destroy him because of this rebellion of idol worship. (II Chronicles 25:20). Fifteen years later, his enemies assassinated him, just as the prophet had said!

All Amaziah would have had to do was to turn from his sin and give God His rightful place in his life and God's first statement to Amaziah would have come true, "The Lord is able to give you much more than this!"

The message for today: Today, God offers you life or death. Choose life! (Deut. 30:19, 20)

Prayer: Dear Heavenly Father, Thank You for providing the best for me. Help me to go after Your ways from now on.

June 11 – Shaking Like a Leaf

Do not be afraid for I have ransomed you. I have called you by name. You are mine. When you go through deep waters and great trouble, I will be with you. When you go through rivers of difficulty you will not drown. When you walk through the fire of oppression, you will not be burned up. The flames will not consume you. For I am the Lord your God, the Holy One of Israel – Your Savior. (Isaiah 43:1-3)

Can you picture yourself in court, waiting for your name to be called? All at once, Isaiah 43:1-3 comes to your mind. You quietly say it over and over, "Do not be afraid…I am Your Savior."

The power of God's Word is so great that circumstances actually change for the better when we believe and claim God's promises. Think of these scriptures in your own situation.

1) God says, "Do not be afraid." That doesn't mean that you will not feel fear. You might be "shaking like a leaf", but you know God is with you.

2) God says, "I have ransomed you." Jesus paid a huge price to free you when He died on the cross.

3) God says that you are special and loved by Him. "I have called you by name. You are mine."

4) God promises three times that He will be with you in great trouble, in rivers of difficulty, and in the "fire of oppression" (when everything goes wrong).

The message for today: The battle is not yours, but the Lord's.

Prayer: Dear Heavenly Father, Thank You for fighting my battles for me.

✝

June 12 – Lord, Break My Will

Rebellion is as the sin of witchcraft and stubbornness is as iniquity and idolatry. (I Samuel 15:23)

It is said that if a child's will isn't broken by the time he is five, he will become a juvenile delinquent. A child must know that his parents won't allow rebellious behavior, or he will continue in it. As he grows, this behavior plays itself out into worse things than childhood temper tantrums. The rude and demanding, mean and disobedient child becomes the rude and demanding, mean and disobedient teenager and adult.

We are exactly the same way when we accept Jesus into our lives. God created us; so when He looks at our life, He says, "I'd better break this child's will before five years go by, because I want his obedience – not his rebellion." We call it Christian growth, but it is really our wonderful heavenly Parent caring enough to make us want to obey. The Bible calls it "chastening" (child training). When the Holy Spirit comes in at salvation, our will (new nature) wants to obey God – not Satan or our flesh.

Our old nature is perverse and rebellious and refuses to be enlightened by God, and the spiritual battle rages until God or Satan wins. The remedy is obedience.

The message for today: The Holy Spirit is your dynamite that blows rebellion out of your life.

Prayer: Dear Heavenly Father, I confess that I am rebellious and want my own way. Please forgive me and help me to obey You.

June 13 – A Cheerful Worker

A cheerful mind works healing. (Proverbs 17:22)

In four small chapters of the book of Ruth, we see God's eternal plan for Jesus, the Messiah, to be born.

Naomi and Elimelech moved from Bethlehem to Moab, and their sons married Moabite women. All seemed to be going well until all three women lost their husbands. Naomi was so depressed that she decided to return to Bethlehem. She told her daughters-in-law to go back to their relatives, but Ruth refused.

After arriving in Bethlehem, Ruth worked in the fields of Boaz, a relative of her former father-in-law. Boaz was a cheerful, generous man.

Boaz cared for his field workers, and his kindness made history because of Ruth, the foreigner who came to "glean" in his fields. Every day she worked hard, picking up the grain that the workers left behind at their boss's request – on purpose. Ruth couldn't understand why he was so kind. When she asked him why he cared so much to provide for her needs, he told her that he had heard about her loving care for her mother-in-law.

Ruth and Boaz later married, and they had a son named Obed. He was Jesse's father, and Jesse was David's father. David was the ancestor of Jesus Christ!

The message for today: A happy heart is good medicine and a cheerful mind works healing. (Proverbs 17:22)

Prayer: Dear Heavenly Father, Help me to show others how wonderful You are every day by my attitude.

June 14 – Yesterday's Gone

I, even I, am He Who blots out and cancels your transgressions, for My own sake, and I will not remember your sins. (Isaiah 43:25)

Many times in our Christian life, Satan tries to bring up our past and make us feel depressed and unworthy. If we listen to him, we live life at a sub-standard level, thinking that we are terrible, in spite of God's goodness to us.

When I got saved, I read the books of Leviticus and Deuteronomy. All my past offences surfaced while reading those books of the Bible, and I confessed them one by one until I knew they were all forgiven. What a freedom I experienced in knowing that God had said in Isaiah 43:25 that He blotted out (forever!!) my sins for His own sake and that He had forgotten them! If He could forget my sins, why shouldn't I? Every time Satan brought my thoughts to how terrible I was, I just told him to get away from me because I was forgiven.

The message for today: Ask God to forgive every known and unknown sin you have ever committed. Ask Him to lead you in the way of everlasting life, and He will.

Prayer: Dear Heavenly Father, Thank You that no one can bring any charge against me because I am Your chosen and acquitted child!

June 15 – Harvest Time

"...let us run with patience the race that is set before us." (Hebrews 12:1)

My friend said something profound to me once. I told her that we reap what we sow, and she added, "But usually not in the same season". Every act in our life usually takes time to produce a result.

Someone has said that insanity is "doing the same thing day after day but expecting different results." I prayed for years to lose weight, but one day I realized that it was not going to happen without changing my routine and eating habits. Last year I started eating more proteins and vegetables, and less bread and pasta. I walked two miles per day, and in 90 days, I had trimmed off 24 pounds! I was excited! By continuing my strict regime with patience, I have stayed exactly the same weight for over six months now, and I feel great.

God showed me II Peter 1:3-8, and three words changed my actions and attitudes regarding why I couldn't lose weight before. I had good intentions but I failed every time, until I read, "Add to your faith, virtue, and to your virtue, knowledge, and to your knowledge self-control, and to your self-control, patience."

There it was! Knowledge, self-control, and patience made my victory possible. Start today, and with God's help, you will see that planning for future results really does work.

The message for today: A farmer doesn't "cram" for a harvest. He patiently plans ahead and waits for it.

Prayer: Dear Heavenly Father, Please give me knowledge, self-control, and patience to continue my race and finish it well.

June 16 – Dare to Dream

Keep on asking and it will be given you; keep on seeking and you will find; keep on knocking and the door will be opened to you. (Matthew 7:7)

I read a plaque many years ago, but I have never forgotten the saying on it:

Successful people are dreamers
Who find their dream too important
To remain in the realm of fantasy
But daily toil in the service of that dream
Until they can see it with their eyes
And touch it with their hands.

After being released from prison, my friend asked God to help her become a successful business woman. She started working as a counter clerk in Church's Chicken. Within two years she became a manager, and today she travels the country, teaching managers how to train new employees to sell chicken!

Why don't you dream a little? Ask the Lord Jesus to direct your paths as you dream. Think within the realm of your skills and desires.

Finish this sentence: If money were no object and I could do anything I wanted, I would _____.

The message for today: Dare to dream, because Jesus loves you.

Prayer: Dear Heavenly Father, I commit my way unto You. I trust also in You. Please bring my dreams to pass in Your perfect time and way.

June 17 – Peace of Mind

Jesus said, "I am leaving you with a gift – peace of mind and heart." (John 14:27)

Confusion and agitation are all around us. Prisoners are used to confusion and spend time with people who know nothing of peace because their up-bringing has been one of hurt and sin.

When I asked Jesus to come into my heart, the Holy Spirit came into my very being and infused it with peace and rest. I could actually feel myself resting in what the Bible said about this supernatural peace.

Jesus said that "In the world you will have tribulation, but I have overcome the world" (John 16:33). After learning that the Holy Spirit was my source of peace with God and myself, things didn't worry me as much. I was told that Satan's main goal is to cause me to doubt, that is to lose my peace. Once I finally realized this, I took control over him by deliberately seeking peace and pursuing it through reading the Word. The Bible comforts when no person can. The Bible gives hope. All Satan comes to do is to kill, steal, and destroy our peace and hope.

Start taking control over the devil by countering every negative, doubtful thought with this verse: "May the God of hope fill you with joy and peace in believing so that you may abound in hope by the power of the Holy Spirit." (Romans 15:13)

The message for today: Nothing is as important as peace in life.

Prayer: Dear Heavenly Father, please give me Your gift of peace.

June 18 – Overflowing Love

I came that they may have and enjoy life, and have it in abundance (to the full), till it overflows. (John 10:10)

Being an experienced inmate gives me opportunities to speak to new residents as they come into the jail system. I share with them the things they will experience in jail, and they know they have a friend in a very unfriendly new world.

After being torn from my family and friends and being incarcerated, I had a difficult time for years. Fear would come upon me, and I felt like giving up on life. But God kept me safe. Now I live my days in joy that no one can take away from me because I have Jesus Christ in my life.

The enemy still creeps in when I become unaware of his trickery and deception; but even in that I have overflowing love for my fellow prisoners. As I share with them, I tell them how much Jesus loves them, and many times they ask Him to be their Savior.

In John 10:10 Jesus said that He came that we may have life and have it more abundantly. He wants us to have life that is full and overflowing with joy, even in prison. Abundant life would not be possible if Jesus hadn't come to save us from our sins. Eternal life is not something we work for. Jesus did all the work on the Cross of Calvary.

The message for today: Every experience we have and every person we meet is God's preparation for a future that only He can see.

Prayer: Dear Heavenly Father, Thank You for the hard times, as well as the good times. Teach me to love You so much that Your life will flow through me abundantly.

June 19 – Don't Miss Your Appointment

The woman said to Jesus, "I know that Messiah is coming, He Who is called the Christ; and when he arrives, He will tell us everything we need to know and make it clear to us." (John 4:25)

Little did the Samaritan woman realize that she was actually talking to The Messiah in John 4! The Bible says that Jesus needed to go through Samaria, a place that was absolutely not frequented by the Jews! But Jesus knew there was a woman there, who needed to know Him personally. Because of her salvation, she caused hundreds of people to believe on Jesus.

Every day when I awaken in prison, I ask the Lord to send me to anyone He chooses that day. I love to watch how He works as I go about my daily routine. One month I asked Jesus to guide me to women who needed to know Him, and two prisoners asked Him into their hearts! I was so humbled and blessed that He would use me!

That's how it is with you. You have influence that no one else has. You can touch hearts that no one else can. God wants to use you daily, but He needs your availability and commitment to Him. If you know Jesus Christ as your true Lord and Savior, ask Him to use you in any way He chooses. You will be amazed at the answers to prayer in just a few months!

The message for today: Don't miss any of God's special appointments to be used of Him.

Prayer: Dear Heavenly Father, Please fill me with Your Holy Spirit today and use me in any way You choose. I am available to You, Lord.

June 20 – A Good Steward

He who is faithful in little things is faithful also in much, and he who is dishonest in little things is dishonest also in much. (Luke 16:10)

We all need God's point of view on managing our time and money, even in prison. God tells us that if we fail to handle any part of our life properly, we keep back His blessings from our lives.

I read a true story about a man who was blessed because of how he took care of things. He couldn't afford a new car. The floor board of his fifteen-year-old car was actually worn through, and he could see the pavement as he drove. He prayed for a new car but kept taking care of the one he had. He washed it and kept it shiny and clean. Then one day a lady at his church asked him if he could use a good car that she didn't want anymore, and she gave it to him!

The Bible tells us that "no servant is able to serve two masters; for either he will hate the one and love the other, or he will stand by the one and despise the other. You cannot serve God and money (or anything in which you trust, and on which you rely)." (Luke 16:13)

Many times our devotion is split between God and the world. We want to have one foot in the world and the other in the Kingdom, and it doesn't work.

The message for today: Get everything the Father wants to give you by seeking first the Kingdom of God and His righteousness. Then everything else will be added to you. I promise.

Prayer: Dear Heavenly Father, Help me to be balanced and manage Your assets well.

June 21 – Don't Forget about Church

Give attentive, continuous care to watching over one
another in noble activities, not forsaking or neglecting your
assembling together as believers, as is the habit of some
people, but encouraging one another... (Hebrews 10:25)

Unsaved prisoners watch everything Christian inmates do so they can judge them when the opportunity arises. In prison there are many temptations for young Christians, so they stick together and go to church every time the doors open. But the unbelievers watch like hawks; and every time a Christian makes a mistake, they are quick to judge and say, "I thought you were supposed to be a Christian! You go to church all the time, and it's not helping at all!"

You have heard the old saying, "I'm not perfect – just forgiven", and how true it is. Romans 8:1 says that "there is now no condemnation to those who are in Christ Jesus, who live and walk, not after the dictates of the flesh, but after the dictates of the Spirit".

In situations where you are talked about, be of good cheer. The Bible says that in order to defeat the flesh you have to feed your spirit, and the only way to do that is to go to church, study the Word of God, and pray constantly. It doesn't matter what others say when you make a mistake. God is the only One who really matters! He's watching over you at all times.

The message for today: Be faithful to church services. You need the encouragement of other believers.

Prayer: Dear Heavenly Father, Help me to be an example of the believers in everything I think, say, and do. Help me to never bring shame to Your wonderful Name.

✝ June 22 – That's Mine!

And as they were loosening the colt, its owners said to them, "Why are you untying the colt?" And they said, "The Lord has need of it." And they brought it to Jesus...
(Luke 19:33-35)

If you were the owner of the colt mentioned in Luke 19, what would you have done when the disciples just started untying your animal and leading it away? I would have probably done more than just ask them why they were taking it. I might have been angry and said, "Hey, you can't take that colt! It's mine!"

Most prisoners are very possessive when it comes to their stuff, but God wants to change their attitudes. He wants them to hold on to material things with a very loose hand. Usually, our problem with giving is that we fear that our possession will not be replaced. We are selfish, fearful people, and God wants to change that.

God's economy is upside-down compared with the world's economy. The world says, "Get, so you can have." God says, "Give, so you can get." Confusing? Yes, because God blesses us with more when we put Him first and give Him 10% of all the money we get.

The world says, "Seeing is believing." God says that "believing is seeing". Hebrews 11:1 makes it all a little clearer: "Now faith is the assurance (the title deed) of the things we hope for, being the proof of things we do not see. (Faith perceives as real fact what is not revealed to our senses)."

The message for today: Give everything you own to Jesus.

Prayer: Dear Heavenly Father, Help me to realize that everything I have is Yours – not mine. It is only lent to me.

June 23 – Pray for Them

*You have heard it said that you shall love your neighbor
and hate your enemy; but I tell you, love your enemies and
pray for those who persecute you... (Matthew 5:43-45)*

In prison you find out who your friends are very quickly. They
stand up for you, even in bad situations.

In Job 42 God delivered Job from the most major trial of his
life. Job finally realized that he had been looking at God with
physical eyes and seeing all his suffering but forgetting that he
needed to look at his situation with spiritual eyes (Job 42:5).
He then asked the Lord's forgiveness for questioning His
judgment in his life.

After talking to Job, God addressed his three "friends", who
were sure they had all the answers, and told them that He was
angry with them for misrepresenting Him and His purposes.
He told them to go to Job and ask his forgiveness and have him
pray for them. When Job prayed for his friends, the Lord
stopped his trial of sickness, poverty, and depression and
restored his family and fortune to him and gave him twice as
much as he had before the trial.

Jesus our Lord prayed for all who would mistreat, deny, and
crucify Him in John 17. He saw beyond the Cross to the very
day that you and I would ask Him into our lives, and He prayed
for us!

We, too, should pray for those who treat us badly because we
are commanded to and because there's a future blessing in it.

The message for today: The arm of flesh will fail you, but Jesus
never will.

Prayer: Dear Heavenly Father, Help me to obey Your
command to pray for the people who have hurt me.

✝ June 24 – Not Me!

Now to Him Who is able to carry out His purpose and do superabundantly, far above all that we dare ask or think, to Him be glory forever! (Ephesians 3:20)

Many prisoners cannot look beyond their failures and see anything great in their future, but God sees great things ahead for those who are obedient to Him.

Moses went from being inadequate and fearful to becoming the deliverer of 3,000,000 Israelites because he was God's chosen man for the job. He never could have done the job without God's supernatural power working in him, and he knew it.

A woman was concerned about a town meeting, in which she had a chance to make a difference by her statements, but she felt inadequate to say the right things. While she was thinking about it, she looked at her watch and saw that it was time to go. She had to leave, or it would be too late to make the meeting. She picked up her coat and gloves, put them on, and hurried out the door. As she was driving down the street, the Lord spoke to her and said, "Your coat and gloves became useful when you put them on. I want to use you, so go and stand up for what you believe right now."

God has placed a power in us that is supernatural. It is His power and doesn't have a thing to do with us, except for the fact that we are available to be used by Him.

The message for today: Assignment comes with God's enablement!

Prayer: Dear Heavenly Father, Thank You for the Holy Spirit in me, Who gives me abilities far beyond what I could ask or think! Use me to do something for You, Father, that will count for eternity.

June 25 – Comfort One Another

Blessed be God, even the Father of our Lord Jesus Christ, the Father of mercies, and the God of all comfort. (II Corinthians 1:3)

When I was twelve, my sister lost her baby. I did not know what to do or say as she cried and refused to be comforted. My mother was away in England and my father was at work, so I called my neighbor and asked her advice. She told me to tell her that God loved her and the baby, but He wanted the baby with Him in heaven. As I shared with my sister, I saw the Lord's comfort come upon her.

Matthew 5:4 says, "Blessed are they that mourn, for they shall be comforted." It is only in God's school of mourning that we learn to better understand the need of those who are hurting.

Most of us try to comfort people with words we think they would want to hear in their time of sorrow; but how can we help them if we have never walked in their moccasins?

The next time you are in a situation where you need to encourage and comfort a hurting person, ask God for His words of comfort. After all, He is the Father of our Lord Jesus Christ, the Father of mercies, and the God of all comfort.

If you are going through a storm and you have no one to comfort you, remember that you are deeply loved of the Father. Do what James 4:8 says. "Draw near to God, and He will draw near to you."

The message for today: God wants to use you to comfort hurting people.

Prayer: Dear Heavenly Father, Help me to show others Your great love by my kindness and my words.

June 26 – A Good Prayer

May He grant you out of the rich treasury of His glory to be strengthened and reinforced with mighty power in the inner man by the Holy Spirit. May Christ through your faith actually settle down and abide, and make His permanent home in your heart. (Ephesians 3:16, 17)

I was talking with my prayer partner in prison, and she shared with me that she prays Paul's prayer in Ephesians 3:16-20 for me daily. She puts my name in the prayer and asks God to strengthen me in my mind and body. She asks God to ground me in His love and cause me to be filled with all His fullness! Now that is a good prayer!

Paul never once prayed for anything tangible like a coat or food. His prayers were so far above my prayers, so I decided to look at them more closely.

In Ephesians 1:16 Paul said that he thanked God for his friends in Ephesus and constantly prayed for them. Then he said something so wonderful that I decided to pray it for my friends also. He asked that God would give unto his friends the spirit of "wisdom and revelation in the knowledge of God" and that their eyes of understanding would be opened and that they would know the hope of God's call on their lives.

In Colossians 1:9-14 Paul prayed that the Colossian believers would be filled with the knowledge of God's will in all wisdom and spiritual understanding and that they might walk worthy of the Lord unto all pleasing, being fruitful in every good work, and increasing in the knowledge of God.

The message for today: Try praying scripture prayers for your friends.

Prayer: Dear Heavenly Father, Use me to pray Your Word for others.

June 27 – God's Call

And we know that God causes everything to work together for the good of those who are called according to His purpose for them. (Romans 8:28)

One day God showed me Ephesians 1:4 where it says that He "chose us in Christ before the foundation of the world that we would be holy and blameless before Him". I cannot understand how God knew me before I was born, but He did.

Stephanie grew up in a Christian home. She got very tired of being forced to go to church; and during her teenage years, she started to hang with the wrong crowd. Her habits of drinking and smoking got worse as the years passed. She had no regard for God or her parents until one December day when she found out that her father had died.

On Christmas, Stephanie opened a present which contained a Bible and a beautiful hand-made cross from her father. She started crying and ran into her mother's arms in repentance for all the things she had done to dishonor her dear parents. The next Sunday she was back in church. The pastor gave an altar call, and Stephanie went forward to talk to him. He told her that the Lord was calling her to something special for Him. As she prayed, she heard the word "missionary". She immediately knew that God had saved her "before the foundation of the world" and called her before she was even born to serve Him on the mission field. Today she serves God faithfully as a missionary and has won many souls to Jesus.

The message for today: Answer God's call on your life.

Prayer: Dear Heavenly Father, Thank You for Your higher purposes and nobler callings. Help me to reach Your calling for me.

June 28 – The Glorious Gospel

For the god of this world has blinded the unbelievers'
minds that they should not discern the truth...
of the gospel. (II Corinthians 4:4)

Why isn't everyone saved? One part of me says that our free will chooses God, and we live "happily ever after." Another part of me says that we have nothing to do with our salvation, because God knows who will be saved and who will be lost. Without the Holy Spirit's help, I would be so confused.

One day I was asking a group of believers to pray for my friend's son, whose life was a mess. One member of the group spoke up and said that I should pray for a "chink" in his armor. I got to thinking about that, and it made sense. In the Old Testament, men were killed by arrows that went strategically right between the parts of their armor where they were not protected.

People who have no time for God need Christians to pray for them. When you get a burden to pray for an unsaved inmate, remember that God has placed that burden on your heart. When you pray, and the person's life starts crumbling all around him, that is when God can really draw him to faith in Jesus Christ. There is a "chink" in his armor against God, because God knows exactly how to get his attention. After fighting God for many years, the person usually gets saved, and the glory goes right back to God!

The message for today: If you have someone on your heart who needs to know Jesus as their Savior, start praying. The results will astound you!

Prayer: Dear Heavenly Father, Please find a "chink" in _____'s armor and save their soul.

June 29 – The Juniper Tree Syndrome

Elijah sat down under a juniper tree and asked
that he might die. He said, It is enough; now, O Lord,
take away my life... (I Kings 19:4)

Do you ever get depressed from being incarcerated? We all experience the enemy's attacks on our emotions.

Elijah got depressed after a huge miracle at Mt. Carmel. James 5:17 says that he was just like us in his feelings and affections.

I Kings 18 tells the story about the 450 false prophets of Baal who had a contest with Elijah to see who the true and living God really was. The false prophets went into a frenzy, trying to get Baal to respond, but there was silence. Then Elijah called on the Jehovah God, and the entire bull, the wood, the stones, the dust, and all the water were consumed by God! He then had the 450 wicked prophets killed.

When Jezebel, the wicked queen, found out what Elijah had done to her prophets, she threatened his life. He ran for almost 100 miles in fear. Then the depression hit him and he wanted to die. This is the same man whom God used mightily and now he was running from a woman's threats!

Discouragement carries several traits with it. Satan uses it to cause us to be pre-occupied with ourselves, our doubts, and our fears. We forget God, and we are the center of our attention. We do not pray as we should; and we run away from the problem instead of going to the Lord for help.

The message for today: Why are you cast down, my soul? Just hope in God!

Prayer: Dear Heavenly Father, Help me to keep my eyes on You and not my problems.

✝
June 30 – The Comforter

When the Spirit of truth comes, He will guide you into all truth... (John 16:13)

The moment we accept Jesus Christ as our Savior, He becomes the Head of our life. Faith, hope and love become a part of our being, and we start changing.

The Holy Spirit comes to live inside us at salvation. I can't understand it, but I accept it, because Jesus said, "I will ask the Father, and He will give you another Helper, that He may be with you forever; that is the Spirit of truth, whom the world cannot receive, because it does not see Him or know Him, but you know Him because He abides with you and will be in you." (John 14:16, 17)

Before I accepted Christ as my Savior in prison, there was fear in me all the time because there was only darkness in my soul, and Satan works in darkness. He rules every unsaved person's life. He is the "god of this world". Jesus told the Pharisees that they were of their father, the devil (John 8:44). They were religious, but lost.

When I started reading the Bible and praying, the Holy Spirit quickened my spirit to start changing. I started to choose righteousness instead of sin. I started to be at peace in my soul, and I started to trust that God was working everything out for my good as I obeyed Him. I found that the Christian life really works!

The message for today: Whoever confesses that Jesus is the Son of God, God abides in him, and he in God. (I John 4:15)

Prayer: Dear Heavenly Father, Thank You for providing everything I need to live the Christian life victoriously!

JULY

July 1 – Heart Blockage

If I regard wickedness in my heart, the Lord will not hear me; but certainly God has heard. He has given heed to the voice of my prayer. (Psalm 66:18, 19)

When I first became a Christian in prison, everything was going well. God answered all my prayers! I was a happy camper! But as I grew in my faith and knowledge of the Lord Jesus and His ways, I found that there was more to the Christian life than I had first thought.

God stopped answering every prayer, and it caused me to step back and take a look at my life. Wasn't this Christian life supposed to be trouble free? I soon learned that God had to start pruning away the bad habits and thoughts from my past in order to give me victory.

God started my "pruning process" by helping me to realize that something was blocking my fellowship with Him. One day I was reading Psalm 66:18 and it hit me hard, "If I regard wickedness in my heart, the Lord will not hear me". There it was. God would not and could not answer my prayers if I was angry with someone or some situation in my life. Sure enough, I had held bitterness toward my parents for many years! I confessed that anger to God, and I was free! He started answering my prayers again.

The message for today: Keep short accounts with God and watch for answered prayer.

Prayer: Dear Heavenly Father, Help me to grow in the grace and knowledge of You and Your Word.

✝

July 2 – Faith is the Victory!

*For whoever is born of God overcomes the world;
and this is the victory that overcomes
the world – even our faith. (I John 5:4)*

Did you know that you are an overcomer? Yes, you! John told us that if we believe that Jesus is the Christ and we love Him, we have overcome the world. Well, then, why don't we feel and act like overcomers? I'm glad you asked.

When I first got saved, I thought that I was inadequate in most areas to conquer anything, but then I heard that God had made me more than a conqueror in every situation of life (Romans 8:37). How could I conquer something if there were never any challenges or problems? So, with each new challenge, I would call on Jesus to help me.

One night in prison, I was in a math class, and the teacher asked me to go to the board and complete the problem. Even though math was my worst subject, on my way to the board, I just kept repeating Philippians 4:13 (I can do all things through Christ who strengthens me!). I did the problem correctly, and conquered my fear by using my faith in Jesus. Now the teacher can't get me to sit down!

I John 5:4 also says that faith is the victory that overcomes the world. Faith, like our muscles, must be exercised in order to work well. Faith says, "I am your servant. I will give you victory every time, but you must use me."

The message for today: Speak faith instead of fear today, and watch it work.

Prayer: Dear Heavenly Father, Please forgive my unbelief. Help me to speak faith with my lips and my actions.

July 3 – Who's on the Throne of Your Life?

...the moment you hear the sound of the trumpet, you are to fall down and worship the golden image that Nebuchadnezzar the king has set up. (Daniel 3:5)

From Daniel 3:5, it is easy to see who King Nebuchadnezzar liked! He made a 90-foot image of himself and commanded the people to bow down and worship it every time a trumpet sounded. Talk about pride!

Most Christian prisoners have a pride problem like the king. We are so self-centered that we cannot even see the needs of others, let alone help them. If we do focus on someone, it is only for a short time. Then our personal interests take over again.

When we are depressed, it stems from pride (self-pity). We (not Jesus) are on the throne of our life again. We concentrate only on our poor, pitiful lives. God tells us to cast those self-centered thoughts down and substitute them with thoughts and words of praise to God (II Corinthians 10:4, 5). When we are on the throne of our life, we push Jesus off, and that is sin.

What have your thoughts been like today? Have you asked the Lord to place someone in your path that you can bless? Have you looked around to find someone in need of prayer or a kind word? They're out there, and God will show them to you. Even if you see someone who is hurting and you privately pray for them, you are performing a godly act.

The message for today: You can't help but love others when Jesus is on the throne of your life.

Prayer: Dear Heavenly Father, Help me to pray for others today and minister to their needs.

✟ July 4 – Celebrate Freedom!

You shall know the truth, and the truth
shall set you free. (John 8:32)

Have you ever been kidnapped? I can only imagine how terrible that would be, and yet there are millions of people who are taken captive by sin. They think they are free to do what they want with no restraints; but sooner or later, their deeds catch up to them and tragedy results.

Today is July 4, a day on which America celebrates freedom. Are you free in your spirit, or are you bound to sin? Jesus died on the Cross to free you from your greatest enemy – sin. The Bible says in I John 3:9 that "no one born of God deliberately, knowingly, and habitually practices sin, for God's nature abides in him."

None of us will ever be perfect in this fleshly body. The flesh wars against the Spirit of God, and the Spirit wars against the flesh. Jesus saves our souls from hell, but our bodies will never be regenerated until heaven. In Romans 7:17 Paul said, "It is no longer I who does the deed, but the sin principle which is at home in me and has possession of me."

Paul asks in Romans 7:24, "Who will release me from the shackles of this body of death?" Then, in a triumphant answer, he cries out in Romans 8:1, "O thank God! He will through Jesus Christ, our Lord! There is therefore now no condemnation to those who are in Christ Jesus!"

The message for today: There is no greater cause for celebration than our freedom in Christ!

Prayer: Dear Heavenly Father, Thank You for freeing us from the greatest captor. You released us from sin and death and set us free to love!

July 5 – A Sacrifice of Praise

Let us continually offer to God a sacrifice of praise.
(Hebrews 13:15)

There was a song many years ago called, Praise the Lord. As I listened to the words, my eyes filled with tears because of the power of the words. It goes something like this:

> Now Satan is a liar and he wants to make us think that we are
> paupers when he knows himself we're children of the King.
> So lift up the mighty shield of faith for the battle must be won.
> We know that Jesus Christ is risen so the work's already done.
> Praise the Lord! He can work through those who praise Him.
> Praise the Lord! For the chains that seem to bind you
> Serve only to remind you, that they fall powerless behind you
> When you praise Him.

Praise is our greatest weapon of spiritual warfare against Satan, but it is the hardest thing to do when we are in the middle of a crisis. Jehoshaphat told God in II Chronicles 20 that he didn't know what to do; he was powerless, but his eyes were on God. God told him to take his position (bowing face down on the ground), stand still and see the deliverance of the Lord who was with him.

The message for today: Sometimes the only thing we can lay at the feet of Jesus is the adoration of our heart toward Him.

Prayer: Dear Heavenly Father, Thank You that Your presence comes the sweetest when I am at my lowest.

✝
July 6 – The Truth

Thy mercy is great above the heavens: and thy truth reaches unto the clouds. (Psalm 108:4)

Have you ever been in a situation where you had to make a decision as to which one of two parties was telling you the truth?

I was in a situation like that when I was growing up. Some articles were stolen out of my book bag in high school, and only two other people were in the room when they disappeared. My teacher made the three of us stand in front of her. Then she asked me to identify the one I thought it was who stole my articles. When I accused one, she would say it was the other one. The "case of the missing articles" was never solved.

When Jesus stood before Pilate in John 18:38, Pilate asked Him, "What is truth?" After he said that, he went out to the Jews again and told them that he found no fault in Jesus. The sad part of that story is that The Truth was standing right there before him, and he could not recognize it.

In John 14:6 Jesus proclaims that He is The Way, The Truth, and The Life. No one comes to the Father, except through Him.

Even in court before a judge, the accused plead their cases and tell the truth; but when it is all said and done, many are unjustly sentenced, just like the Lord Jesus. Just remember, though, God knows your innocence and He will make a way where there is no way.

The message for today: Speak the truth, no matter what happens.

Prayer: Dear Heavenly Father, Sometimes Your truth is revealed in the darkness of my storm. Remind me of this when I pray for the storm to end.

✝
July 7 – God's Mercy

Be merciful, just as your Father is merciful.
Do not judge, and you will not be judged...
Forgive, and you will be forgiven. (Luke 6:36, 37)

Almost everyone knows the Bible verse that says, "Judge not that you be not judged", and it is quoted freely in anger. But have you ever read the verses before and after Luke 6:37?

Jesus was teaching His disciples throughout Luke 6. He taught them the Beatitudes (how to be blessed). He warned the rich, who took comfort in their money instead of God. He taught His disciples how to be generous and loving to everyone, no matter how they were being treated. Then Jesus said that they should not judge or condemn others, but instead they should give up resentment and forgive others.

Usually, we judge others when we see them committing sins that we personally haven't committed, so we feel superior to them. We might think because we are in prison for shoplifting, it isn't as bad as our cell mate, who is in for murder; but daily we ought to say to ourselves, "But for God's grace, there go I."

The message for today: What if God judged us with the same judgment we give others?

Prayer: Dear Heavenly Father, Help me to see my own faults before I judge the faults of others.

✝
July 8 – Who's First in Your Life?

If anyone intends to come after Me, let him forget,
ignore, disown, and lose sight of himself and his own
interests, and take up his cross follow Me. (Mark 8:34)

It has been said that the only way to live a victorious Christian life is to put Jesus first, others second, and yourself last. That equals J O Y.

It sounds easy, but it is difficult to put others first all the time. Many insecure people fear that putting others first means being a doormat and letting people control and cheat them, so they lead selfish, cold, and unhappy lives.

Jesus told the truth to the disciples when He said that we have to forget about ourselves and serve Him totally. John 3:30 says that He must increase, and I must decrease.

In 1 Kings 17:13 Elijah asked the widow who was about to make a cake for her and her son and then die, to make him a cake first. That sounds selfish, but God was using Elijah to prove the woman's faith and create a miracle of blessing in her life. She trusted Elijah and did what he said.

In I Kings 17:15-16, we see the miracle she received by putting Elijah first instead of herself, "…and she went and did according to the saying of Elijah: and she and her house, did eat many days. And the barrel of meal wasted not, neither did the cruse of oil fail, according to the word of the Lord, which he spoke by Elijah."

The message for today: When you put others first, you are really putting God first in your life.

Prayer: Dear Heavenly Father, Please forgive my selfish spirit, and help me not to fear putting others first.

July 9 – Little by Little

And the Lord your God will clear out those nations before you, little by little... (Deuteronomy 7:22)

It would be so nice if God saved us, cleaned us up, and sent us on our way as a mighty warrior all in one day. Unfortunately, that does not happen. It takes many years to become the man or woman of God that you want to be.

The Holy Spirit is the One who makes us know truth, and truth sets us free from the bondages of our past.

A fellow prisoner told me about the generational curse of alcohol that was over her husband's family. One day someone shared with her that God breaks bondages over people, so in simple faith she prayed for Him to break the curse of alcoholism over her husband. She started praying daily for him and showing him that he was special, even when he treated her badly. One day, two years later, he started vomiting blood. He immediately called for his wife and asked her to pray for him. She did, and he got better within hours! Six weeks later he asked his wife to pray for him to be saved. Within a month, he decided that drinking was bad, and he quit!

God will drive out the bondages of your past "little by little". It doesn't happen quickly, but He makes sure it happens as we stay in His Word and keep growing in Christ.

The message for today: I may not be where I want to be in my Christian life, but thank God I'm not where I used to be!

Prayer: Dear Heavenly Father, Thank You for helping me grow day by day in my Christian life until I see the bondages of my past disappear.

✝ July 10 – It's Our Choice

So come out from among unbelievers and separate yourselves from them, says the Lord, and touch not any unclean thing; then I will receive you kindly and treat you with favor. (II Corinthians 6:17)

The Bible is full of great advice given by the hand of God to protect and strengthen us as believers. In II Corinthians 6 Paul talks to the Christians and tells them lovingly that they should not marry unbelievers or hang out with them because there can be no harmony between God and Satan.

Your body is the temple of the living God if you are saved, but Jesus Christ wants to settle down in your heart and body. He cannot be at ease if you are living a double lifestyle with one foot in the world and one foot in Christianity. Paul goes on to urge the people in II Corinthians 6:17 to separate themselves from the sinful world.

Sharon had the flu but went to school anyway. The kids stayed away from her because she was so sick, and it made her sad. Her mother reminded her that she had a contagious infection so it was natural for the kids not to want to be with her. Sin is the same way. If you are a believer and hang out with sinners everyday, you will start sinning, too, because sin is also contagious – just like the flu.

Isaiah 52:11 says to "cleanse yourselves and be clean…"

The message for today: We are the ones who have to choose righteousness over sin.

Prayer: Dear Heavenly Father, Help me to be so pure that there is nothing in my life for You to change. Help me to grow daily in my knowledge of You.

July 11 – The Green-Eyed Monster

Be on the watch to secure God's grace in order that no root of resentment causes trouble and bitter torment...
(Hebrews 12:15)

Have you ever been jealous? Have you ever seen the consequences it brings when it is allowed to take root in your life?

Jealousy stems from insecurity and fear, and it makes us compare ourselves with others. We fear that someone else will get what is ours, so we let people know that we are angry and jealous. It is a dangerous tool that Satan uses in people's lives.

Cain and Abel were brothers. Abel was a shepherd and Cain was a farmer. They were the first two children of Adam and Eve; but because sin had already entered the human race through Adam, things got out of hand.

One day Cain brought an offering of vegetables to God, and Abel brought the firstborn lamb of his flock. God required a blood sacrifice, but Cain did not care. He chose to bring vegetables instead of the blood sacrifice, and God was not pleased.

Cain was very jealous of Abel and committed the first murder in the human race. Sin had been crouching at the door of Cain's heart through jealousy, and he listened to his angry, resentful heart and acted out that anger. Cain went away from the Lord's presence and became a wanderer for the rest of his life.

The message for today: If we allow jealous behavior to take root in our thought life, it causes pain for us and others.

Prayer: Dear Heavenly Father, Help me to be so secure in You that I won't be jealous of others.

✝ July 12 – A Happy Ending

With respect to the promise of God, Abraham did not waver in unbelief but grew strong in the faith, giving glory to God, knowing that what God had promised, He was also able to perform. (Romans 4:20, 21)

A friend told me a story about her husband not trusting anyone. Bob grew up in a hostile environment where his mother and father divorced when he was two. Since his mother had to work 12 hours a day, she placed Bob and his sister in an orphanage. For two years, he never got any love or attention. Only his basic needs of food and clothing were met. His mother then remarried and took the children out of the orphanage into a home with a mean step-father. The only words spoken to the children were critical and condescending. He said he was told hundreds of times that he was stupid and would never amount to anything. In short, the children were nuisances. When Bob was 19, his step-father was killed in a trucking accident. Bob said he never shed one tear.

Bob's life has a happy ending, though. He asked Jesus to be his Savior. Today, he is a successful business man who is happily married and well adjusted because of God's transforming power!

The message for today: Let God heal you every where you hurt.

Prayer: Dear Heavenly Father, Help me to see Your hand in my past, present, and future and trust Your promises as Abraham did.

July 13 – Don't Forget

After you have suffered awhile, God will perfect, establish, strength, and settle you. (I Peter 5:10)

I heard a story about an old couple, Arthur and Patricia. They loved people and never met a stranger. It seemed as if their whole life had been sweet and peaceful, but such was not the case.

Arthur had worked in the steel mills in Pennsylvania and contracted lung cancer when he was 64. He was not expected to live, but God had another plan. Through Arthur's suffering, God drew him to Jesus and he became a Christian. Patricia believed also.

Within two years, Arthur was healed of the cancer. One day a lady who was visiting them saw a plaque on their wall which said, "Please, Lord, teach us to laugh again; but God, don't ever let us forget that we cried." When she inquired about that beautiful saying, Arthur told her about his and Patricia's terrible days as alcoholics. In fact, they met each other in a weekly AA meeting. They had both lost their homes, their families, their self-respect, and their health because of alcohol. They later married and made a life together, having learned some hard lessons.

If you have been through a lot because of life and the curves it throws you, remember that God loves you and He will bring laughter back to your life if you ask Jesus to be your Savior; but He will never let you forget your tears. They are what forms character.

The message for today: God bottles our tears and remembers every one of them. (Psalm 56:8)

Prayer: Dear Heavenly Father, Help me to laugh again. I give my life and all my sin to You. Please start me on the right path by Your grace.

July 14 – God Cares

...Your Father knows what you need before you ask
Him. (Matthew 6:8)

We have all heard that God provides for our ev ery need, no matter what it is. He created us and He longs to give us good gifts because of His great love for us, but some of the responsibility is on our part, too.

Matthew 10:29-31 says that birds don't fall to the ground without God's consent and notice. It tells us that God even knows the exact number of hairs on our heads! It is hard to imagine that God loves me that much, but He does.

God told the Israelites in Deuteronomy 8 about keeping His commandments and entering the "good land" that He had promised them, but He gave some stipulations which still apply to us to get our needs met, too:

1. Keep God's commandments from the Bible.
2. Remember how God has provided in the past for you.
3. Know that God's discipline develops godly character.
4. Put into practice what you learn from God.
5. Be thankful!

Read Dueteronomy 8 today and write down your blessings.

The message for today: What have you thanked God for today?

Prayer: Dear Heavenly Father, Thank You for every one of my blessings. Help me to know how much You care for me.

July 15 – God's Ways are Best

Repay no one evil for evil… (Romans 12:17)

God does not want us to take personal revenge. At times in prison, if we are not careful, we take matters into our own hands and the consequences are always bad.

God wants us to deal with people from His perspective – not ours. In Leviticus 19:18 He tells us not to take revenge or bear any grudge against our neighbors. Jesus quoted this verse in Matthew 5:43-46 when He told the disciples to love their neighbor as they loved themselves. He said for them to love their enemies and pray for those who persecuted them.

Deuteronomy 32:35 says that vengeance belongs to God, and He will repay people for the wrong they have done to you. It's not your job.

While I was in prison, an inmate hit me in the face. My first instinct was to return evil for evil. I sat for days planning how to get her back; but God pointed me to many scriptures, which changed my thinking. I knew I had to allow Him to deal with my situation, so I started praying for her.

A few months later, she was transferred to another prison where she started fighting and was badly beaten. Because the prison could not control her, she was transferred yet again to another facility. I really started praying this time for peace in her life, and I realized that God had taken the resentful spirit away from me and she was in His hands now.

The message for today: Pray for everyone who hurts you.

Prayer: Dear Heavenly Father, Please forgive me for wanting personal revenge against _____. Help them to come to know You as Lord of their life and help me to love them, too.

July 16 – God's Interruptions

And we know that all things work together for good to those who love God, to those who are the called according to His purpose. (Romans 8:28)

In some situations we receive news that breaks our heart. When I found out that I had to go to prison, my heart was broken. Reality hit me hard when I realized that my children would now have to live without their mother. I have never been so sad.

In prison I discovered that God used my misfortunes and bad choices to capture my attention, my mind, emotions and attitudes. God saw a diamond in the rough when he looked at my life. He knew He could not use me as I was so He intervened in my life and chose radical means to make eternal changes in my life.

God told Hosea to take a prostitute as his wife (Hosea 1:2, 3), and he obeyed. He was a godly man, and it must have been difficult for him to marry a harlot and have children with her; but God wanted the Israelites to learn a lesson from this marriage. God's chosen people were offering sacrifices to idols and sinning greatly. Gomer, Hosea's wife, was used to show God's love for His unfaithful people.

Even when we are unfaithful to God, He is still faithful to us. He uses whatever means He must to draw us back to Himself. God works all things together for our good – even prison time – to make us into the pure, clean vessels He can use.

The message for today: God only allows us to go so far, and then He intervenes.

Prayer: Dear Heavenly Father, Thank You for interrupting my life and putting me on the right path.

July 17 – One is the Loneliest Number

Two are better than one, because they have a good reward for their labor; for if they fall, the one will lift up the other...a threefold cord is not quickly broken. (Ecclesiastes 4:9-12)

God usually chose two people to accomplish His work. When He created the earth, He placed Adam and Eve in the Garden of Eden. God told Noah to bring two (male and female) of every animal into the ark. Jesus told His disciples to go out "two by two".

Matthew 18:19, 20 says, "If two agree on earth about anything that they may ask, it shall be done for them by My Father...for where two or three have gathered together in My name, I am there in their midst."

Proverbs 27:17 says that "iron sharpens iron; so one man sharpens another."

Here's the message: We need each other.

Ecclesiastes 4:9-12 says it so well. Two are better than one. We miss so many blessings when we are too fearful to be friendly. In prison I hear people say that they don't trust anyone in the whole world. They can make it on their own, and they don't need anyone. The exact opposite is true.

The message for today: The three-fold cord equals you, your friend, and Jesus.

Prayer: Dear Heavenly Father, Please bring a special friend into my life who sharpens my faith in You. Help me to be the friend You want me to be, too.

July 18 – Be Thankful

In everything give thanks, for this is the will of God in Christ Jesus concerning you. (I Thessalonians 5:18)

I was watching a television program one night in which a young couple was in a car accident. A telephone call from the husband to the wife was shown. He was kind and asked how she was, and all she could do was complain. She could have said, "I'm not well yet, but praise the Lord, I still have my life. I am so thankful that you are alive, too."

Every situation can be taken in a positive or negative way. It's up to us how we react to life and its problems.

The Apostle Paul puts most of us to shame in his attitude. In II Corinthians 4:8, 9 he writes, "We are troubled on every side, yet not distressed; we are perplexed, but not in despair; persecuted, but not forsaken; cast down, but not destroyed." Now that is faith in Jesus Christ!

When I am troubled on every side, can I remain in peace? When I am confused and perplexed about things, do I start worrying? When I am persecuted from wicked people, do I act as if God doesn't care? When I am depressed and unhappy, do I wish I could just die?

Choices…every single day we are faced with them. How are we going to react to bad things? If we are walking in the Spirit, we will go to the Word of God; we will pray; we will praise God for what we do have and stop complaining about what we don't have.

The message for today: Give Satan a fit by choosing to concentrate on your blessings!

Prayer: Dear Heavenly Father, Help me to practic e being thankful in every situation.

July 19 – God's Sure Promises

God's promises are His performances. (see Romans 4:21)

Psalm 37 is full of God's promises. Let's count nine of the promises in this one psalm alone.

Promise 1 — Don't worry about bad people, because they shall surely be cut down (37:1, 2)

Promise 2 — Trust in the Lord, and you will dwell in a good land and be fed (37:3)

Promise 3 — Delight yourself in the Lord, and He will give you the desires of your heart (37:4)

Promise 4 — Commit your way unto the Lord; He shall bring it to pass (37:5)

Promise 5 — Cease from all anger and worry. The evil doers shall be cut off (37:7, 8)

Promise 6 — Those who wait upon the Lord shall inherit the earth (37:9)

Promise 7 — The meek shall delight themselves in the abundance of peace (37:11)

Promise 8 — The Lord knows the days of the upright and their inheritance shall be forever (37:18)

Promise 9 —I have been young and am now old; yet I have not seen the righteous forsaken or his seed begging for bread (37:25)

The message for today: Stand on every promise of God.

Prayer: Dear Heavenly Father, Thank You for each promise in Your Word.

July 20 – Lord, Do You Know I'm Here?

But if from there you will seek the Lord your God, you will find Him if you truly seek Him with all your heart, mind, soul, and life. (Deuteronomy 4:29)

I felt so fearful and suicidal as I endured every day of incarceration. To get relief from the loneliness, confusion, and fear, I started praying. I didn't know too much about God and prayer, but I thought it was worth a try. I prayed about everything, from my roommate (a mental patient, who caused me to stay awake all night in fear) to new sneakers. I started seeing that God cared about me, a Jamaican with no one in the world except Him.

Every traumatic situation in our lives has three parts to it: shock, acceptance, and re-adjustment. After the initial shock wore off, I accepted my lot in life and started mentally re-adjusting to my surroundings. I read Deuteronomy 4:27-31, and it changed my life. God told His people that they would be scattered to a place that He would drive them to because of their sins; but from that terrible place, God would hear their prayers as they turned away from sin to Him. It goes on to say that "the Lord your God is a merciful God; He will not fail you or destroy you or forget His covenant with you."

My faith took hold and I found that God really was a very present help in trouble.

The message for today: God's grace is sufficient for any situation you find yourself in.

Prayer: Dear Heavenly Father, Today I draw on Your mercy and grace to help me through one more day.

July 21 – Peace amidst the Storm

Thou wilt keep him in perfect peace, whose mind is stayed on Thee, because he trusts in thee. (Isaiah 26:3)

On my arrival at the county jail, I saw despair in the eyes of the residents, and they saw the same in mine.

I felt as if the world was closing in on me and crushing me in its vice, one day at a time. I was so lonely; but after a few days, I tried to get acquainted with other people.

I was put in jail because of my former lifestyle of stealing, selling drugs, lying, and cheating. I had no peace because I had no God. As the months went on, I kept so busy with activities that I didn't have time to think about my spiritual life. I tried to make friends and talk to them all the time. But there was always night time when I had to be by myself with my own thoughts.

God whispered peace to my heart one day when I read Isaiah 26:3. I knew it was time to make peace with Jesus Christ, who had died for me. I bowed my head and asked Him to be my personal Lord and Savior. A supernatural calming force came into my life that day. The peace of God started guarding my mind from terrible thoughts and actions. It amazed me!

The message for today: Know God, Know Peace – No God, No Peace.

Prayer: Dear Heavenly Father, Thank You that You are the Prince of Peace when we trust You to guide our lives.

July 22 – Where's Your Treasure?

Give, and it will be given to you. They will pour into your lap a good measure – pressed down, shaken together, and running over. For by your standard of measure it will be measured to you in return. (Luke 6:38)

Prison is a good place to practice giving, but most of the time, the givers are not cheerful. Inmates do not give away anything willingly. If they do, it is because they have a selfish motive in mind.

I know a female inmate who is a true believer in Jesus Christ. One day she asked Jesus how she could tithe in prison, and He showed her a most unique way, which she now practices weekly. She gives her sandwich away three times a week and fasts what she normally would eat for lunch. She blesses other residents when they least expect it. They just look at her and wonder why she is so unselfish. Then she has the opportunity to tell them of her Lord and Savior, Jesus. She has led many people to Jesus because of her practice of giving.

Matthew 6:21 says that "where your treasure is, there your heart will be also". If we only treasure "stuff" like the rich fool in Luke 12:13-33, God cannot bless us, as He longs to do. Examine yourself today and ask the Lord to help you trust Him for your next need.

The message for today: Make your Heavenly Father happy today by being generous.

Prayer: Dear Heavenly Father, Thank You for giving the greatest gift, Jesus, to us. Help us to be cheerful givers.

July 23 – The Cure for Sadness

He who conceals his transgressions will not prosper,
but he who confesses and forsakes them will find
compassion. (Proverbs 28:13)

How do you know if you are concealing a sin? I don't mean a
sin like gossiping or lying, but a deep-seated sin that you've
never been able to talk about. Sometimes it is something
that constantly nags at you day and night, and you try to
rationalize that it "wasn't that bad".

When we conceal our sin, our lives stop prospering. We feel
depressed and just "out of sorts". Every day is empty and
lonely. The problem is that we are living outside of God's
fellowship. You know the feeling.

There is a remedy for this sadness. Confess your sin to the
Lord and renounce it. Confess means to "agree with God".
Renounce means to "turn from it and give it up". A sure way to
renounce your secret sin is to share it with a friend and tell
them that you are going to change. Your pride will tell you not
to share it with anyone, but that is Satan's trick to keep you in
bondage to that very sin. Telling another person about it will
give you new power to say no to it in the future.

The message for today: Be free today by confessing and
renouncing your hidden sin.

Prayer: Dear Heavenly Father, Please show me what is keeping
me in bondage and set me free today from my sin of
_____. I praise You, Jesus,
for forgiveness of this sin. Help me to find the right person to
share this decision with and be accountable for never committing it again.

July 24 – What Do You Know?

Take My yoke upon you and learn of Me...
(Matthew 11:29)

Jesus asked His disciples to learn all they could about Him. That was a big command, because it is said in John 21:25 that if everything Jesus did was recorded in books, the world itself could not contain them!

Every day in prison I try to learn something new from the Bible. As I constantly read it, my mind is being changed by the Holy Spirit. It is being conformed to the things of Christ, even if I don't realize it at the time.

I Peter 4:7 says that since the end of all things is near, Christians should stay sound-minded, self-restrained, and alert. We should have intense and unfailing love for one another and practice hospitality with everyone who crosses our path, without complaining! We should do everything to the glory of God.

What is consuming your mind today? Do you long to bless other people? Do you ask Jesus for opportunities to show love to the unloved? Do you commit your day to Christ every morning, and no matter what happens, you have a peace that He has ordered your steps throughout the day?

I read a tract that challenged me to love others more. It said that we should let our "interruptions" become God's "invitations" to blessing.

The message for today: Why not try to live today with God directing your steps and plans?

Prayer: Dear Heavenly Father, I pray that Christ will be formed in me as I learn more about Him daily. (Galatians 4:19)

July 25 – Relax a Little

And God rested on the seventh day from all His work.
(Genesis 2:2)

In prison and out of prison, Sunday is no different than any other day of the week. People no longer regard it as a sacred day when they rest and refresh themselves in mind and body. It is starting to show in our lives, too. Some people work seven days a week and wonder why they have health, marital, and family problems. Duh!

I never realized that when I go to church on Sundays, I actually sit down and rest for a couple hours. God has already made provision for me to relax during that time when I choose to honor Him and His Word.

We are the ones who control our schedules, and in today's world we are not doing a very good job of it. One lady was complaining because she had so much to do. She prayed about it and told God how overworked she was. All at once, she heard a still, small voice saying, "My child, you are the one who makes your schedule. Stop complaining and start controlling."

The message for today: Follow God's example and get some rest.

Prayer: Dear Heavenly Father, I pray that You would help me to trust in You and rest in Your unfailing love for me.

✝
July 26 – Humble Me, Lord

A man's pride will bring him low, but he who
is of humble spirit will obtain honor. (Proverbs 29:23)

Pride is a tricky thing. It is all tied up in self-importance, conceit and smugness. However, there is an opposite side of pride which hurts just as much. It is called shame.

Pride says, "I'm the best! There's no one better!" Shame says, "I'm the worst. There's no one lower than me." Both attitudes are sinful and hurt our walk with God.

Satan had a BIG pride problem, and God had to cast him out of heaven. True, he was the most beautiful angel and the best song leader, but this attitude went to his head and he messed up, big time! Isaiah 14:12-14, the famous "fall-of-Satan-because-of-pride" passage, tells us about his five "I wills". Satan said, "I will ascend into heaven. I will exalt my throne above the stars of God. I will sit upon the mount of assembly in the uttermost north. I will ascend above the heights of the clouds. I will make myself like the Most High."

Jesus died on the cross to give us self-esteem. He became sin, sickness, poverty, and bondage so that we might be free. When someone doesn't know who they are in Christ, Satan robs them of their "freedom blessings". They walk around confused when someone talks badly about them or treats them badly, instead of shaking it off and going on because Jesus will take care of it.

The message for today: The better you know Jesus, the less you worry about being "accepted".

Prayer: Dear Heavenly Father, Help me to know You so well that my pride will shrink daily. You love a humble spirit, so I now surrender my pride to You.

MESSAGE FROM GOD

July 27 – God is Always There

*In all your ways acknowledge God, and
He will direct your paths. (Proverbs 3:6)*

Psalm 139 talks about God's omnipresence (He's everywhere). He keeps track of every one of us from "before the foundation of the world".

God thinks about us all the time. In Psalm 139:17, 18 He shows His amazing love and caring for us. (This would be a good scripture to memorize, my friend.) It says, "How precious also are Your thoughts unto me, O God! How great is the sum of them! If I should count them, they are more in number than the sand; when I awake, I am still with You!"

I remember how I used to act, and I shutter to think what would have happened to me if God hadn't been watching out for me and protecting me – even when I didn't know it. God has brought back to my mind the things I used to do. I should have died a couple times, but His hand was on my life. How I praise Him and appreciate Him for that!

God watches over His children who are in prison. Going through even one day without getting treated badly by a correction officer or another inmate is a miracle! One day an inmate tried to sell me some perfume; when I said, "No", she hit me as hard as she could! I started to hit her back, but God stopped me short. I later praised Him for helping me because we both would have been locked down if I had fought with her.

The message for today: Nothing escapes God's all-seeing eye!

Prayer: Dear Heavenly Father, Thank You for protecting me, even in the most terrible circumstances.

July 28 – Abandoned

Jesus said, "I will never leave you or forsake you."
(Hebrews 13:5)

When I was sent to prison, it was the worst time of my whole life. My thought life was terrible, and I wanted to die every day. The worst thoughts were about my family. I couldn't call them; and when I got enough money to buy a stamp and paper, I would write to them, and they never responded. They turned their backs on me, and it hurt me so deeply! I started getting angry and resentful against God and my family. It was a horrible time in my life. I just wanted a shoulder to cry on – someone to understand how I felt, but there was no one.

When a family supports a relative in prison, it makes things so much better. Joseph was looking for his brothers' support when he told them that he had a dream. (Read Genesis, chapters 37-50 when you get a chance.) But instead of supporting him, they turned their backs on him and sold him into slavery in Egypt! God kept them from killing him because He had a much larger plan for Joseph than he could see at the time.

A friend told me that for over five years she wrote to an inmate whom she had met at a jail church service. When asked what meant the most to her while she was in jail, she said, "It was the letters from my family and friends."

The message for today: When there's no one else, there is Jesus to comfort us.

Prayer: Dear Heavenly Father, I pray for the inmates who have no one to love and support them. Please touch them with Your presence.

July 29 – A Good Soldier

No soldier entangles himself with the affairs
of this life, so that he may please him who has chosen
him to be a soldier. (II Timothy 2:4)

It is hard to stand up for our Christian faith in prison. Everywhere we turn, there are residents who think that it doesn't matter what you believe.

I was not a Christian before I went to prison; but a few weeks after my incarceration, I began to seek God. The women who knew me before I accepted Jesus Christ into my heart found it very difficult to believe that I had changed. After I learned more about the Bible and my faith in Christ, I tried to share the scriptures with them. All they could do was bring up my past and tell me that I had "jail house religion"; but after a few months, they saw that my faith was real, in spite of what they said.

One day in jail I was confronted by an inmate from a religious cult for using the name of Jesus and calling Him God. She only knew what the cult had taught her, and "Jesus is Lord" was not one of the things she ever heard. She told me off, and I knew then that Jesus wanted me to enter the "fellowship of His suffering," and sometimes it would mean offending people and being misunderstood.

Paul and Silas were misunderstood, but they didn't care. They were beaten; then they sat in jail singing hymns at midnight! They lived above their circumstances as good soldiers of Jesus Christ.

The message for today: Those who would live godly will suffer persecution.

Prayer: Dear Heavenly Father, Help me to stand up for You in faith and power.

July 30 – Keeping Good Company

Do not be bound together with unbelievers, for what partnership has righteousness with lawlessness, or what fellowship has light with darkness? (II Corinthians 6:14)

In prison there is no such thing as choosing your roommate or your dinner partner. That is why it is important to learn to recognize people with sinful spirits. If you associate with them too much, you will get into trouble quickly.

Satan has a plan for each of us, just as God does. He is the "accuser of the brethren", and he walks about "like a roaring lion, seeking whom he may devour". He and his demons are very busy and successful when it comes to ruining lives.

Satan does not know what is going to happen because he is not God. He is a created being, and God is in control – not him – but he has a general idea of what is going to happen if a person gets saved and starts reading the Bible. He starts putting that person in the same cell or at the same dinner table with unsaved people.

II Peter 2:14 talks about wicked sinners who are controlled by Satan, and they cannot stop sinning. They trick "unstable souls" (i.e., untaught Christians) and pull them into cults. Cults have some truth, and people who don't know the Bible think there is nothing wrong with them. But soon their eyes are off Jesus and on to the works of the flesh.

The message for today: Don't be deceived. Bad company corrupts good morals. (I Corinthians 15:33)

Prayer: Dear Heavenly Father, Please help me to learn Your Word and not be tricked by the Devil and his lies.

July 31 – Good Communication Skills

Pray without ceasing. (I Thessalonians 5:17)

When Jesus was teaching the disciples about prayer in Matthew 6:7, He warned them not to use memorized prayers only (vain repetitions). Then in Matthew 6:9-13 He gave them The Lord's Prayer as a guide.

Religion says that we must repeat the same words over and over again to get God's attention, but Jesus tells us that our prayers have to come from our hearts. Our prayers shouldn't be "grocery list" prayers like, "God, I need this and this and this." God is not our "heavenly butler" who jumps at our every command. Until we learn that, we will be selfish in our prayers and not see the answers we want.

Our Father God is high above every limitation. He is so big we cannot limit Him. We are also not to limit ourselves with God. We are to be available at all times to speak to Him and to be attentive to His commands. When we actually learn more about Jesus Christ and love Him more than anything, our prayers change dramatically.

As I have grown in my Christian faith, I have learned scripture, which I pray back to God. He honors His Word above His name (Psalm 138:2)! Psalm 119:49, 50 says, "Lord, remember Your word to your servant, upon which You have caused me to hope. This is my comfort in my affliction, for Your word has given me life."

The message for today: Learn five verses, and pray them back to God in your own words. He loves it!

Prayer: Dear Heavenly Father, Help me to know You better as the months go by, so that I will know that with You, all things are possible!

Notes

AUGUST

August 1 – Depending on God

Be merciful unto me, O God for my soul trusts in Thee; yes, in the shadow of Thy wings will I make my refuge until these calamities are passed. (Psalm 57:1)

When things are going well in prison, we are all quite confident. We don't need God. But let things start going downhill in our lives, and all at once we start praying and begging Him to help us. All of a sudden, we become "spiritual". That is how God has planned it. He puts us in terrible circumstances to force us to come to Him.

I read a story about a woman who was in a terrible trial and found it so difficult to trust the Lord. She doubted His provision every day. One day she said to her friend, "I guess I've done everything I can do. Now all I can do is trust God." The other lady looked at her and said, "Oh, no! Has it come to that?"

Trusting God is voice activated. We have to speak words and scriptures of trust, even when we are in the deepest problems of our life. However, doubt (negativity) is also voice activated. We can have it either way in our lives. We can trust God or doubt Him. It's our choice.

When I finally knew that God was in control of every situation in my life, I started praising Him for the way He would work out every trial – big or small. Hebrews 11:6 says that without faith, it is impossible to please God. The opposite is also true, "With faith, God is well pleased."

The message for today: Speak faith!

Prayer: Dear Heavenly Father, I know that doubt is sin. Forgive me and help me to trust You and not my own thoughts.

August 2 – Wait Expectantly (Part 1)

Wait on the Lord; be of good courage, and He shall strengthen your heart. Wait, I say, on the Lord.
(Psalm 27:14)

Waiting is spoken of in Isaiah 40:31 with the idea of expecting good things to happen and being filled with hope as we wait. God says that while we wait we shall "mount up with wings as eagles". That means that we can live above our problems and be close to God during trials. When the Word says that we "shall run and not be weary and shall walk and not faint," it means that during any tribulation, God will give us supernatural strength to keep going – no matter what.

We suffer when we don't wait on God, but take matters into our own hands. My friend used to pray for a husband; but instead of waiting on God and seeking His perfect mate for her, she married the wrong man. Because she was so unhappy, she started doing drugs. She wanted out, but she wouldn't let God make her way of escape.

For many years I knew nothing of being patient. I thought the world revolved around me and no one else. Why did I have to wait in grocery lines? Why did I have to wait my turn at the doctor's office? I was a selfish, impatient person, but God knew how to teach me to be more long-suffering. He sent me to prison where I learned what it means to "wait on the Lord".

The message for today: Troubles are God's messengers to make us patient.

Prayer: Dear Heavenly Father, Please teach me to be patient in all things.

August 3 – Wait Expectantly (Part 2)

Wait on the Lord; be of good courage, and He shall strengthen your heart. Wait, I say, on the Lord.
(Psalm 27:14)

There are many scriptures in the Bible which counsel us on learning how to wait on God to answer prayer or for things to change in our lives. Many times we wait, but we are nervous and edgy with no peace or confidence in our Lord.

God makes us wait on purpose. Patience is developed as we have to wait on God to fix things. Paul says in I Corinthians 10:13 that "there hath no trial taken you but such as is common to man, but God is faithful, who will not allow you to be tested above that you are able, but will with the temptation also make a way of escape that you may be able to bear it."

God makes perfect ways of escape if we allow Him to. We could never arrange our circumstances to turn out as well as He can orchestrate them.

Are you waiting today for something to change in your life? Does it seem as if it never will? Well, take heart, my friend. As you submit yourself to God and don't try to tell Him how to run your life, you will be rewarded richly with His presence and His deliverance when He is ready.

The message for today: Rest in the Lord and wait for Him. Don't worry. Everything's under control.

Prayer: Dear Heavenly Father, Help me to wait with hope that You are working out my situation. Thank You for loving me so much.

August 4 – Breaking Down Walls

Jesus is our peace and has broken down the walls between us and Him. (Ephesians 2:13, 14)

I grew up in a terrible neighborhood. The children of the neighborhood were exposed to violence, gang wars, political factions, and mean neighbors. As a child, I never knew why people hated each other and fought all the time.

In Jesus' day, it was no different between the Jews and the Gentiles. They hated one another and would not even speak, but Jesus came to change that attitude. In Mark 2:16, 17 the disciples asked Jesus why He was mingling with the tax collectors and sinners. He told them that He came to preach the gospel to the poor, heal the brokenhearted, preach deliverance to the captives, to open blinded eyes, and give freedom to everyone who wanted it. What a deal!

Jesus came to teach us to stop looking down on others and give them a chance. It is amazing how people respond to real love! When someone knows they are loved, their whole attitude and behavior changes. I have seen hardened criminals break into tears when someone showed them the least amount of Christ's love.

I John 3:18 gives Christians a precious command as to how we should treat others when it tells us to not just love with words, but love others by doing kind deeds and being truthful with them.

The message for today: Break the walls of hatred with the love of Jesus.

Prayer: Dear Heavenly Father, Please help me to give Your love to those people You bring across my path.

August 5 – Read the Instructions

I was brought low, and He helped me. (Psalm 116:6)

Instructions are made to be followed. Warning signs are meant to help us to be alert, but sometimes we think we can beat the odds. The sad part is that we cannot beat the odds every time, and punishment awaits us.

God gave us His Word to warn us about many things. In Romans 1, He warns us against homosexuality. It is not according to God's laws of nature; but because people think they can commit this sin and not get caught, God must allow them to bear the penalty in their bodies. Literally, AIDS is the mark which homosexuality has left in the bodies of its victims.

No matter what the sin, there are consequences to ignoring our Lord's instructions in His Word. We take second best when we go our own way. God wants to give us His best as we love and obey Him.

As you start reading the Bible, ask the Holy Spirit to reveal truth to you. It is richly contained in God's Word. Keep reading every day, and soon you will come upon something that will minister to your heart. The Bible says that the Word of God is quick and powerful and pierces our hearts exactly where they need awakening. That's a good thing!

My heart was cold and sad when God started working on me in jail. Slowly but surely, He opened my heart to love Him. Now I ask Him to soften my heart and reveal sin to me daily as I try diligently to follow His instructions.

The message for today: God's Word is our owner's manual for life.

Prayer: Dear Heavenly Father, Help me to listen to You and obey Your commands and instructions.

August 6 – The Results of Praying

Confess your sins to each other and pray for each other so that you may be healed. (James 5:16)

I read a story about Stonewall Jackson, and I was thrilled as I thought about it. He said that he found great pleasure in prayer, and one of his favorite things to do was to include a written prayer in every letter he wrote. It became his personal way to share his faith in Christ. Later on, those who responded started putting prayers in their letters, too.

James 5:13-18 talks about the power of prayer in our lives. We need to reach out to others by praying for them every chance we get. James asks, "Are any among you suffering? They should keep on praying about it; are any among you sick? They should call for the elders of the church and have them pray over them..." James says that prayer offered in faith will make them well and sins will be forgiven! Prayer has power!

Elijah was a man just like us; and yet when he prayed that no rain would fall, it didn't rain for 3 years! When he prayed for rain, down it poured! God longs to answer the prayers of a believing saint. All we need to do is – pray.

What kind of method do you use to spread the gospel of Jesus? Do you pray for others; do you study the Word with others; do you sow love and kindness everywhere you go? Practice your own special gift with the world.

The message for today: Practice praying for others.

Prayer: Dear Heavenly Father, Please bring people across my path and help me pray for them.

August 7 – What's Your Faith Level?

Let me make just one more request. Allow me one more test with the fleece. (Judges 6:39)

Gideon was very much like us. He walked around in fear and doubt, but God saw great potential for this young man – just like He sees in us.

The angel of the Lord appeared unto Gideon while he was working and said unto him, "The Lord is with you, mighty man of valor." I can see Gideon looking up and replying, "Who, me? I'm a chicken!" (Judges 6:12, 13). Gideon needed his faith developed, just like we do; so God went to work by using the three levels of faith that we all need to learn.

Level One Faith is being able to believe only when we see a sign from God. Gideon asked that the fleece be wet and the ground dry just so he would really know God was with him. God granted that request. When we are immature Christians, we need to see God work. Our emotions get in the way of every prayer we pray. Like Gideon, we feel the fleece and are only able to trust God if it is wet. This is imperfect faith, even though it is genuine. Level One Faith believes only when emotions are favorable.

Level Two Faith believes even when all emotions and feelings are absent but still doesn't quite believe that God "loves me enough to answer my every prayer".

Level Three Faith believes God's Word when emotions and common sense seem contrary to what is happening in our life.

The message for today: Trust God's Word, even when every other sign points the opposite way.

Prayer: Dear Heavenly Father, Help me to have Level Three Faith.

August 8 – You're in Good Hands

...the Lord protects those who are loyal to Him.
(Psalm 31:23)

Psalm 46:1 tells us that God is our refuge and strength – a very present help in trouble. Proverbs 18:10 says that the name of the Lord is a strong tower. The righteous run into it and they are safe.

God is our wonderful Protector every moment of every day. He never gets tired or sleeps.

Every night I ask God for His mercy and protection through the night. When I awaken, I praise Him for His hand of safety and ask Him to guide the new day as only He can do. These prayers are especially needful for prisoners because every day brings new challenges that only God's grace is equipped to handle.

Joshua was filled with some fear of new challenges after Moses died, and he was appointed by God to lead the Israelites into the final phase of their wilderness, Promised-land journey. Even though he had "not passed this way before", God told him to be strong and very courageous, and He would protect him and all the people. We don't know how each day will turn out because "we have not passed this way before", but God has!

God's protection over me in jail has been a testimony to many people. They do not know Jesus, but they know someone is watching out for me. David said in Psalm 31:19, "Your goodness is so great! You have stored up great blessings for those who honor You. You have done so much for those who come to You for protection, blessing them before the watching world."

The message for today: God is the best body guard!

Prayer: Dear Heavenly Father, Thank You for Your great protection throughout my entire life.

August 9 – Psalm 32

*Therefore, let all the godly confess their rebellion
to You while there is time. (Psalm 32:6)*

A little story is told about a person thanking God that she hadn't gotten angry or been impatient with anyone that day. Then, the next line is "but I'm getting up now and I'll really need Your help!"

Meditate on Psalm 32:1-8 all day and let it sink deeply into your heart. Read it three times in succession and be blessed as I was this morning. Let's look at it together:

1 Oh what joy for those whose rebellion is forgiven, whose sin is put out of sight!
2 Yes, what joy for those whose record the Lord has cleared of sin, whose lives are lived in complete honesty!
3 When I refused to confess my sin, I was weak and miserable, and I groaned all day long.
4 Day and night Your hand of discipline was heavy upon me. My strength evaporated like water in summer heat.
5 Finally, I confessed all my sins to You and stopped trying to hide them. I said to myself, "I will confess my rebellion to the Lord," and You forgave me! All my guilt is gone!
6 Therefore, let all the godly confess their rebellion to You while there is time, that they may not drown in the floodwaters of judgment.
7 For You are my hiding place, and You protect me from trouble. You surround me with songs of victory.
8 The Lord says, "I will guide you along the best pathway for your life; I will advise you and watch over you..."

The message for today: Oh the joy of forgiven sins!

Prayer: Dear Heavenly Father, I confess my sins to You, Lord. Please return Your joy to me.

August 10 – Failure Isn't the End

I keep my body under subjection, lest by any means, when I have preached to others, I myself should be disqualified. (I Corinthians 9:27)

Have you ever tried something and failed? Failing is not a good experience; but someone has said that when we fail at something, we know what not to do the next time. Failure teaches us some good lessons that we could learn no other way.

Adam and Eve failed in the Garden of Eden and were cast out because of disobedience to God's one command. The greed of Judas ended in his committing suicide because of his guilt. Disobedience in God's Kingdom brings failure and sadness. Disobedience to natural laws brings bad results. When we disobey physical laws, we fail. When we obey all these laws, there is a reward.

I heard about a man who is facing life in a wheelchair because of overeating. He weighs 350 pounds and now can't walk more than a few steps. He disobeyed God's law of "moderation" in all things and is now literally paying the price. A gastric bypass to surgically stop him from overeating costs over $40,000, and his insurance won't pay for it. God still loves him, and His mercy will help him, but he is paying a painful price for disobedience and lack of self-control.

How do we do what Paul said and keep our bodies under control? How do we stop lying and stealing? It is only by a radical change from within. Jesus Christ is the only answer to all failure.

The message for today: Failure isn't the end. It could produce a new beginning.

Prayer: Dear Heavenly Father, Help me to take baby steps of control in my life.

August 11 – Change

When I am afraid I will trust in God.
(Psalm 56:3)

What type of personality do you have? Are you always smiling? Are you easy going and laid back? Are you supportive of others and always try to help? Or are you a stern, serious leader type?

We all fall into one of these categories. The person who falls into the supportive group usually hates change the most. Fear of the unknown makes people afraid of change. Instead of a spirit of adventure, they have a spirit of fear. They are always asking, "What if?" So many wonderful opportunities have been missed because of this timid attitude.

When I accepted Jesus into my life, He started showing me that He was the One who went ahead of me. Deuteronomy 31:8 says that "the Lord, He it is, who goes before you. He will not fail you or forsake you, so don't fear or look anxiously around." He did not say that we wouldn't feel fear. Fear is a very real emotion because it perceives hurt. Since we don't want to get hurt, we back down many times from great opportunities. God tells us to remember that He goes before us; and He will protect us, so we should not look around, expecting failure or hurt. We should "do it afraid".

When something you can't control happens, trust God to help you. He is the One who creates the circumstances of our lives. If He knows we need change, He will orchestrate it. It could be good or bad, but He will protect us through every change.

The message for today: There is nothing as permanent as change.

Prayer: Dear Heavenly Father, Help me to trust You during the changes of my life.

August 12 – God's Whispers

Ah, Lord God! Behold, Thou hast made the heaven and the earth by Thy great power and stretched out arm, and there is nothing too hard for Thee. (Jeremiah 32:17)

God allows us to enjoy so many good gifts because He is a good God. He does not give us anything bad until He sees us straying away from Him. Then He gives Satan permission to do what it takes to get us back to serving Him. God knows how to back us into a corner!

Most times when we have problems, we run to God for refuge and help. Then, when things are going well, we end up feeling as if we have everything under control and we don't need God.

C.S. Lewis wrote, "God whispers to us in our pleasures, but He shouts to us in our pain." If we refuse to listen to Him when He whispers, He may have to shout to get our attention. I always want to stay close enough to my Lord to hear His whispers – His still, small voice that is undetectable to most people.

Although God had given the Israelites a land flowing with milk and honey, they turned from Him and started sinning; so He caused calamity to come upon them. He really did them a favor because His goodness in punishing them drew them back to Him. That is what Romans 2:4 means when it says that "the goodness of God draws men to repentance."

The message for today: Sometimes God has to shout because we won't obey His whispers.

Prayer: Dear Heavenly Father, Thank You that You have my best at heart, and You will use any way You must to get my attention.

August 13 – What Can I Do?

Whatever your hand finds to do, do it with all your might. (Ecclesiastes 9:10)

A lady named Joyce decided to take a brisk walk around her neighborhood every morning. One Spring morning as she was walking, she was prompted by the Holy Spirit to pray for every home she passed. Sometimes she would walk the block and say hello to everyone she met. Through the months, she got to know a few of the neighbors by name. People soon started responding to her the moment they saw her, and she made many friends. Even though Joyce didn't recognize what was happening, she started seeing some of these same people at her church. God had answered her prayers because He saw her heart of love. She used what she had, and God rewarded it.

Mary lost her husband and sat in her friend's home crying. "It's all over! My life is over." Her friend looked at her and lovingly asked, "What do you like to do, Mary?" "Well, I love to bake pies, but what good is baking pies when there's no one to share them with?" Her friend suggested that she open a little pie shop and restaurant in the front of her home. She decided it was worth a try, and today (10 years later), Mary has a very successful business. Hundreds of friends pass through her town and always stop to have a piece of Mary's pie!

The message for today: What do you love to do? Offer God what you have, and He will use it.

Prayer: Dear Heavenly Father, Please use me in others' lives to make an eternal difference.

August 14 – Loose Him!

And he who was dead came forth, bound hand and foot with grave clothes; Jesus said unto them, "Loose him, and let him go." (John 11:44)

In John 11:1-6 Mary and Martha sent word to Jesus that their brother, Lazarus, was on the brink of death. Instead of rushing right over to Bethany, Jesus purposely waited two days to go to him. When He got to Bethany, Lazarus had died, and Mary and Martha were a little miffed at Jesus. "If You had been here, our brother would not have died," they moaned (John 11:21, 32). Jesus wept (because of their unbelief), but He asked them to take Him to the tomb where Lazarus lay.

Jesus told the grave keepers to remove the stone. Everyone gasped in unbelief (again) because they knew that his body would stink after four days, but Jesus looked at them and said, "Did I not tell you that if you would believe, you would see the glory of God?"

Jesus thanked His Heavenly Father that this would cause the people to believe and called Lazarus out of the tomb. (Someone has said that Jesus had so much power that if He had not called Lazarus by name, every single dead person would have come out of the grave!)

All at once, everyone saw Lazarus (wrapped in the grave clothes) come walking out of the tomb – alive and well! Jesus told the people to "loose him and let him go".

If there is something in your life that needs released from bondage, give it to Jesus.

The message for today: Jesus will loose anything that binds us – if we believe.

Prayer: Dear Heavenly Father, I believe that You can do all things. Help my unbelief.

August 15 – Solid as a Rock

The Lord is my rock and my fortress, my deliverer.
(II Samuel 22:2)

Jesus is called "The Rock" for good reason. When He comes into our life, He becomes that firm foundation on which we can stand in confidence. All through the Bible, God is portrayed as the Solid Rock of our faith.

If we build our relationship on Jesus Christ, our life takes a turn for the better. We still will have problems, because that is part of life; but we will be able to cope better because of Jesus. It's been said that Jesus Christ is no security against storms, but He is perfect security in storms. He has never promised us an easy passage, only a safe landing.

A friend of mine was working on the company computer when she accidentally deleted an old program. It was gone, and she couldn't recover it. She knew that she would probably be fired and she worried all day. She said that she was walking down the hall and the she heard the words, "I am Jesus and I will not fail you. You will not be fired, so don't let Satan tell you that you will." God allowed her to realize that He was in control – not the devil. She went back into the office and told her boss what had happened. Even though she had lost a whole data base, it was able to be retrieved from the main server! Jesus had brought her to a "safe landing" once again!

The message for today: Don't forget the Rock of your salvation. He's a sure foundation.

Prayer: Dear Heavenly Father, Help me to know that no problem is too big for You. You are my Rock, my Fortress, and my Deliverer!

August 16 – The Lord is with You

Joseph's master put him in prison…but…the Lord was with him…and gave him success in whatever he did. (Genesis 39:20, 21, 23)

In foreign countries people are placed into dark, cold prisons without enough to eat because of their stand for the Gospel of Jesus Christ.

When God allows people to go to prison because of their service to Him, it is nearly the most blessed place in the world they could be, because He goes with them. Joseph probably knew this truth very well. He did not sulk or become discouraged or mean. He didn't pity himself by thinking, "Everything is against me!" If he had done so, the prison warden would never have trusted him.

If you want favor in prison, you must bear some of the responsibility. At first, when I went to prison, I wanted to scream every day. It was so terrible to be incarcerated, but I soon realized that Jesus Christ was with me right there in that prison. He had no plans of leaving or forsaking me. He loved me enough to mold my character and help me become the child of God that He knew I could be, and it was because of prison.

If we allow self-pity to set in, we will never be used by God again until it is fully removed. Joseph simply placed everything in joyful trust upon the Lord; and as a result, the prison warden placed everything in Joseph's care!

When the prison door closes behind you, keep trusting in God with overflowing joy that He is in control.

The message for today: You can truly be free – even in prison.

Prayer: Dear Heavenly Father, Help me to see the brightness of Your face, even in the darkness of sorrow.

August 17 – Success

Be strong and very courageous and obey
all the law…turn not from it…so that you may
prosper wherever you go. (Joshua 1:7)

When Moses died, God appointed Joshua to be the leader of the Israelites – a very big job! How would you like to lead 3 million people across a desert? Only God could be the strength that Joshua needed!

God is a God of success. He wants us to succeed in all we do, and He has given us guidelines for victory in our lives. God gave Joshua three secrets of success for leading the Israelites. They apply to our lives, too.

1. Be strong and brave. God thought this was important enough to repeat it three times because He knew that any time we accept a challenge to do anything that honors Him, it will bring opposition. If we don't exercise our faith, we will give up without successfully completing the challenge.
2. Obey all the laws of God and do not turn away from them. This insures success in our challenges. Isn't it funny that we look at success as having control of someone or something, but God equates success with being controlled by Him? He tells us that to succeed we must live godly lives that are in obedience to His law – the Bible.
3. Constantly study and meditate on God's Word in order to know God's mind regarding your challenges. When we become uncertain of what to do, knowledge of God's Word is what keeps us focused on the right path to success.

The message for today: Success is on our doorstep as we obey God.

Prayer: Dear Heavenly Father, Help me to use all the keys to success, which You have given me.

August 18 – The Trinity

*The grace of the Lord Jesus Christ and the love of God
and the fellowship of the Holy Spirit be with you all.
(II Corinthians 13:14)*

The Christian faith is so difficult for our human minds to comprehend. It is argued fiercely by cults and Eastern religions that there is only one god, and his name is Jehovah or Allah. How could he possibly be a three-part being? According to man's understanding, there is no way for God to be a trinity (Father, Son, and Holy Ghost).

The Trinity cheers us on in our race of life. Each member has His own special place to play in our Christian life.

Did you know that the "grace of the Lord Jesus Christ" cheers you on? Grace shows God's unmerited favor to us sinful humans. It gives us a behavior that is excellent toward others. It gives us strength during trials.

Did you know that the "love of God" cheers you on? God's love is so awesome that we cannot comprehend how He could ask His Son Jesus Christ to sacrifice His life on the cross for you and me; but He did, and Jesus won the victory over Satan for time and eternity. We are victorious because Jesus was victorious over the devil!

Did you know that the "fellowship of the Holy Spirit" cheers you on? The Holy Spirit always points people to Jesus Christ, our Savior. He is not an "influence". He is the Third Person of the Trinity who comes to live inside our very bodies when we ask Jesus to be our Savior.

The message for today: How can we fail with so much power behind us?

Prayer: Dear Heavenly Father, Thank You for being the great Three-In-One God!

August 19 – Think Big

I know that You can do all things and that no thought or purpose of Yours can be restrained or frustrated. (Job 42:2)

Have you ever been in a situation that looked impossible? When I first was sentenced to go to prison, all I heard the judge say was, "17 years". My life crumbled before me. How could this happen? My small thinking told me that I could never make it. I never once thought about God and how all things are possible to us if we believe His Word. Instead of asking God what He was going to do, all I could think about was, 'What am I going to do?'

I wish I had known Matthew 19:26 at the time, and I would have said out loud, "But Jesus looked at them and said, 'With men this is impossible, but all things are possible with God.'" One day as I was praying about my sentence, God let my spirit know that I would never serve 17 years in prison. Soon after that, my attorneys came in and told me that my sentence would probably be cut in half!

God delivered the children of Israel by doing many miracles right before their eyes; but their small thinking wouldn't allow them to look beyond the giants of the new land. They should have known that when their feet touched the border of the Promised Land, the giants would disintegrate!

The message for today: "Impossible" is not in God's vocabulary.

Prayer: Dear Heavenly Father, I give You my giants. Help me to trust You and speak faith over them.

August 20 – A New Season

...as the heavens are higher than the earth, so are My ways higher than your ways, and My thoughts than your thoughts. (Isaiah 55:8, 9)

My friend was so confused after a failed missionary journey. She asked the Lord why He would permit such a failure, and the words of Isaiah 55:8 came to her mind. God assured her that He had a plan she could not understand then; but in time He would reveal why He allowed the failure. She hung on to that for years, and one day as she was reading the Word, she read that if we are not willing to give up houses and lands for the sake of the Gospel, we cannot be God's followers (Matthew 19:29). At that moment, the Lord revealed to her how pleased He was to know that she and her husband were willing to obey, even though it meant certain failure. He had given them a test, and they had passed!

Jeremiah saw a branch of a tree when he looked around (Jeremiah 1:11). God told him that He had appointed him to root out the wickedness and to destroy and overthrow it, as well as to build and plant. Jeremiah's tree branch, which signified the emblem of alertness and activity, blossoming in late winter, was God's spiritual Springtime coming!

Sometimes in the dark Winter seasons of our life, we cannot see the good things that are coming; but just as one season has to give way to another, a new day is coming.

The message for today: No matter what season you are in, better days are ahead with Jesus as your Leader.

Prayer: Dear Heavenly Father, Even if I can't understand Your ways, help me to trust Your hand in my life.

August 21 – Dispel the Darkness

The people who walked in darkness have seen a great Light; those who dwelt in the land of intense darkness and the shadow of death, upon them has the Light shined. (Isaiah 9:2)

A pastor reported to his congregation about his visit to an African village where missionaries had never gone. He and his team arrived in the middle of the night with a huge truck filled with beans and rice. The truck was unloaded and left, leaving the village in total darkness. The moon and stars were not out that night. Because of their intense hunger, the people started grabbing at the team in the hope that they would somehow find the food they needed so much. He said he was never so afraid in his whole life. He went to his tent and sat there until dawn. Someone yelled out, "Chicken!" He told the congregation that if they had been there, they would have done the same thing.

That pastor took the Light to that tribe, though. Three chiefs and the whole village accepted Jesus as their Savior! God had prepared them to respond to the invitation of Jesus!

Consider for a moment that you are a candle whom Jesus has sent to light other prisoners' lives.

Jesus talked about our Christian testimony right after He gave the Beatitudes in Matthew 5. He said that, "You are the light of the world. A city set on a hill cannot be hidden. Nor do men light a lamp and put it under a basket, but on a lamp stand, and it gives light to all in the house."

The message for today: Let your light so shine before men that they see Jesus. (Matthew 5:16)

Prayer: Dear Heavenly Father, Please use me in people's dark lives.

✝ August 22 – Our Soul Man

For all that is in the world – the lust of the flesh, the lust of the eyes, and the pride of life – these do not come from the Father but are from the world. (I John 2:16)

All through our life we tend to listen to our "soul man", our fleshly desire that gets us in trouble. In the Bible, there are many examples of people listening to their flesh with terrible results.

Genesis 3 talks about how Satan tricked Eve into taking the apple from the forbidden tree. He wasn't an ugly snake like we picture him; he was a beautiful creature whom she had no reason to fear. Since the curse of Adam had not entered the human race yet, Eve knew nothing of fear, so she listened to his words and gave in to the temptation he offered her. When she gave the fruit to Adam and he ate it, the whole human race from then on was "under sin". Sin entered the whole world through one man, Adam.

If Adam and Eve had not listened to their flesh, sin might not have entered the world then; but Satan would have kept trying because he hated God for expelling him from heaven. Through the ages, he has caused people to sin because he hates Jesus Christ and His atoning death for us.

Our soul man causes us to sin. Sin makes us want our way instead of God's way; and when we act independently of God, disaster results.

The message for today: Walking in the Holy Spirit is the only way to counteract Satan's desires for our life.

Prayer: Dear Heavenly Father, Help me to walk in the Spirit and not fulfill the lust of my flesh.

August 23 – God's Beauty Contest

...beauty is vain because it is not lasting, but a woman who reverently and worshipfully fears the Lord, she shall be praised. (Proverbs 31:30)

My parents wanted me to grow up and be beautiful, but I didn't turn out as pretty as they would have liked. When I was growing up and even now, people don't classify me as beautiful; but the last time I checked the Word of God, He said that I am fearfully and wonderfully made in His likeness.

With the Holy Spirit living in me, God sees beauty and perfection. When I first read II Corinthians 4:7 I was so happy! It says, "For we have this treasure in earthen vessels that the excellency of the power may be of God and not of us." I'm just the container for the Holy Spirit, and it's what is inside that counts!

God even says that my feet are beautiful! In Romans 10:15 Paul says, "How beautiful are the feet of those who bring glad tidings!" If I walk in His ways and obey His Word, my feet will take me places that the world can't take me. God will lead me in the "paths of righteousness for His name's sake." He will lead me to the unsaved who need Him.

We do not need people's acceptance to know we are beautiful in Jesus' eyes. He made us in His image, and His main concern is our soul – not just our looks. How beautiful is your soul today?

The message for today: You are the apple of God's eye (Psalm 17:8), and He hides you under the shadow of His wings.

Prayer: Dear Heavenly Father, Help me to see myself as You see me – beautiful!

August 24 – Growing in Faith

As for the man who is a weak believer, welcome him into your fellowship, but not to criticize his opinions or pass judgment on his scruples or perplex him with discussions. (Romans 14:1)

Romans 14 tells us not to dislike people who are different from us. That is a big command for prisoners because we come in contact with all different kinds of people. Some say they believe in Jesus, but they aren't taught to act like Him. When you meet someone who is a baby Christian, it is your job to build them up – not tear them down or judge them.

Paul gives good advice to the believers of Galatia when he says, "Brethren, if any person is overtaken in misconduct or sin of any sort, you who are spiritual should set him right and restore him without any sense of superiority and with all gentleness, keeping an attentive eye on yourself, lest you should be tempted also." (Galatians 6:1)

As we grow in our faith, God teaches us to love others and take their feelings into account. He knows where we are in our Christian walk, and He helps us to love people supernaturally.

The life of faith means submitting to God and learning what He expects of us. Be patient if you feel that you have not "arrived" in your Christian growth. You will not arrive until the day Jesus Christ takes you home to heaven! We never stop learning and growing. God never stops teaching and stretching us.

The message for today: Love others, no matter where they are in their faith.

Prayer: Dear Heavenly Father, Help me to walk obediently in the light You have given me and not judge others because they are not like me.

August 25 – Addictions

Let your moderation be known to all men.
(Philippians 4:5)

The word addiction comes from the original word "addictus", which means "to surrender". When a person is addicted to something, he has literally surrendered to its power.

Addictions come from Satan. He lures people with a little bait and then reels in the line tighter and tighter until they are held captive and have "surrendered" to their lifestyle. The addicted person lives an out-of-balance life. We can get addicted to drugs and alcohol, or the addiction can be more subtle. It can be anything from chewing gum, to overeating, to watching TV. Here are some suggestions to stopping addictive behavior:

1. Admit to yourself that you have a problem with _____.

2. Tell someone close to you about your problem. You will be amazed how this helps!

3. Be accountable to a close friend. Report once a week to the person and tell them how things are going.

4. Keep a journal of your successes and failures. Sometimes you will fail, but more times than not, you will succeed if you know you will have to write it down.

The message for today: Jesus is the remedy to any obsessive behavior.

Prayer: Dear Heavenly Father, Please deliver me from my addiction to _____. Help me to help myself by Your grace.

✝
August 26 – Shut the Door

And they went away in a boat to a solitary place by themselves. (Mark 6:32)

Jesus Christ knew the secret to power with people. He regularly spent quiet time with His Heavenly Father. His ministry could not have succeeded without taking this time alone. His inner strength came from quiet times with His Father.

It is difficult and almost impossible in prison to find a quiet place to be with the Lord, but God tells us to purposely spend time with Him daily in His Word in quietness.

Every day I try to live according to the following advice...

> Find a place to be alone with God – a quiet place with no pressure and noise, and God will meet you there. He awaits your coming, for He longs to pour out His blessings on you. He longs to give you power and revelation.

> Be very still before God. Don't let the toils and cares of the day rob you of this sweet fellowship with Him, for He knows what you need and is concerned about your every duty and responsibility.

You will find your cares vanished and your load lightened by an Unseen Hand. He will bring His power to you so that your work will produce a two-fold measure of success!

The message for today: Get alone with God – rest in Him and wait on Him to reveal great things to you.

Prayer: Dear Heavenly Father, Please help me to get alone with You every day and draw strength from You for my day.

August 27 – Humility 101

*Blessed are the poor in spirit (the humble,
who rate themselves insignificant) for theirs is
the kingdom of heaven. (Matthew 5:3)*

The first beatitude describes how to be blessed in the Christian life, but it's not a simple thing. We can easily say, "I'll be blessed if I'm humble," but humility is not an easy trait to attain. We are all so proud and independent. Jeremiah 17:9 says something quite sad about all of us. It tells us that "the heart is deceitful above all things and desperately wicked. Who can perceive, understand, be acquainted with his own heart and mind?"

Many prisoners find it difficult to rely on God. It is easier to manipulate or force people to do what they want them to do than to be humble and trust God.

God tells us that He should mean everything to us – not just be a crutch when we need Him. We will be greatly blessed and be a part of God's kingdom for eternity if we strive to please God first in our lives. Anything else is "second best", and God doesn't want us to only have what is "left over".

Today, rid yourself of pride and self-reliance by asking Jesus to help you read the Bible and pray daily. Seek to know God so intimately that there is perfect harmony between you and Him. Start watching for blessings as you put Him first.

The message for today: When we grow spiritually, we start thinking less of ourselves and more of God.

Prayer: Dear Heavenly Father, Help my life to show forth Your power – not mine.

August 28 – Treasure Hunting

For where your treasure is, there will your heart be also.
(Luke 12:34)

In the Bible, Jesus teaches us how to get our priorities straightened out, but in prison, that is not an easy task. It is easy to see where prisoners' hearts are as you listen to or watch them trading their possessions for something they want more. Jesus says that our attitude toward possessions shows where our priorities are.

Read Matthew 6:19-22, 24:

Do not gather and heap up for yourselves treasures on earth, where moth and rust and worm consume and destroy, and where thieves break through and steal. But gather and heap up and store for yourselves treasures in heaven, where neither moth nor rust nor worm consume and destroy, and where thieves do not break through and steal. For where your treasure is, there will your heart be also...No one can serve two masters; for either he will hate the one and love the other, or he will stand by the one and despise and be against the other. You cannot serve God and money (deceitful riches, possessions, or whatever is trusted in).

Psalm 37:16 says that "it is better to be godly and have little than to be evil and possess much." Do you get the point? God wants to bless our lives "abundantly", but He can't until we hold our money and possessions loosely. It is not our stuff; it is God's, and we are just the stewards of it.

The message for today: Things take wings and fly away, but no one can steal your spiritual riches.

Prayer: Dear Heavenly Father, Help me to treasure Jesus more than material things.

August 29 – From Darkness to Light

At midnight Paul and Silas were praying and singing hymns to God. (Acts 16:25)

There are many things we can do at midnight, especially in the secular lifestyle. Before I became a Christian, I used to do things that were unlawful, ugly, and sinful at night.

Before Paul accepted Jesus Christ, he persecuted Christians mercilessly; but when he met Jesus he did those things that pleased Him. His behavior changed from darkness to light.

Because I am in prison, I don't have the temptations that I would have if I were free, and I am so glad about that. In prison, I don't have to worry about robbing a bank. However, Satan makes prisoners' temptations much more subtle. He attacks our thought life and attitudes. I have to be constantly alert to his influence on my mind, but I see God daily molding me and making me after His will. I praise Him for my environment and for His mighty knowledge that I needed it!

It might be "midnight" in your heart right now, and you are tired of all your sins. They are no longer fun. Everything seems at its darkest, but there is a loving, merciful God Who is waiting for you to turn from your sinful deeds and trust Jesus as your Savior. When you do, your night season will turn to day. God will bring you inexpressible joy, even in prison. Jesus is the Light of the World and is a real Savior who lights up your life.

The message for today: Let the light from heaven shine down on you!

Prayer: Dear Heavenly Father, Thank You that Jesus shed His blood for me on that cross so that I could experience light in my soul!

August 30 – It's No Big Secret

With God all things are possible. (Matthew 19:26)

In the 50's, a radio host named Stuart Hamblem poked fun at a young preacher holding a revival in Hollywood. To further hassle him, Stuart showed up at one of the meetings. In the service the preacher announced, "There is one man in this audience who is a big fake." Hamblem was convinced that he was the "fake". He showed up drunk at the preacher's hotel room around 2:00 a.m. demanding that the preacher pray for him. But the preacher refused, saying, "This is between you and God, not between you and me." However, he invited Stuart in, and they talked until 5:00 a.m. — at which point Stuart dropped to his knees and with tears, cried out to God for salvation.

Because of Stuart's conversion, he lost his job at the radio station, and hard times were upon him.

A friend named John told him that all his troubles started when he "got religion" and asked if it was all worth it. Stuart answered, "Yes". John asked him how he could give up his lifestyle so easily, and his response was, "It's no secret. All things are possible with God." "That's a catchy phrase. You should write a song about it," said John. So Stuart did…

"It is no secret what God can do; what He's done for others, He'll do for you.

With arms wide open, He'll welcome you. It is no secret what God can do!"

Incidentally, the friend was John Wayne, and the young preacher who refused to pray for Stuart Hamblem was Billy Graham.

The message for today: Come to Jesus. He'll welcome you.

Prayer: Dear Heavenly Father, Thank You for rescuing me from my sin.

August 31 – Growing Up

But grow in grace and in the knowledge of our Lord and Savior Jesus Christ. (II Peter 3:18)

Once there was a little boy who was tired of his mother's instructions. "Why can't I be treated like an adult?" he asked. His mother replied, "Because you have to learn how to be a good child before you can be a good adult." She went on to tell him that he would always have teachers who would instruct him in the things of life.

There's a saying that "every expert was once a beginner". Every pilot was once a passenger on a plane. Every teacher was once a student. No one starts out being an expert without prior experience. Remember the old saying, "Experience is the best teacher." Bad experiences teach us what to do differently next time; good experiences teach us confidence.

God doesn't give up on His children in prison. He lovingly teaches us every lesson through circumstances which come into our lives. In Psalm 139 David said that no matter where he went he could not get away from God. He asked God, "Where shall I go from Your Spirit, or where shall I flee from Your presence? If I ascend up into heaven, You are there; if I make my bed in hell, behold, You are there!" (Psalm 139:7, 8).

Is God trying to get His point across to you today in some area of your life? Allow Him freedom to mold you as He pleases. It will bring rich rewards!

The message for today: Every level of spiritual growth teaches us something new. Keep on learning.

Prayer: Dear Heavenly Father, Help me to get Your lessons the first time and not have to repeat the course.

Notes

September

September 1 – Anticipation

And now, little children, abide in Him, that when He shall appear, we may have confidence and not be ashamed before Him at His coming. (I John 2:28)

God told Simeon that he would not see death until he saw the Messiah, Jesus Christ. His waiting paid off when he walked into the temple one day and saw Mary and Joseph and their child, Jesus. He took him in his arms and thanked God and said, "Lord, now You can let me die in peace for my eyes have seen Your salvation!" He had waited so long and finally saw Jesus, the Savior of the world! He waited because he knew that what God had promised, He would perform.

Is there anything you are waiting for today? Perhaps you are eagerly waiting for a court date or word from your attorney about your release. The most important thing we could ever wait for is the soon-coming return of our Lord Jesus. All other waiting pales in comparison to that wait.

The message for today: Plan your life as if Jesus isn't coming back for 50 years, but live as if He's coming back today.

Prayer: Dear Heavenly Father, Help me to live a holy life so that I will be eagerly anticipating my Savior's return.

September 2 – Putting Down Roots

And the man who delights in the Lord shall be like a tree firmly planted by the streams of water, ready to bring forth its fruit in due season. Its leaf shall not fade or wither, and everything he does shall prosper. (Psalm 1:3)

The verse for today contains a promise. Did you see it? If you delight yourself in the Lord, He will make everything you touch successful! Most of us in jail or prison don't really believe that, because we have bought Satan's lies. "Things just never turn out right for me" is what most of us say, and our words come true; but God has an excellent future for us as we put Him first.

Read Colossians 2:6-8 from The Living Bible and let it speak to your heart.

And now, just as you trusted Christ to save you, trust Him, too, for each day's problems. Live in vital union with Him. Let your roots grow down into Him and draw up nourishment from Him. See that you go on growing in the Lord and become strong and vigorous in the truth you were taught. Let your lives overflow with joy and thanksgiving for all He has done. Don't let others spoil your faith and joy with their philosophies, their wrong and shallow answers built on men's thoughts and ideas, instead of on what Christ has said.

God really wants you to prosper spiritually, emotionally, socially, physically, and financially. Don't believe anything else.

The message for today: God is able to make every favor and earthly blessing come to you in abundance as you put Him first. (II Corinthians 9:8)

Prayer: Dear Heavenly Father, Help me to believe that You want me to be blessed.

September 3 – You are Being Followed

Surely goodness and mercy shall follow me
all the days of my life. (Psalm 23:6)

Psalm 23 is full of promises for prisoners. This psalm was written by David, a former shepherd boy, who sat at night and looked into the heavens. There were no street lights or distractions – only the serene quietness of the atmosphere. It must have been wonderful!

Sometimes in prison, I long for quietness. I wish I could turn off the loud voices and noise; but since I can't, I meditate every time there is even a hint of "quiet" around me.

If the Lord is your Shepherd, the Bible says that you will not want for anything. That doesn't mean that you won't have any needs but that Jesus will be your portion in all circumstances.

If the Lord is your Shepherd, He will bring your soul to a place of quietness. He will make you lie down in green pastures beside the "still" waters.

If the Lord is your Shepherd, He will be with you in trouble – in the valley of the shadow of death. He will give you confidence – you do not need to fear because Jesus is in the trial with you.

God loves us so much that we cannot comprehend, no matter how hard we try, to grasp that love. Goodness and mercy follow us everywhere we go! I have been very glad for God's mercy following me when I should have had judgment.

The message for today: Memorize Psalm 23 to get a better picture of our Heavenly Father.

Prayer: Dear Heavenly Father, Thank You for Your provision for my every need!

September 4 – The Prodigal Son

And when he came to himself, he said, "My father's
hired servants have bread enough to spare, and
I perish with hunger!" (Luke 15:17)

We have all been prodigal sons at one time or another, and we are still capable of becoming one again. The choices we make can lead us down the road that takes us to prison where God can bring us closer to Him, in spite of our incarceration.

My friend shared a letter that she received from a broken-hearted woman whose husband had left her for another woman. Listen to her hurt.

"I want to let you know that God is at work in some way in John's heart. He has begun to weep over his actions, yet is still very much connected with his girlfriend, Brenda. The battle rages on for John's release from Satan's lies. Your fervent prayers are needed at this time for the whole situation.

Please pray for God to continue to press hard on John's and Brenda's hearts until their relationship is totally destroyed. Pray that John will come to his senses and return in genuine repentance to his heavenly Father and will allow God to heal him and change him."

A line from "Growing Young" by Rich Mullins —

And everybody used to tell me big boys don't cry.
Well, I've been around enough to know that was the lie
That held back the tears in the eyes of a thousand prodigal sons.

The message for today: Your Father still waits, and He watches down the road to see you coming back to Him again.

Prayer: Dear Heavenly Father, Please forgive me for turning from Your love. I return in repentance to You. Thank You for loving me so much!

September 5 – Here's My Plan, God

A man's mind plans his way, but the Lord directs his steps and makes them sure. (Proverbs 16:9)

Helen had her day planned out perfectly! She had an important job interview. She got ready with great anticipation for the day. She decided that since she had extra time she would go by her favorite store and buy a dress for her first day on the new job.

While Helen was in the dressing room of the store, she heard an angry male voice demanding everyone to lie down on the floor. She froze with fear. She would be discovered in that dressing room! She breathed an urgent prayer, "Please help us, Lord", and then it happened. The man burst into her dressing room and demanded that she get on the floor with the others.

Helen did something then that is totally out of character for a hostage. She looked at the man and said, "No, I will not get on the floor! In the mighty name of Jesus Christ, I command you to leave us alone and not harm one of us!" The surprised man wanted to kill her, but instead, he turned and ran out of the store!

Jesus had given her a holy boldness that was just what was needed in the critical situation, but Helen was never the same after that day! She had her day planned, but God interrupted her plan with His mighty lesson that needed to be taught.

The message for today: Do you know how to make God laugh? Tell Him your plans.

Prayer: Dear Heavenly Father, I have not passed this way before and I don't know what this day will bring, so I'm giving it to You to direct as You see fit.

September 6 – Learning to Fly Alone

As an eagle that stirs up her nest that flutters over her young, God spread abroad His wings and took them and bore them on His wings. (Deuteronomy 32:11)

God uses natural stories in the Bible to allow us to see His love for us. Can you picture a mother eagle making the nest very uncomfortable for the two eaglets who want to stay there? Every time they get the least bit comfortable, she messes up the nest again! She then pushes each one out of the nest! Sounds cruel, doesn't it? But that is the only way the tiny chicks will learn to fly on the wind thermals that are waiting for them. The mother eagle knows the exact time to start this behavior, because God has placed within her a marvelous pre-patterned behavior to know when to stir up the nest.

As the tiny chick is panicking, the mother comes underneath it and lets it rest on her giant wings. Then she releases it yet again, and soon the eaglet gets its "flying wings" and is confident. This learning experience has gone on since the beginning of time. Each mother eagle produces strong, confident birds of prey.

God also uses the eagle's strategy in teaching us to "fly on our own". When He decides to change our circumstances, He does some tough stuff in our lives to force us to "fly". We think these things are mean and cruel, but God relentlessly works with us (His children) to teach us the lessons we must know in the Christian life to survive.

The message for today: Has God been ruffling your nest lately?

Prayer: Dear Heavenly Father, Help me to know that You only have my best in mind when my circumstances change.

September 7 – Thank You, Lord!

Praise be to the Lord, to God my Savior,
who daily bears my burdens! (Psalm 68:19)

Praise is the substitute for negative thinking. Every time I am down, I start praising God with my mouth. I have listed some of the ways I praise my Lord, using His names, which show His attributes. In prison, this is a great release when you feel like screaming at someone.

As the Word dwells richly in you, God will start re-programming your mind for victory!

1. I praise You today, Lord, that You are my Jehovah-jireh – my Provider. You make grace abound and generously provide all I need. (II Cor. 9:8)
2. I praise You today, Lord, that You are my Jehovah-shalom – the Lord my Peace. You are my God of peace who will soon crush Satan under my feet! (Romans 16:20)
3. I praise You today, Lord, that You are my Jehovah- rapha – the God who heals. You heal me physically, spiritually, and every other way! (Isaiah 53:4)
4. I praise You today, Lord, that You are my Jehovah- shammah – the God who is present with me, even in jail. You are with me always and You will never forsake me. (Hebrews 13:5)

The message for today: Everything we will ever need is found in our God!

Prayer: Dear Heavenly Father, Thank You for being everything I need at every moment of my life.

September 8 – Who's in Control?

Pray for all who are in positions of authority that you may live in peace. (I Timothy 2:2)

America has lost its respect for all authority figures, both spiritual and governmental, because we are in the last days before Jesus Christ returns.

Being a prisoner, I hated to pray for our government authorities because they put me in prison. When I was living my sinful lifestyle, I was constantly aware of the police. I know now that it was because I had something to fear – getting caught.

God has placed the police in control. Many members of the police force are unsaved and love to "catch" people doing wrong, but God is still in control. The Bible says that He sets up and tears down rulers.

Paul, who spent a lot of time in prison, wrote to us in Romans 13:1-5 some very thought-provoking commands:

Let every person be loyally subject to the governing authorities. For there is no authority except by God's permission, and those authorities exist by God's appointment. Therefore, he who resists the authorities resists what God has appointed and arranged. And those who resist will bring down judgment on themselves. For civil authorities are not a terror to people of good conduct but to those of bad behavior. You would have no dread of him who is in authority if you were doing right. For he is God's servant for your good; but if you do wrong, you should dread him and be afraid for he does not bear and wear the sword for nothing.

The message for today: Obeying authority pleases God.

Prayer: Dear Heavenly Father, Help me to pray for all those in authority over me and obey You fully.

September 9 – It's Almost Time

For the Lord Himself will descend from heaven with a
loud cry of summons, with the shout of an archangel,
and with the blast of the trumpet of God...
(I Thessalonians 4:16)

The Church Age is about to end, folks. Jesus, our Lord, is about to return for the true believers. As one person put it, "We are sitting of the second hand of Jesus' return." Picture it being 11:59 p.m. and Jesus is returning at midnight!

The Word tells us that in the last days, bad things will happen and be out of control. Let's look at those things. Do any of them sound familiar in your prison life?

> "...in the last days perilous times will come. People will be utterly self-centered, lovers of money and greedy, proud and boastful. They will be abusive, disobedient to parents, ungrateful, unholy and profane. They will be unfeeling and contract breakers; they will be false accusers and troublemakers with no patience and loose morals and conduct. They will be uncontrolled and fierce, haters of good."
> (II Timothy 3:1-3)

Even though things are getting worse, Deuteronomy 28:1 says that if we accept Jesus Christ as our Lord and Savior and strive to obey Him in all we do, we will experience all the blessings He has for us in these troubled times.

The message for today: Be ready when the trumpet sounds!

Prayer: Dear Heavenly Father, Thank You for Your promise of Christ's return!

September 10 – Who Are You Hangin' With?

I wrote to you in my previous letter not to associate closely and habitually with unchaste and impure people... (I Corinthians 5:9)

You have heard the old saying, "You take on the characteristics of the people you're around". It is truer than most of us would like to admit. Paul says that "evil companionships corrupt good morals", and he is so correct. (I Corinthians 15:33)

I have found it very difficult to think and act right in prison. No matter where I turn, there is a sinful attitude or action going on. After praying much about this, the Lord showed me that, although external things are negative, it is possible to keep my heart and mind on Jesus Christ and His example to me.

Romans 12:1-3 tells us how to keep our attitudes and actions pure, even in a less-than-desirable environment. "I appeal to you therefore, brethren, and beg of you in view of all the mercies of God, to make a decisive dedication of your bodies and minds as a living sacrifice, holy and well pleasing to God. Do not be conformed to this world, but be transformed by the entire renewal of your mind by its new ideals and its new attitude..."

If you know Jesus as your Savior, the Holy Spirit lives inside you, and He can supernaturally transform your thinking and your actions with your cooperation. He did it for me! He will do it for you!

The message for today: Jesus was a friend of sinners, but they never once influenced His walk with His Father.

Prayer: Dear Heavenly Father, Show me how to influence others for good.

September 11 – No Fear

*Moses brought the people from the camp to meet
God, and they stood at the foot of the mountain.
(Exodus 19:17)*

God had some very strict rules for the Israelites in their exodus from Egypt to the Promised Land. When they came to Mt. Sinai, they were not allowed to go up the mountain or touch the border of it, or they would die.

Our minds cannot begin to comprehend the power of the God of creation. Hebrews calls Him a "consuming fire" because of the awesome power He possesses. He spoke and our entire solar system came into being. He sustains the universe daily and yet loves each one of us as though we were the only person in the world! That is a powerful God!

Hebrews 12:18 talks about the Israelites at Mt. Sinai and compares New Testament Christianity to the Old Testament Law. The writer tells us, "You have not come as did the Israelites in the wilderness to a material mountain that can be touched, a mountain ablaze with fire where you will be stoned to death if you touch it. But rather, you have come to Mount Zion, even to the city of the living God, the heavenly Jerusalem, and to countless multitudes of angels in a great gathering."

We serve a merciful, loving God who wants to bring us to His heavenly Kingdom someday.

The message for today: Learn to know the loving and faithful God who wants nothing but the best for you.

Prayer: Dear Heavenly Father, Teach me more about You and Your love.

September 12 – The "Now" God

And God said to Moses, "I am who I am". Tell Pharaoh "I AM" has sent you. (Exodus 3:14)

In our small minds, everything has to have a beginning and an end. We look at our time in prison as if it will never end, but one day it will.

God is a present-tense God. He is not the great "I will be". He is not the great "I was", but He is the great "I AM". When we call on Him, He is there "now". He hears and answers our prayers according to His great mercies.

What do you need now? If you need a friend, He wants to be that Friend. If you need a lawyer, He will fill those shoes perfectly. The Word says that "we have an advocate with the Father, Jesus Christ the Righteous." (I John 2:1)

When Jesus was healing people, He seldom told them to "wait a minute". He was always there for them the moment they needed Him. He touched them, and they were healed instantly. Jesus is the same yesterday, today, and forever (Hebrews 13:8). He is a "now" God.

God is not limited by time and space as we are, but He understands our needs. He answers prayer when He knows we need it – not necessarily when we want it. God is never early, never late, but always on time!

The message for today: Let God's timing order your life today. Just settle down and relax. He has everything under control.

Prayer: Dear Heavenly Father, Thank You for being the great "I AM" who knows exactly what I need.

September 13 – How to Win the War

It is true that I am an ordinary, weak human being, but I don't use human plans and methods to win my battles. I use God's mighty weapons, not those made by men, to knock down the devil's strongholds. (II Corinthians 10:3, 4)

Are there any "situations" in your life that are bothering you? Have you thought about every conceivable way to solve those problems, and you still can't come up with answers? We all have experienced the "common sense" route, and sometimes we come up with nothing but confusion.

What are God's weapons? How does He knock down the devil's plans against us?

In prison we must fight battles everyday, but God gives us every weapon we need to win every battle in Ephesians 6:11-17. Since we fight spiritual battles, God protects our mind, will, and emotions with His weapons of the helmet of salvation, the breastplate of His righteousness, the belt of truth, the gospel sandals of peace, the Sword of the Spirit (the Bible), and the shield of faith (which quenches all the fiery darts that Satan hurls at us).

When we immerse ourselves in the Bible and seek the Lord with all our hearts in prayer on a regular basis, a marvelous transformation takes place, and we start to win the war over Satan. Jesus already accomplished the victory over Satan on the cross. We just need to put the armor on and fight him!

The message for today: Your armor won't jump onto your body. You must pick it up and put it on to win battles.

Prayer: Dear Heavenly Father, Thank You for your mighty weapons of warfare!

September 14 – You Can Make It

God has given me plenty of room for my steps under me, that my feet would not slip. (Psalm 18:36)

The Living Bible gives a great translation of Psalm 18:32, 33 when it says, "He fills me with strength and protects me wherever I go. He gives me the surefootedness of a mountain goat upon the crags. He leads me safely along the top of the cliffs."

All through the verses of Psalm 18, there is a winning combination of power and strength sent to us from our God. David tells us that, as Christians, God gives us the "surefootedness" of a mountain goat (18:32) and the power and strength of "the strong horn of a mighty fighting bull" (18:2).

Our steps are sure and steadfast in the Lord because we stand on the solid Rock, Jesus Christ. God gives us power and strength that is beyond our greatest expectations when we let Him fight for us. He will fight for you today in prison, because He loves you – no matter what you come up against.

David tells us that he was in real trouble in Psalm 18. He had Saul's armies chasing him, and it looked as if he would be killed at any moment; but he praised the Lord for the almighty strength that was his. He praised and he prayed. Instead of cowering away in a cave, David met the enemy head-on with God's power fighting for him.

We have the same exact power that God gave David. We just need to start praising Him for a victorious outcome – no matter what the horizon looks like.

The message for today: God will deliver you from all your enemies!

Prayer: Dear Heavenly Father, With Your help I can make it. Help my unbelief.

September 15 – Get up!

We who live for Christ are constantly experiencing being handed over to death for Jesus' sake, so that His resurrection life also may be evidenced through our flesh...
(II Corinthians 4:11)

Jesus' resurrection life in us is seen daily by the way we handle tough situations in prison. We either break down and cry or we stand up and fight. Satan would love it if we just fell apart every time something went wrong. Paul knew how to adopt an attitude of victory every time something went wrong. He said,

> "We are pressed on every side by troubles, but not crushed and broken. We are perplexed because we don't know why things happen as they do, but we don't give up and quit. We are hunted down, but God never abandons us. We get knocked down, but we get up again and keep going!" (II Corinthians 4:8, 9)

At the end of the day, no matter what you may have gone through in jail, it doesn't even begin to compare to Calvary and what happened there for you. Simply said, "Don't measure yourself by how many times you have been knocked down, but by how many times you got back up. As long as the 'getting up' outnumbers the 'getting knocked down', you are going to make it!"

Paul knew that God would bring him through because of his ability to use the faith God gave him. All he wanted to do was to "win the race" and not be disqualified because he doubted God's ability to rescue him.

The message for today: Don't give up. Jesus didn't.

Prayer: Dear Heavenly Father, Help me to get through every trial victoriously with You.

September 16 – What Did You Say?

May the words of my mouth and the meditation of my heart be pleasing in your sight, O Lord. (Psalm 19:14)

When you really get angry, what do you say? Most of us say every slang word that comes to mind.

In prison, it is so easy to get caught up in swearing because everybody does it.

Why is profanity so common today? Because the movie industry uses it excessively, people are "desensitized" to it. Foul language serves no purpose, even though Hollywood would like to say it does.

The Bible talks a lot about our language and the effect it has on us and others. Ephesians 4:29 says, "Do not let any unwholesome talk come out of your mouths, but only what is helpful for building others up according to their needs, that it may benefit those who listen."

Does your talk build others up or tear them down? Jesus says that we should talk about wholesome, good things. Ephesians 5:4 goes on to say, "Nor should there be obscenity, foolish talk or coarse joking, which are out of place, but rather thanksgiving."

A Christian friend of mine constantly said, "Oh, my God" in her conversation. One day I told her that she was using the Lord's name in vain. She said that she wasn't using it in anger, so it wasn't wrong. As our friendship went on, I noticed that she stopped using it. It was very refreshing.

The message for today: The way we talk shows how much (or how little) we respect our Heavenly Father.

Prayer: Dear Heavenly Father, I ask You to help me talk in a wholesome, godly way.

September 17 – Bearing Fruit

I am the Vine; you are the branches. Whoever lives in Me and I in him, bears much fruit. (John 15:5)

Jesus gave us some good information about how our Christian lives can be happier. He said that He is like a vine, from which all of us grow. Every day in jail as I awaken, I think about my attachment to Jesus, and I pray that my life will show it.

Paul tells us about the "fruit of the Spirit" in Galatians 5:22-24. This spiritual fruit produced in our lives contains nine beautiful characteristics, which are evident because of Jesus' presence in us.

1 — Love
2 — Joy
3 — Peace
4 — Patience
5 — Gentleness
6 — Goodness
7 — Faithfulness
8 — Meekness
9 — Self-Control

The message for today: Start bearing fruit and get blessed.

Prayer: Dear Heavenly Father, Help me to show every characteristic of the fruit of the Holy Spirit.

September 18 – Brian's Miracle

Jesus said, "Loose him and let him go." (John 11:44)

Miss Appleton, Brian's first-grade teacher saw all the signs of physical abuse in his life. He was violent and aggressive. She asked her friend Tom to be a mentor for Brian. Tom was a Christian man who had experience with abused children and agreed to mentor Brian.

One day Tom noticed that Brian was especially agitated and upset, so he asked him what was wrong. Brian trusted Tom, so in tears he told him the whole story of his father beating his mother the night before. Tom knew the time had come for the authorities to remove Brian from his home so he made the necessary calls, and to his delight they offered him the opportunity of caring for Brian.

After three years with Tom, Brian's father was killed in an accident, and Brian was allowed to return to his mother. During his time with Tom, Brian had learned that Jesus truly did love him and he asked Jesus to be his Savior.

Brian became a well-mannered student, and no one could deny the change God had made. Tom kept mentoring him and was his best friend. Brian went on to be a spiritual young man and a normal adult, all because one person cared enough to reach out to him.

Prisoner, if you have been physically, sexually, or emotionally abused, only the mighty power of Jesus can release you. He's ready and waiting to heal your wounded soul.

The message for today: Satan has tried to ruin your life, but Jesus Christ came to rescue you!

Prayer: Dear Heavenly Father, Please come and heal my wounded soul from the abuse of my childhood.

September 19 – God's Grace

He said to me, "My grace is sufficient for you, for my power is made perfect in your weakness."
(II Corinthians 12:9)

Many years ago, a man was put in jail for his faith and almost starved to death. One day the Lord placed an idea in his head, and he practiced it every day for three years until God released him. Because he was so weak, it took everything he had to stand up; so he told the Lord that he would purposely stand up in his cell for ten minutes a day and praise God for all His blessings! Some days he would fall down in weakness, but up he got again! He said that he finally knew that "grace" that was more than a word on a Bible page!

Meditate on and practice the prayer below daily!

The message for today: Use God's promises as realities, and you will find them powerful as you believe them.

Prayer: Dear Heavenly Father, I praise You that even as my heart wavers, I am learning that Your grace is sufficient for me: because Your strength is made perfect in my weakness. So I will gladly glory in my infirmities, that Your power may rest upon me. Therefore I rejoice in the infirmities You allow to grip me, in the reproaches that reach me, in necessities that make me look to You, in persecutions, in distresses for Christ's sake; for when I am weak, then am I strong because I see the power of the resurrected and living Christ working in me. Thank You, Father, that even in this I can see Your victory rising. Thank You that I will never be strong enough, but You will always be exceedingly abundantly strong enough in every situation.

September 20 – Stay Put!

If the spirit of the ruler rises up against you, do not leave your place or show a resisting spirit; for gentleness and calmness prevent or put a stop to great offenses. (Ecclesiastes 10:4)

I never knew this scripture was in the Bible until one day after a deputy was verbally cruel and rude to me. That night, as I read the Word, God knew I needed to hear that He really cared about me as a prisoner.

So many times, prisoners are forgotten after awhile, and the lack of love from others becomes a major identity issue. Unless God intervenes, life can be terrible!

Even when we are mistreated, we can act wisely and behave ourselves as David did if we only go to the Word of God and do what it says.

Every problem we have is a "wisdom problem". If we steal, we lack wisdom of how to get things honestly. If we lie, we lack wisdom of the blessings of speaking the truth. Wisdom keeps us from every sin we are tempted to commit.

In Proverbs, Solomon wrote 54 times in 31 chapters about God's wisdom working in us. Proverbs 4:7 says it all. "Wisdom is the principal thing; therefore get wisdom…"

The message for today: Wisdom is like a gushing stream – sparkling, fresh, pure, and life giving. (Proverbs 18:4)

Prayer: Dear Heavenly Father, Help me to build my life with Your wisdom and know how to respond when I am treated wrongly.

September 21 – Pools of Blessing

When they walk through the valley of weeping, it will become a place of refreshing springs where pools of blessing collect after the rains. (Psalm 84:6)

Psalm 84 shows God's protection, plans, and provision for prisoners.

"Happy are those who are strong in the Lord, who set their minds on serving God and reaching their Jerusalem!" (Psalm 84:5) The secret to being happy is to have a goal. Remember… "if we aim at nothing, we usually hit it." As we daily love and obey Jesus, there is great peace and happiness in our souls.

Strong, spiritually healthy people go through trials much differently than the unsaved or spiritually immature. Psalm 84:6 says that when strong believers encounter trouble — the Valley of Baca (weeping), — they become even stronger because they know their God will change and mature them in some way not possible without the trial.

After it is over, and even during a trial, we can draw refreshment and hope from Jesus; and the storm in our life produces "pools of blessing". Psalm 84:7 says these people grow stronger through their trials in preparation for seeing Jesus in heaven.

The message for today: My worst day with Jesus is better than my best day without Him!

Prayer: Dear Heavenly Father, Help me to trust in You and be truly happy! (Psalm 84:12)

September 22 – The Course of Time

To everything there is a season and a time to every purpose under the heaven. (Ecclesiastes 3:1)

Solomon said in Ecclesiastes that there is a season for everything in our lives. Where are you today? Is your season in prison getting you down? There is hope that this "season" will end.

There is:

A time to be born and a time to die;
A time to plant and a time to harvest;
A time to weep and a time to laugh;
A time to mourn and a time to dance…;
A time to embrace and a time to refrain from embracing;
A time to get and a time to lose;
A time to keep silent and a time to speak.
A time to love and a time to hate;
A time of war and a time of peace.

Whew! Our lives go through many changes! Today you might be in the "time to keep silent" or the "time to weep", but as we see above, Solomon (led by the Holy Spirit) said that a different time will emerge as the days go by.

Be encouraged as you sit down today and read the whole book of Ecclesiastes.

The message for today: Make time for Jesus today.

Prayer: Dear Heavenly Father, Help me to know Your timing in my life today as I seek You.

September 23 – What's Important?

Be earnest and steadfast in your prayer life, and pray for us also, that God may open a door to us for the Word, to proclaim the mystery concerning Christ on account of which I am in prison... (Colossians 4:2, 3)

Prison life is no picnic. Often inmates go to great lengths to pursue appeals in the hope of being released or perhaps getting a new trial. For many, freedom is the biggest thing on their mind; everything else is of less importance.

Paul was jailed on many occasions and endured much suffering. He was beaten and treated cruelly by people, including high officials; and yet he never was deterred from God's purpose for his life – to spread the gospel to the Gentiles and anyone who would listen.

Release from prison was not Paul's all-consuming thought. Even in chains, he could glory because – whether in life or death – he knew the gospel continued unfettered.

Paul used his time wisely by writing letters to the Philippians and Colossians to encourage and correct the error present in the churches. While he may have been chained, Paul was still an apostle whose heart had been set free!

I use my time in prison to write, to speak, to pray, and to live for Christ. If Paul could do it, I can do it. Paul didn't care that he had chains around his legs. He only cared that he was making a difference in the kingdom of God. What a lofty goal for all prisoners and those who are free, as well!

The message for today: Bloom where you are planted.

Prayer: Dear Heavenly Father, Help me to redeem the time because the days are evil.

September 24 – Run, Forrest, Run!

But you, O man of God, flee these things and pursue
righteousness, godliness, faith, love, patience, gentleness.
(I Timothy 6:11)

What do you think of when you think of a "godly" person?
Do you think of a priest or a missionary? Do you think of
your mama? We all have different perceptions of what a
"godly" person is.

The truth is, every born-again Christian who is "godly", has
the ability to sin because of Adam's famous "fall" in the Garden
of Eden and his passing the sin nature to every one of us who
were ever born after that. But when God redeems a soul from
Hell, He changes us from the inside out and we become "new
creations in Christ Jesus". However, let me explain something
of huge proportion. We do not lose our ability to sin. So many
untaught people think that once we accept Jesus, we become
new and we cannot sin. That is why unsaved people do not
respect Christians who act poorly at times. They believe that
God is a joke, because they think that Christians should act and
be perfect. You have heard the saying, "Christians aren't perfect
– just forgiven!"

I John 1:8, 9 is written to Christians and it says, "If we say
that we have no sin, we deceive ourselves, and the truth is not
in us. If we confess our sins, He is faithful and just to forgive us
our sins and to cleanse us from all unrighteousness."

The message for today: Run as fast as you can away from sin!

Prayer: Dear Heavenly Father, Help me to love You so much
that I run from ungodly practices and pursue You with all my
strength.

September 25 – Do You Work Full-time?

For bodily exercise profits a little, but godliness is profitable for all things, having the promise of the life that now is and of that which is to come. (I Timothy 4:8)

Paul urged his young protégé, Timothy, to pursue godliness for good reason, i.e., it is profitable for every part of our life. No matter what we come up against, if we are in fellowship with our Lord, the challenge is less threatening than if we are fearful and untaught.

Whenever our perspective in life switches from the present to the future, our priorities change. While living for today may be pleasurable, living for God today and tomorrow impacts our souls (and the souls of others) for eternity. Seeking to live a godly life isn't just for us. It is also for those around us who need to see the love of God pouring out of us.

God has not asked us to give Him our lives for occasional service, but for full-time service. That doesn't mean that we have to go to Africa as a missionary or work full-time in a church, but it does mean that "for us to live is Christ" – 24 hours a day.

During the daily routines of our days in prison, moment by moment, God can change our hearts and transform us to be the people He has intended us to be all along — godly people who love and serve Him for the sake of the gospel and the saving power that comes from knowing Jesus Christ.

The message for today: The dividends paid from serving God are eternal.

Prayer: Dear Heavenly Father, Help me to be profitable to You and Your kingdom.

September 26 – Do Unto Others

*That in the ages to come He might show the
exceeding riches of His grace in His kindness toward us
in Christ Jesus. (Ephesians 2:7)*

The word "grace" in the Old Testament Hebrew has the
meaning of "free and spontaneous willingness to bestow good
on those who are destitute of it, either in a way of kindness or
compassion."

The meaning excludes all ideas of merit (deserving it).
Grace is not, "I feel obligated to help you because you helped
me." It is simply and act of favor, mercy, or compassion
initiated by the one who is kind. It is unmerited favor – not a
favor returned.

God shows this exact love and compassion to us. II Peter
3:18 tells us to "grow in grace". No one comes by grace
naturally. We have to learn to be kind and compassionate. Not
one of us was born loving Jesus. Someone told us of His love,
and we accepted Him as our Savior. If we had been in the
crowd that took Jesus' life, we would have yelled, "Crucify
Him!" But He loves us anyway. When that love opens our heart,
we then know how much we need a Savior.

Does your life in prison reflect God's grace, or do you need
some work in being kind, loving, and giving?

If you know someone who is defensive and insecure, try
showing free and spontaneous love. That is grace. As you
continue to be kind and considerate, watch the person
respond. Love begets love.

The message for today: Mama used to say, "You catch more
flies with honey than with vinegar."

Prayer: Dear Heavenly Father, Help me to show others the
kindness that I would like shown to me.

September 27 – Graduating with Honors

Jesus turned to Peter and said, "Get thee behind me, Satan! You are a dangerous trap to me. You are seeing things merely from a human point of view and not from God's." (Matthew 16:23)

In Matthew 16 we can learn some lessons about ourselves. Peter learned much about himself as he spent time with his Savior. Jesus asked him one day, "Who do people say that I am?" Without hesitation, he said, "You are the Messiah, the Son of the living God." Jesus showed Peter at that moment that God had to be the One to have revealed that answer to him.

Peter listened to Jesus as He shared about His death and resurrection, but then his mouth really got him into trouble. This is the same mouth that spoke wisdom a few days before. Peter decided to "set Jesus straight" about what the future held, and Jesus had to put Peter in his place with hard words.

Peter grew spiritually as he spent much time with Jesus; but only when the Holy Spirit energized him did his tongue and actions start changing. His whole life became a trophy for Jesus to use, and thousands were converted because of Peter. He wrote two books of the Bible – all because he surrendered to God's plans for his life. He graduated with honors!

What would Jesus say to you today if He analyzed your words and actions over the last 24 hours? Would it be, "God has revealed this to you" or "Get thee behind me, Satan"?

The message for today: Give Jesus first place, and watch your thoughts, words, and actions change.

Prayer: Dear Heavenly Father, Thank You for the taking time every day to teach me the lessons I need to learn.

September 28 – Looking Back

*Oh, what a wonderful God we have! How impossible it
is for us to understand His decisions and methods!
(Romans 11:33)*

A lady sat in church one day listening to the sermon, "It's
Possible with God". All was well with her soul and her life was
at peace. At the end of the sermon, the pastor sang some words
from an old chorus:

> Got any rivers you think are uncrossable?
> Got any mountains you can't tunnel through?
> God specializes in things thought impossible.
> He does the things others cannot do!

All at once, she remembered that song from 25 years before
and broke into tears. How far she had come in 25 years! She
remembered thinking that God didn't care, and nothing would
ever change after her divorce, which ripped her life apart. She
remembered how God had picked her up and carried her when
she didn't think she could make it another day.

She cried, just rehearsing the blessings God had graciously
and lavishly poured on her during her life.

God gave her a wonderful husband of 15 years. She had
been reconciled with her son and daughter. She had led her
new daughter-in-law to Jesus and was seeing her develop into
a good wife for her son.

Yes, her rivers were humanly uncrossable, but God intervened by caring enough to make her remember when she
heard that little chorus!

The message for today: Count your many blessings. Name them
one by one, and it will surprise you what the Lord has done!

Prayer: Dear Heavenly Father, Thank You for Your wonderful
love for Your children!

September 29 – Great Benefits

Commit your way unto the Lord; trust also in Him, and He shall bring it to pass. (Psalm 37:5)

There are three major reasons why we should wait on God's timing in prison. He has a plan that demands waiting, even though it is difficult.

I wait on God because:

1. My steps are ordered by the Lord (Psalm 37:23) and I am His pleasure.

2. My God will not let me down (Psalm 37:24). When others leave and abandon us, He lifts us up. Psalm 37:39 says, "He is my strength in the time of trouble." He never lets me down. He stays around when others leave.

3. My needs will be met (Psalm 37:25, 26). Even as an old man, David never saw God forsake him. If we play by God's rules, He cannot forsake us. God meets every physical, spiritual, material and relational need in our lives! God sees next week and next year, and He is ordering our steps as we trust Him. We don't have to figure it out; God will.

The message for today: You will wake up one day exactly where God wants you!

Prayer: Dear Heavenly Father, Thank You for providing for all my needs.

September 30 – Excuses, Excuses

When Jesus saw him and knew how long he had been ill,
He asked him, "Would you like to get well?" (John 5:6)

Jesus walked by a man one day, who was waiting to get into the Pool of Bethesda. Blind, lame, and paralyzed people came there daily to get into the pool. When an angel stirred up the water, anyone who was in the pool got healed.

Jesus asked the man if he wanted to be healed. The man didn't answer the question but said, "Everyone always gets in ahead of me, and no one will help me into the pool." This had been going on for 38 years! Basically, the man said, "I haven't received the breaks that other people have, and it is other people's faults that I'm still here waiting."

Had this man become comfortable with his daily routine of sitting around, watching others? Did he really want to be well, or did he enjoy the freedom from responsibility that his sickness gave him? He was a victim, and his words proved it.

Satan knows that if he can keep a person thinking he is a victim and no one cares, that the person will never amount to anything for Jesus. The truth is that when Jesus comes along and saves us, we are set free from the authority of darkness. The new nature of Christ enters us and along with it come seeds of greatness.

Who will you identify with – the past with all that imprisons you, or with Jesus who can make you victorious?

The message for today: As we choose to identify with Jesus, powerful things happen.

Prayer: Dear Heavenly Father, Help me to stop blaming others and trust You.

OCTOBER

October 1 – How you Doin'?

But the godly will flourish like palm trees and grow strong like the cedars of Lebanon, for they are transplanted into the Lord's own house. They flourish in the courts of our God. (Psalm 92:12, 13)

After all my years of sinning and running from the Lord, I asked Jesus to be my Savior in prison. I never knew much about being strong and flourishing like a healthy "palm tree in the Lord's house" until God "transplanted" me into His kingdom. A whole new life emerged with new and exciting opportunities – even in prison!

The long, dreary days became shorter and easier to live. My incarceration gave me time to meditate on and learn God's ways. New-found joy and excitement rule my life now.

I have found that there is a huge difference between "existing" and "flourishing". One lady told me that she hated food and only "ate to live", but one day she discovered that healthy eating made her feel good and have more energy. Within three months, she looked so healthy! She started "flourishing" because of her good eating habits.

If you have been transplanted into God's kingdom through salvation, it is your heritage to "flourish."

The message for today: Let your roots grow deeply in Christ and start flourishing in the courts of the Lord.

Prayer: Dear Heavenly Father, Thank You for helping my roots to grow deeper in You.

✝
October 2 – There's Still Time

Seventy years are given to us. Some may even reach eighty, but even the best of these years are filled with pain and trouble; soon they disappear, and we are gone.
(Psalm 90:10)

If we could see time as God sees it, we would know why He tells us that our life is "like a vapor" – a little mist that flows into the air and disappears!

Psalm 90:4 says, "For you, Lord, a thousand years are as yesterday! They are like a few hours!" So, as we look at our short 70 or 80 years, they must seem as nothing to God; but He certainly packs a lot of teaching and training into those years!

If you are like I am, you had to waste 20 or 30 years before you finally got it: I'm a sinner and I need a Savior. I can't live this life successfully without Jesus!

Moses asked God to help us to start making the most of our time so that we may grow in wisdom (Psalm 90:12) and show us His unfailing love so that we may sing for joy to the end of our lives (Psalm 90:14).

A good prayer is: "Give us gladness in proportion to our former misery! Replace the evil years with good…May the Lord show us His approval and make our efforts successful!" (Psalm 90:15-17)

If your life has been ruined by your bad choices to sin, take heart! You are still alive and Jesus is still waiting to redeem your life and re-make it. Why not give Him the chance today? There's still time.

The message for today: God's love never stops reaching down to redeem His children.

Prayer: Dear Heavenly Father, Please give me Your salvation and a long life to serve You.

October 3 – All Alone

And Elisha saw Elijah no more. (II Kings 2:12)

There comes a time when each of us must go through something alone in our Christian life. The friends seem to have vanished and there is no one there but God.

One day Lottie's closest friend moved away. She had relied on her for everything spiritual. A few months later, the doctor informed Lottie that he had found cancer cells in her body. He told her that he would freeze the cells and scrape them away. She was petrified and cried out to God, "Where is my friend when I need her? I'm alone here, and I can't do this!" God gently whispered in her ear that she wasn't alone because He was with her. She endured the long procedure and prayed a lot. A few weeks later, God showed her that from now on she would be alone.

God showed Lottie a cycle of life that Christians must experience. When He knows we need to advance spiritually, He removes a close friend or Christian mentor on whom we have heavily relied. When we are forced to grow, we become strong and help others. Then we are taken from their life and they are forced to grow spiritually.

If God has removed someone dear from your life, He wants you to be strong and stand alone. The Holy Spirit prays for you and through you. He makes groanings to Jesus which cannot be uttered or understood. He knows how to pray for exactly what you need.

The message for today: For we do not know how to pray as we should, but the Spirit Himself intercedes for us… (Romans 8:26).

Prayer: Dear Heavenly Father, Help me to feel Your presence when I feel so abandoned and alone.

October 4 – Courageous Faith

Though the fig tree does not blossom and there is no fruit on the vines; though the product of the olive fails and the fields yield no food, though the flock is cut off from the fold and there are no cattle in the stalls, yet I will rejoice in the Lord. I will exult in the victorious God of my salvation! (Habakkuk 3:17, 18)

There was a prophet named Habakkuk in the Old Testament, who was confused as to why God would let the Israelites be in such trouble. In Habakkuk 1:2, he asks, "Lord, how long shall I cry for help and You will not hear, or cry out to You of violence and You will not save?" God answers him in 1:5 and says, "Look around you, Habakkuk, and be astonished and astounded! For I am putting into effect a work in your days such that you would not believe if it were told you!"

In 2:1 Habakkuk gets a clue and repents to God. He says, "Oh, I know I have been rash to talk out plainly this way to God!"

By chapter 3, this man of God even had a vision from God (3:7), and knew He would spare His chosen ones. He concludes with the faith-filled verses of 3:17-18, which say in effect, "No matter what, Lord, I will rejoice in You!"

If you trust God in your problems, He will put into effect a work that you won't believe!

The message for today: When the storms of life get the worst, it is time to praise; but most of us think of everything but praising when we are going through deep waters.

Prayer: Dear Heavenly Father, I promise You now that I will praise You, even in my problems.

October 5 – U Are Important

And you shall call his name Jesus for He shall save His people from their sins. (Matthew 1:21)

The following poem is one we should take to heart.

The U in Jesus

Before U were thought of or time had begun,
God even stuck U in the name of His Son.

And each time U pray, you'll see it is true –
You can't spell out JesUs and not include U!

You're a pretty big part of His wonderful name;
For U He was born and that's why He came.

And His great love for U is the reason He died.
It even takes U to spell crUcified.

Isn't it thrilling and splendidly grand;
He rose from the dead, with U in His plan?

When JesUs left earth at His upward ascension,
He felt there was one thing He just had to mention.

"Go into the world and tell them it's true,
that I love them all – just like I love U."

The message for today: Jesus is the sweetest name I know!

Prayer: Dear Heavenly Father, Thank You that I know You. Help me to show others the way to knowing Jesus as their Savior.

October 6 – Change Your Mind

It is the Lord who goes before you…He will not fail you or forsake you; fear not… (Deuteronomy 31:8)

Listen to a story by my friend, Kristi.

"For many years my life was filled with doubt and fear, because I never had positive affirmation or love as a child. I also had no Christian training as a child and adolescent, so my decision-making powers were non-existent. I ignored relationship problems and I would not confront them.

I accepted Jesus at age 19 and I started changing, but the childhood years and conditioning had taken their toll. I let life tell me what to do instead of taking control of the situation.

One day (at age 30) I sat praying and saw a familiar road in my mind. This road had to be accessed by going in a loop from west to east. Without a word from God, I knew He was saying, 'It's time to do the opposite of what you have been doing all these years. I want your total life – not a piece of it.' That day I purposely made the decision to serve Jesus Christ 100% at all times and never turn back.

God showed me through the years that I had let Satan control my thoughts and actions instead of taking them captive to the obedience of Jesus. I started substituting scripture for sadness, victory for vanity, and faith for fear! How I praise God for His persistent love in teaching me what no one else had!"

The message for today: Be still before the Lord, and He will teach you what you need to know.

Prayer: Dear Heavenly Father, I surrender my total life to You today. Do with it as You will.

October 7 – The Cost of Living

I press toward the mark for the prize of the high calling of God in Christ Jesus. (Philippians 3:14)

Prisoners do not worry about the economy of the nation and the cost of living. The government pays all the bills for food, electricity, and water.

Have you ever really thought about the "cost" of living your life? As long as you are alive, money will have to be spent. Dead people incur no bills, need no money, or care about the economy.

A preacher was talking about the large amount of money needed to maintain the growing and thriving ministry of his church. He said that the congregation should be glad for the big bills because "life" created them. Dead churches have very few extra bills because they maintain the same programs with no vision and no power – usually no new people either.

The church at Sardis in Revelation 3:1-6 looked alive, but God said it was almost dead. He told them to wake up and strengthen what little remained of life, because death was coming if they didn't start serving Jesus with true and active service. God urged them to return to their "first love" of Christ and hold onto it firmly. What good advice!

Today, dear prisoner, return to your first love of Christ and start practicing "life". If you think your service to Jesus in jail doesn't matter, wake up and ask Jesus for a new zeal. He will give it! Life produces life, and the opposite is true, too. Your testimony does count for more than you could ever imagine.

The message for today: God can resurrect anything dead in your life!

Prayer: Dear Heavenly Father, Help me to wake up and get firmly grounded in You.

October 8 – Creation or Evolution?

O, Lord, what a variety of things You have made!
In wisdom You have made them all. The earth is full of
Your creatures. (Psalm 104:24)

Every time I watch a nature TV program, I always say, "God has such an imagination!" It goes beyond my human mind how He created insects, animals, and birds with perfectly unique characteristics for the region and climate they live in!

You have probably heard the word "evolution" where Darwin said that every living thing (including man) started as a sea organism and then lost its fins and came on to land and "evolved" into a lizard, bird, monkey and man!

Why would a creative God like ours need to go through this million-year process when He could simply speak the word "zebra" and a black and white striped horse would appear? God spoke, and our earth was inhabited with every living organism after its kind!

Cows cannot produce dogs. God placed in the cow only the seed to produce cows. The Bible says that the "seed" of an apple contains apples. That is His protection of the species because He's a great God! I believe He doesn't even care if the races intermarry, because humans produce humans!

If you have asked Jesus into your life, you contain the "seed" of the Holy Spirit and God can use you to "produce" Christians by your consistent witness for Him. We are all pre-programmed to act as we do, and with God inside us, we should show forth His characteristics – not those of the world.

The message for today: Before the foundation of the world, you were meant to be you.

Prayer: Dear Heavenly Father, Thank You for your creative power. Thank You that we didn't just randomly evolve!

October 9 – Take Cover!

He stilled the storm to a whisper; the waves of the sea were hushed. (Psalm 107:29)

Sometimes the "roar" of the storms of life gets very loud, and we can't see how it will ever end. But in the midst of every trial, we can trust that Jesus cares about us, and His command will still all our discouragement, sickness, fear, weariness, and anxiety to a whisper. It is as if Jesus comes to your jail cell or to your sick room and says, "Hush up, storm! Be still!"

God had to say those words to my life when I was sent to prison. I could see no earthly reason why God couldn't teach me some other way than prison; but He knew me better than I knew myself. He had to get me away from the mainstream of society and put me in a world of structure and routine in order to get my attention. And He got it! I bowed low before Him one day and gave my entire life to Jesus Christ. I told Him that no matter what happened, He was my Savior and I would serve Him and no one else.

Someone has said that the shortest distance between a problem and a solution is the distance between your knees and the floor. As I prayed that day during my storm, I realized that Jesus Christ was my covering. He had placed me under His strong protection, and nothing could come into my life except what He had first filtered through His fingers of love.

The message for today: Let Jesus be your covering today. Ask His help in all your trials.

Prayer: Dear Heavenly Father, Help me to understand that You do not have my worst in mind, but my best.

October 10 – Five Secrets

And they continued steadfastly in the apostles'
doctrine and fellowship, and in breaking of bread
and in prayers...praising God and having favor
with all people. (Acts 2:41-47)

Acts 2:41 gives five secrets of a power-filled life for the Christian. The Holy Spirit was sent to believers in the book of Acts, and great things happened. If your life is dull, and you want some power, why not try these five suggestions for holiness?

1) Continue steadfastly in the apostles' doctrine (the Word of God). If we do not establish a time with Jesus every day, our consistency in the Christian life will be lacking.

2) Continue in fellowship and in the breaking of bread (with other Christians). We need prayer partners and precious friends who love Jesus as we do.

3) Continue in prayer (alone and with others). When we see prayers answered, we are thrilled for others and ourselves. Learn to pray out loud, even if your fear tells you not to do it.

4) Give your time and money to Jesus. People who are not generous with their money are not right with God and have no strength to fight the Devil. (See Acts 2:45)

5) Continue praising God! Even if you don't feel like it, say words of praise to the Lord.

The message for today: Be an Acts 2:41 Christian.

Prayer: Dear Heavenly Father, Teach me Your disciplines for my Christian life.

October 11 – God Understands

But deal well with me, O Sovereign Lord, for the sake of Your own reputation! (Psalm 110:21)

Have you ever hated someone for betraying you? In prison, betrayal is practiced daily.

David asks God for terrible things to happen to the wicked in Psalm 109:6-15. He prays for someone evil to turn on his enemy. He asks for his enemy to go on trial and be pronounced guilty. He prays for his enemy to die young and his family to become destitute. He prays for the enemy to become homeless and hated and for his children to die and the family to have a tainted reputation.

God understands when we are at the bottom. He hears all the mean things we say as we vent our anger about others to Him. We cannot shock God, no matter how hard we try. However, I would be very afraid to pray vengeance like Psalm 109 on someone.

God knows our every thought. Besides, as we pray, God will change our heart; and He will take vengeance on those who hurt us. In Psalm 109:21-31, David regains his correct frame of mind and asks the Lord to help him. He says that the Lord stands by the needy, ready to save them from those who condemn them (109:31).

The message for today: If you feel like David, you are no surprise to God. Confess how you feel and ask His help.

Prayer: Dear Heavenly Father, I pray for all those who have betrayed and hurt me. I forgive them and know that You will deal with them much better than I could.

October 12 – Miracles Still Happen

*The righteous do not fear bad news; they confidently
trust the Lord to care for them. They are confident and
fearless and can face their foes triumphantly.
(Psalm 112:7, 8)*

A young man named Tony was wrongfully accused of four counts of child molestation because he had angered a 14-year-old girl whom he refused to date. In retaliation, she told her parents that he had raped her. He was hunted down by the police and put in jail. His family and friends at church prayed night and day for him. There was no way for him to get out on bail because of the severity of the charge and the huge amount of bail needed. For seven days prayer went to heaven for Tony. At 3:30 a.m. on the eighth day, a rich man in their church had a dream in which he saw Tony's face. He couldn't forget the dream, so he went to the jail and put his $500,000 home up as a property bond for Tony! Upon release, Tony's life changed dramatically, but a t rial still lay ahead. For 14 months the people prayed with delay after delay, but God was working.

Tony finally went on trial with very little human hope for an acquittal. The jury trial was held for three days. Tony maintained his peace, in spite of all the bad reports. When the verdict came in, Tony was acquitted of all counts and proven innocent! Songs of joy and victory were sung in the camp of the godly that day! (Psalm 118:15)

The message for today: The righteous cry and the Lord hears them and delivers them from all their troubles! (Psalm 34:17)

Prayer: Dear Heavenly Father, Please help me to trust You – no matter what.

October 13 – Walking Our Talk

He who walks uprightly walks securely...
(Proverbs 10:9)

The Bible talks much about how our actions speak louder than our words. Many prisoners talk about how much God means to them. They go around telling everyone about God. They corner people and ask them if they "know Jesus".

The above is wonderful if the Holy Spirit is doing the leading, but I have found that many times it is not God doing the leading, but the "sales person" in us trying to sell Jesus to the unfortunate and unsaved so that we can put a check mark on our long list of souls for Jesus.

If we are in love with our Savior, our very behavior shows forth His Spirit in us with more than words! In a sense, we are all "preachers" of the gospel.

Calvin Miller wrote to preachers about the power of their sermons:

"I am convinced that most people want Christ to permeate the sermon because He has already permeated the life of the preacher. It is a matter of the preacher's hunger for Jesus. When the preacher gets hungry for Jesus, the hunger of those who come to church will be automatically satisfied." (*Great Preaching* 1999)

The message for today: Be one of those whose very countenance shows our lovely Lord!

Prayer: Dear Heavenly Father, Help me not to preach so much, but to "live Christ" more.

October 14 – A Pick-Me-Up

Some trust in chariots and some in horses, but we trust in the name of the Lord our God. (Psalm 20:6)

David had every reason to be sad and have the "blahs" in I Samuel 30:1-6, but he won in the end. Read some of his story...

1 Now when David and his men came home to Ziklag, they found that the Amalekites had made a raid on the South and on Ziklag and had struck Ziklag and burned it with fire,

2 And had taken captive the women and all who were there. They killed no one, but carried them off and went on their way.

3 So David and his men came to the town, and behold, it was burned, and their wives and sons and daughters were taken captive.

4 Then David and the men with him lifted up their voices and wept until they had no more strength to weep.

5 David was greatly distressed for the men spoke of stoning him because the souls of them all were bitterly grieved, each man for his sons and daughters. But David encouraged and strengthened himself in the Lord his God.

The story goes on to say that the Lord assured David that he would recover everyone whom they had lost, and they did! (I Samuel 30:8). God was on his side!

The message for today: Being Bored – Blah, blah, blah. Seeing answered prayer – Priceless!

Prayer: Dear Heavenly Father, I praise You for encouraging me when I'm down!

October 15 – Move On Up

The Sovereign LORD is my strength; He makes my feet like the feet of a deer; He enables me to go on the heights. (Habakkuk 3:19)

My friend's family has lived in the same area for over 150 years! There is hardly a person they don't know. When my friend and her husband decided to leave the area, her sisters were angry and never spoke to her again. They tried to hold her down, but they couldn't. God was leading her away, and they weren't happy!

Jesus was the same way. People wanted Him to linger with them and never leave, but He couldn't stay in one place long because He had too much to do for His Father.

We could apply this principal to our spiritual lives, too. How long have you stayed in the same place spiritually? Do you know any more today than you did five years ago? Have you changed your location to a higher plain with Jesus?

An old church hymn says, "Lord, lift me up and let me stand by faith on heaven's table land — a higher plain than I have found. Lord, plant my feet on higher ground." It goes on to say, "My heart has no desire to stay where doubts arise and fears dismay; but still I'll pray till heaven I've found, 'Lord plant my feet on higher ground!'" (Johnson Oatman, 1898)

We can see things more clearly every day when we walk in total surrender to God's wonderful ways.

The message for today: As we move higher, heaven gets closer.

Prayer: Dear Heavenly Father, Help me to desire higher ground with You.

October 16 – More than Enough

And they cut down a cluster of grapes and they carried it on a pole between them. (Numbers 13:23)

Moses sent twelve spies to explore the Promised Land before they actually took possession of it, and what a story they told when they returned! Ten of the spies gave a negative report and told Moses that the people who lived in that land were strong giants and their cities were very large and fortified (13:28). They told Moses that they were not able to go up against the people of Canaan for they were as grasshoppers in their sight. (13:31, 33)

Caleb and Joshua gave a much different report. Caleb had God's perspective of the land, and he quieted the people and tried to get them to see their success; but all they could see were the "giants". Caleb said, "Let us go up at once and possess it; we are well able to conquer it." He knew that the land was sufficient for everyone, but still the Israelites doubted.

God gave our prison prayer group a word one morning, which related directly to this story. He said that we were to go out and get our blessings and bring them back to the church for a testimony of His great goodness.

Others cannot see Christ through our doubts and fears. They can only see Him through our spiritual power!

The message for today: In seeking and trusting God, our blessings appear.

Prayer: Dear Heavenly Father, Bless me and enlarge my border, because I know You are with me.

October 17 – Stay Faithful

And when the Lord brings you into the land with houses
full of all good things which you did not fill and...
vineyards and olive trees which you did not plant, and
when you eat and are full, then beware lest you forget
the Lord...Who brought you out of bondage.
(Deuteronomy 6:10-12)

God knows our human trait of being complacent when things are going well and crawling back to Him when things get bad. It takes much Christian growth to remain constantly in fellowship with Him during the good times and the bad.

God wants us to be overcomers – not victims of Satan's schemes. Revelation 2:26 says that "he who overcomes is victorious and he obeys My commands to the very end, doing the works that please Me; to him I will give authority and power...He who is able to hear, let him listen to and heed what the Holy Spirit says to the churches".

God gives good advice when He also tells us that "those who honor Me I will honor, and those who despise Me shall be lightly esteemed" (I Samuel 2:30). If we highly esteem God, there will be so many blessings overtaking us that we have to run to keep up with them because He is faithful to His promises.

I don't like the other side of the coin, but it must be mentioned. God will not withhold judgment from His born-again ones who put Him in last place and deliberately commit sin against Him. When Christians continue to sin, they crucify Jesus again and put Him to open shame. (Hebrews 6:6)

The message for today: Don't put Jesus to shame.

Prayer: Dear Heavenly Father, Help me to honor You and Your Name in everything I do.

October 18 – Pray for Me

Trouble and anguish have taken hold of me; yet Your commandments are my delight. (Psalm 119:143)

Psalm 119 contains 176 verses of love for God's holy Word.

Put a friend's name in the following verses, and practice "praying" the Bible out loud. It will revolutionize your life. Let's say you are praying for me (Thank you!) in the following verses:

4   You have commanded Marcia to keep Your precepts, that she should observe them diligently.

5   Oh, that Marcia's ways were directed and established to observe Your statutes (hearing, receiving, loving and obeying them)!

12   Blessed are You, O Lord; teach Marcia Your statutes.

34   Give Marcia understanding, that she may keep Your law with her whole heart.

38   Establish your Word and confirm Your promise to Marcia.

59   Help Marcia to consider her ways and turn her feet to obey Your testimonies.

80   Let Marcia's heart be sincere and blameless in Your Word, that she may not be put shame.

133 Establish Marcia's steps and direct them by means of Your Word; let not any sin have dominion over her.

165 Help Marcia to have great peace because she loves Your Word; let nothing offend her or make her stumble.

The message for today: Praying the Word means praying with power!

Prayer: Dear Heavenly Father, I ask for a burden to pray for others who need Your help.

October 19 – A Higher Calling

Moreover, whom He did predestinate, them he also called, and whom He called, them He also justified, and whom He justified, them He also glorified. (Romans 8:30)

A story is told of a man in a bar who was drunk, but he heard God's voice telling him to go to the prisons and preach!

The drunken man had no time for prisoners and always judged them for getting into trouble, so he tried to avoid what he had heard, and he continued to drink and run from God's calling. The alcohol made him forget that he had accepted Jesus as a young boy; but when it wore off, he always remembered!

Finally, he started listening to God. He was undisciplined and uneducated, but God wouldn't let him alone. Someone told him that God chooses the "weak things of the world to confound the things which are mighty," and he was chosen – period. None of his excuses worked, and he finally gave himself to the Lord fully and pursued God's calling for all he was worth.

Today he is a famous man of God and is on the board of pastors for prison ministry. His very presence in a room shows Jesus Christ, and hundreds of prisoners have come to know Jesus because of his genuine witness for his Lord.

If you are saved, you are called; and God will remove you from drugs, homosexuality, and prisons in order to use you. You have a special place in God's heart, and He wants you to fulfill your part of His great puzzle.

The message for today: Surrender your life to Jesus now and let Him use you.

Prayer: Dear Heavenly Father, I surrender myself to Your service. Show me where You want me, and I will go.

October 20 – Peace at Last!

He has redeemed my life in peace from the battle that was against me... (Psalm 55:18)

If our minds are stayed on Jesus, He will keep us in perfect peace because we trust Him. Each time we take our minds off Jesus, we are defeated in some area.

Psalm 55:18 says that, even though there are many people against us, God can keep us in great peace from the battle that rages outside. God will take care of those who hate us and hurt us; therefore, we can rest in Him.

When you trust God, you have a "heavenly host" around you. He controls all the angels (good and bad). Nothing can come to you that our Father has not allowed in His great sovereignty.

Psalm 46 is one of the most comforting psalms in the Bible because it reminds us that "the Lord of Hosts is with us; the God of Jacob is our Refuge (our Fortress and High Tower)." His protection is constant for His children. The writer reminds us in Psalm 46:10, 11 that we need to "be still" and know that He is God; and once again, it repeats, "The Lord of Hosts is with us; the God of Jacob is our Refuge (our High Tower and Stronghold). Pause...and think about that."

Take time today to read Psalm 46 and Psalm 55, and personalize them for your situation.

The message for today: Cast your burden on the Lord, and He will sustain you and never allow you to be moved. (Psalm 55:22)

Prayer: Dear Heavenly Father, Help me to trust in, lean on, and confidently rely on You. Help me to believe that You are with me every moment.

October 21 – Dad's Present

*Fathers, do not irritate and provoke your children
to anger, but rear them tenderly in the training and
discipline and the counsel and admonition of the Lord.
(Ephesians 6:4)*

Two very different lessons were taught to a father and son one day. Dad and Desmond spent the day fishing together. Then they decided that they would stay overnight and camp out – just the guys! It was going to be a good day!

They fished, talked, laughed, and played games together all day. When it was time for bed, both Dad and Desmond were thinking about the day.

Dad's thoughts went this way: 'I am disappointed that I brought my son all this way and we didn't catch any fish! I hope he's not sad about that.'

Desmond's thoughts: 'This was the best day of my life! It was so cool being with my dad and not having to share him with Mom or anyone! I'll never forget this day!'

We cause disappointments to our Heavenly Father sometimes, but each day we spend with Him is a joyous day in His sight. We might think, "I am such a failure today! I hate it when I sin and disappoint God." But when God hears that, I imagine He says, "This was a good day. My child learned about My forgiveness and love, and I am pleased."

The message for today: Spend some quality time with your Father today.

Prayer: Dear Heavenly Father, Thank You for loving me the way You do.

October 22 – Words of Wisdom

The sovereign Lord has given me his words of wisdom, so that I know what to say to all these weary ones. Morning by morning He awakens me and opens my understanding to His will. The sovereign Lord has spoken to me and I have listened. I do not rebel or turn away. (Isaiah 50:4-6)

Because the sovereign Lord helps me, I will not be dismayed. Therefore, I have set my face like a stone, determined to do his will, and I know I will triumph. He who gives me justice is near…the sovereign Lord is on my side. Who will declare me guilty? If you are walking in darkness without a ray of light, trust in the Lord and rely on your God. (Isaiah 50:7-10)

The wonderful passages of scripture above are overflowing with hope and direction for prisoners. Isaiah 50:4-6 is a beautiful picture of Jesus Christ, hundreds of years before He was born as a human, but it also is true of us as God's obedient servants.

Obedience gives us peace, determination, and victory in our Christian lives. Obedience gives us justice because God is on our side. Revel in and meditate all day today on these encouraging scriptures. Say them out loud to God. They give so much hope to prisoners!

If you feel as if you are a person walking in darkness without a ray of light, God offers it…"Trust in the Lord and rely on your God."

The message for today: Get peace and victory by being determined to be obedient.

Prayer: Dear Heavenly Father, I will be energetic today and determined to live in victory!

October 23 – Our Real Father

For even if you had ten thousand others to teach you
about Christ, you have only one spiritual father.
(I Corinthians 4:14)

Who led you to Jesus? That person is your spiritual mother or father, and God used them to bring you to the light of the glorious gospel of Christ. That person has a special place that no one else has. As you go on in your Christian life, you will have many teachers but only "one father".

As we grow in our Christian life, we sometimes stop thinking about that special person who told us of Jesus; and at that point, we can go into error if we are not properly tutored. Paul wrote I and II Corinthians in the Bible to help the baby Christians to understand that what they were doing was in direct disobedience to the true Word of God. We also need to be very careful that what we are taught lines up with God's Word. If we aren't careful, we will go to a cult or some other bizarre group that preaches "another gospel" that doesn't present Jesus as God.

God wants us to know the truth, and He deals with us in truth. He separates the "performance" from the "performer" when looking at our sin. In real life, if God sat us down to talk to us, He would probably say, "Your lying must be punished, but I still love you dearly."

Satan condemns the sinner. He would say to us, "You're bad because you lied. Shame, shame!" We must learn God's Word and listen to the right voice.

The message for today: Listen to your Heavenly Father; He knows best.

Prayer: Dear Heavenly Father, Thank You for the one who led me to Jesus! Help me to continue in the truth.

✝ October 24 – Just Do It!

By faith these people overthrew kingdoms, ruled with justice and received what God had promised them…their weakness was turned to strength.
(Hebrews 11:33, 34)

Hebrews 11 is the summary of some of the greatest believers in history. God approved of their faith so highly that He devoted a complete chapter to them. He even commented that the world was not worthy of them (11:38). Because of their faith in the Living God, we benefit. They proved that God can be trusted in every bad circumstance of our lives.

Dear prisoner, have you exercised your faith in Christ lately? Faith like a muscle, which must be used, or it weakens and becomes useless. When it is used daily, it gets strong and vibrant!

Have you stepped out of the boat and trusted Jesus for something difficult? Most of us want to see our way through something new before even starting it. Seeing is not faith, but reasoning. Common sense reasoning says that it can't be done, but God says differently. If we could see our way from beginning to end, our faith could never develop. God forces us to trust Him so that we will take one baby step at a time and gain experience using our faith.

We each have been given a "mustard seed" faith. Even using that tiny seed of faith, we can see great results. It is when we refuse to even use our "little faith" that God cannot work to show us greater things. If God has asked you to use your faith, just do it.

The message for today: God will never let you down when you step out in faith.

Prayer: Dear Heavenly Father, Forgive my lack of trust in You. Help me to go in Your Word and power.

October 25 – Undeniable Truth

And who is the great liar? The one who says that Jesus is not the Christ... (I John 2:22, 23)

One of Satan's greatest tricks is to make well-meaning people think that there is more than one way to get to heaven. The lie has been voiced for hundreds of years that "we're all on the same road; and as long as we believe in God, we'll get to heaven." NOT!

Jesus Christ was emphatic when He said in John 14:6, "I am THE way, THE truth, and THE life. No man comes to the Father except through Me." Paul said in Galatians 1:8 that anyone who teaches any doctrine, other than Jesus being God, is wrong; and he had some harsh words for those teaching "another gospel". He said that they would be cursed by God.

Revelation 22:18, 19 says that anyone who adds to or takes away from the Bible will suffer eternal consequences. Jesus Christ is Lord God Almighty all through the Bible, but in Revelation, the Bible shows His great power at the time of the very end of the world.

Jesus said in John that anyone who referred to Him, referred to God. (John 14:7)

Hebrews 1:8-10 calls Jesus, "God". "But unto the Son God says, 'Thy throne, O God, is forever...and Thou Lord in the beginning has laid the foundation of the earth.'"

In Exodus 6:3, God is called Elohim (I AM that I AM) and the word is plural! The Hebrew proves that God the Father, God the Son, and God the Holy Spirit are Three-in-One!

The message for today: Jesus Christ is Lord!

Prayer: Dear Heavenly Father, Help me to shun all teaching that says that Jesus is not God.

October 26 – Good Advice

Be strong in the Lord and the power of His might.
(Ephesians 6:10)

Ephesians 6 is loaded with examples of Spirit-filled believers living their daily lives in power.

Power Thought 1 —
Paul deals with our attitude toward authority in Ephesians 6:5-9, and he says that our godly behavior toward our authorities will show whether we are humble or arrogant and willful.
- Be obedient to authority, as if it were Jesus asking you to do something. Until we learn to submit to all authority in our life, we will lose spiritual battles.

- Be enthusiastic in your work and do it unto the Lord… as the servants of Christ, doing the will of God from the heart. (6:6)

- Watch for God's reward to your submission to authority. Knowing that whatever good thing any man does, the same shall he receive of the Lord, whether he is in prison or free. (6:8)

Power Thought 2 —
Ephesians 6:10-17 says that Christians fight a spiritual battle against Satan. Paul says that we are winners if we put on the whole armor of God. If we don't, we will lose the battles we must fight. Do you have your six pieces of armor on?

The message for today: The whole armor of God helps us to obey authority.

Prayer: Dear Heavenly Father, Help me to live my daily life in submission to You and Your commands.

October 27 – May I Have Your Attention?

He took him aside, away from the crowd. (Mark 7:33)

John Bunyan, the author of Pilgrim's Progress (the greatest selling book, aside from the Bible) was in prison in England. His outside voice was silenced; but while he was hidden away, he said, "I was at home in prison, and my great joy led me to sit and write and write." The darkness of his long prison term became a wonderful tool to light the path of millions of weary pilgrims!

If you are in prison, think about what you can do for the Lord today. It may be small and insignificant in your eyes, but God sees everything you do for Him. He has shut you away to get your attention. Praise Him for the good plans that He has for you. He can teach you many things as you get away from the clamors of society. He can give you new opportunities to learn about Jesus and grow in your Christian life.

Madam Guyon, a sweet French Christian, spent a long time behind prison bars, and music began to rise in her soul. She wrote beautiful songs, which have traveled far beyond her prison walls and encouraged thousands of hearts.

Paul called himself "a prisoner for the Lord" (Ephesians 4:1). He knew that even prison was in God's plan.

The message for today: Be a "prisoner for the Lord" and make the most of your time "aside".

Prayer: Dear Heavenly Father, Thank You for taking me aside and away from the crowd for now.

October 28 – Keep the Pressure On

To him who knows to do right and does it not,
to him it is sin. (James 4:17)

I have talked to many prisoners who knew that they needed to change their lives. Many made the decision to follow Jesus and live for Him; but within a few weeks, they were back to their old life, wondering why the Christian life didn't work. They became disillusioned, thinking there was no way they could ever change. Their lives became ineffective and useless for God.

In order to change our lives permanently, four important things need to happen:

1. Knowledge that change is needed. Most of us readily admit that our lives fall short of God's standards. When our lives intersect with God's holiness, we realize we need Jesus and we accept Him. We are enthusiastic beginners and want to become "super Christians".
2. Attitude toward change either makes us or breaks us. If there is no one to help us grow in our Christian life, we sink back into our old patterns and think we are failures.
3. Personal Behavior is the first real sign that we have been saved. We actually have to do something. James says, "Be ye doers of the Word and not hearers only." (James 1:22)
4. Public Behavior proves to be the biggest challenge. How we behave around others shows whether or not we have really been saved.

The message for today: Keep the pressure on yourself every day to change. It's worth it to be a victorious, maturing Christian!

Prayer: Dear Heavenly Father, I pray that others will see my inward change by my outward actions for Jesus.

October 29 – Two Types of People

And we know that all things work together for good to those who are the called according to His purpose.
(Romans 8:28)

There are two types of people in this world: The Driven and The Called.

"Driven" people are self-serving. They want to have everything their way. They have no desire to serve the Lord or help others. Because driven people are self-consumed, they have very little intimacy with God or people. Driven people are sometimes supervisors or bosses, and they tend to make others' lives miserable because they fear vulnerability.

In prison I have met many "in-charge" people who are actually cruel. Pride and fear keep them from caring for people. Driven people make poor "leaders" if their lives are not sold out to Jesus.

"Called" people are a different story. They have their priorities right and it shows. They treat others with dignity and want to serve them. Called people in leadership positions develop others around them to have self-esteem and confidence. They are secure and loving.

Jesus said He came to do His Father's will – not His own (John 5:30). His humility and love showed.

Which are you – driven or called? Jesus makes the difference!

The message for today: Humility is not thinking less of yourself but thinking about yourself less.

Prayer: Dear Heavenly Father, Help me to act as Jesus would act and make my calling and election sure.

October 30 – Enjoy the Good Life

For the happy heart, life is a continual feast.
(Proverbs 15:15)

As a prisoner, I never knew how to live my life happily content and secure until God showed me a wonderful truth, "It's not about me; it's about Jesus." Life took on a whole new meaning when I asked Jesus to be my Savior. I realized that I could be content – no matter what the circumstances were. God started changing me.

God changed my mouth. Look what Solomon says about our words in Proverbs 15:

15:4 – Gentle words bring life and health.

15:7 – If I am wise, I give good advice to people.

15:23 – Everyone enjoys a fitting reply. I will have wisdom to think before I speak.

God changed my attitude. He brought joy where there had been sadness. I started to look forward to the blessings He would bring my way each day. Look at a few from Proverbs 15:

15:8 – The Lord delights in the prayer of the upright.

15:9 – The Lord loves those who pursue godliness.

15:13 – A glad heart makes a happy face!

15:17 – A bowl of soup with someone you love is better than a steak with someone you hate.

The message for today: Godliness with contentment is great gain. (I Timothy 6:6)

Prayer: Dear Heavenly Father, Please help me to have Your outlook on life.

October 31 – Don't Panic

And when you hear of wars and insurrections, don't panic. Yes, these things must come, but the end won't follow immediately. (Luke 21:9)

Jesus taught with so much authority that people knew there was something different about Him, compared with the scribes and Pharisee teachers they heard all their lives. In Luke 21 Jesus foretold the future with specific instructions on how Christians should behave before His second coming at the end of the Church Age.

His first coming was as a baby in a manger, who took on "flesh" and changed the world through twelve men whom He mentored for three short years; but His second coming will be much different! He will come in power and great glory as the King of kings and Lord of lords. In preparing the disciples and readers of the Bible, He made some comforting statements, which we should heed.

Jesus said that nations would proclaim war against each other right before His coming (Luke 21:10). We see that more and more now with Iraq, Israel, and North Korea.

Jesus said that when we hear of great earthquakes, famines, epidemics and terrifying happenings, His coming is near. As we listen to the news every day, it is easy to see all these things happening. But Jesus comforts His people with powerful words of peace, too. He promises us that He will always be with us, even to the end of the age.

The message for today: Don't worry about the future. Jesus is already there.

Prayer: Dear Heavenly Father, I praise You that I will be raptured and rescued from the coming Tribulation since I know Jesus as Savior.

Notes

NOVEMBER

November 1 – I'm Way Ahead of You

But the Lord your God will cross over ahead of you like a devouring fire to destroy them...just as He promised. (Deuteronomy 9:3)

In reading many scriptures over the past few years, I have discovered an amazingly wonderful thing about God. He always goes before us. Nothing ever catches Him off guard or by surprise. Nothing is too hard for God. He's in perfect control!

When Moses told the Israelites to enter the Promised Land, he said that the Lord Himself would cross over ahead of them (Deuteronomy 31:3). He told them to be strong and trust God because they were in His mighty care. Moses urged them not to be afraid or discouraged because God was with them to deliver them.

All of us fear the "next step". We are uncomfortable trusting our future to a God we can't see or touch, but the Bible assures us that Jesus is the Lord of all space and time. He always has been and He always will be. Our part in the Christian life is to trust; His part is to work.

If you are not trusting God today, it is because you do not know His Word. As you memorize scriptures on trust and faith, you will become confident that God has gone ahead of you.

The message for today: Don't be afraid to follow God anywhere He leads.

Prayer: Dear Heavenly Father, Thank You for going ahead of me every day.

✝
November 2 – Good Morning, Lord

My voice shall You hear in the morning, O Lord...
and I will look up. (Psalm 5:3)

Through divine intention, God created our bodies to need up to eight hours of sleep each night. During that quiet time, which Shakespeare calls "death's counterfeit", our bodies repair themselves and are strengthened for the next day. When we awaken, our minds are quiet, as is the new morning. There's a fresh beginning and a clean slate. We have not sinned. It is at this quiet time that we need to spend time with God our Father.

The day will be blessed when the morning is set apart for God. I heard a pastor say that Christians who want to grow spiritually and be powerful should spend at least 15 minutes with God the moment their feet touch the floor every morning, so I tried it. I told God as David did, that He would hear my voice in the morning. I would look up first thing and direct my thoughts and prayers to Him. I have been blessed to be doing this for three years now, and my life has changed for the better.

Many things can keep us from spending quality morning time with God. If we do not get enough sleep, we are tired and don't want to spend time with God. David gave me a verse which I repeat every night. It says, "I will lie down in peace and sleep, for You, Lord, only make me dwell in safety." (Psalm 4:8)

The message for today: Exchange human voices for the voice of God.

Prayer: Dear Heavenly Father, Help me to regulate my days and nights so that I make my time spent with You a priority.

November 3 – Solitude (Part 1)

Be still and know that I am God. (Psalm 46:10)

In order to be effective in your walk with God, you need five important things in your life. I want to look at these five disciplines and our Lord's example in each, over the next five days.

SOLITUDE –

Most noise comes from human contact. When Christians spend time alone in solitude, we escape from noises to spend time with Jesus. Solitude should be spent not talking constantly. We should read God's Word and be quiet for extended time periods. This "alone", quiet time breaks old habits and forms Christ's character in us.

Jesus needed solitude for spiritual renewal and strength, and so do we. He built up His inner self and found peace and purpose in His alone times.

Matthew 4:1-11 – Jesus spent forty days alone in the desert when He was preparing for the test of public ministry.

Luke 6:12 – Jesus spent an entire night alone in the desert hills before He chose the twelve disciples.

Try spending time alone with God this week. When you get alone, sit down with your hands (palms down) on your knees. In your mind, lay down everything that you are trying to control or that worries you. Then, turn your hands palms up, and quietly picture yourself receiving all God has for you. Have no expectations of what God will give you. Meditate on your blessings.

The message for today: God will not compete for our attention. As long as we are "in charge", He will keep His distance.

Prayer: Dear Heavenly Father, Help me to stop Being Under Satan's Yoke (BUSY) and spend more time with You alone.

✝ November 4 – Prayer (Part 2)

Do not be anxious about anything, but in everything, by prayer and petition, with thanksgiving, present your requests to God. (Philippians 4:6)

PRAYER –

When we are baby Christians, we say panic prayers. Our worry and panic take over and we beg God to help us after we have done something stupid. But as we grow in Christ, we learn that we commit each day to Jesus with all its problems, which we have not yet encountered, and He plants a deep peace in our souls. When the problems come, we remember our morning prayers; and we handle the crisis with God's help – not our own panic.

As we make prayer a priority in our lives, our conduct changes. Our public and private behavior show that we "have been with Jesus". The results of spending time with the Creator of the universe cannot help but have an obvious and striking effect on us and others.

When you pray, try using the ACTS method. ACTS stands for Adoration, Confession, Thanksgiving, and Supplication. Start by Adoring God and praising Him for who He is. Then Confess your sins to Him honestly and openly. Thank Him next for specific blessings and answers to prayer. Then make Supplications (prayers) for others.

The message for today: Prayer should be our first response – not our last resort.

Prayer: Dear Heavenly Father, Mature me so that I will pray according to Your will and not my own.

November 5 – Scripture Memorization (Part 3)

All scripture is God-breathed and is useful for teaching, rebuking, correcting, and training in righteousness, so that the man of God may be thoroughly equipped for every good work. (II Timothy 3:16)

SCRIPTURE MEMORIZATION –

Paul tells us in Ephesians 6:13-17 to put on the whole armor of God. He tells us that one of the main pieces of spiritual armor is the Sword of the Spirit, the Word of God. We can't let Scripture (our sword) lie in the closet. We must put it on daily and use it daily, or it can't help us in the battle.

Jesus quoted Scripture back to Satan when he tempted Him in the wilderness. Satan knew Jesus was hungry, so he used His hunger to tempt Him. Satan knew Jesus had power so he used His position to tempt Him.

You will be tempted many times in life. If Scripture is part of your mindset, it will come back to you just when you need it. If it is not part of you, there will be no well to draw from, and your crisis will be twice as big as it needs to be.

If you start today to store up knowledge of God's Word, you will be able to use it to help others in their times of need. The old saying, "You can't give what you don't have" is so true. It's time to learn a Bible verse a week!

The message for today: Crawl out from under the covers of your complacency and laziness and replenish your spiritual resources by learning God's Word.

Prayer: Dear Heavenly Father, Help me to use my time learning Scripture instead of worrying.

November 6 – Unconditional Love (Part 4)

For God so loved the world that He gave
His one and only Son... (John 3:16)

The fourth discipline that we as Christians must learn is how to love others when they hurt us.

UNCONDITIONAL LOVE —

Many prisoners grew up in homes where love wasn't practiced or talked about. They never heard "I love you" or "I'm proud of you", so their self-esteem and self-worth were never developed.

Many parents abandon their children physically, but more abandon them emotionally. Some parents have so many problems that they have no time to care about anything or anyone but themselves. They live in their own self-pity and depression, and the precious children are left to fend for themselves. As the children grow, they believe that they are unimportant and unloved. This behavior goes with them all their lives; and we wonder why they get into trouble with the law and go to jail.

When someone tells them of Jesus and His great love, they remember back to their own parents and think Jesus will be just like them.

There are millions of us who have never experienced unconditional love, so we can't understand God's great love; but once we accept Jesus as our Savior, we realize that He loves us with no strings attached.

The message for today: God's love never fails.

Prayer: Dear Heavenly Father, I accept Your unconditional love for me. I forgive those who didn't know how to love me unconditionally.

November 7 – Support & Accountability Relationships (Part 5)

As iron sharpens iron, so one man sharpens another. (Proverbs 27:17)

The fifth discipline is difficult because it is hard to accept the truth about ourselves.

SUPPORT AND ACCOUNTABILITY RELATIONSHIPS –

When we rely on our own perspective of how we are doing, we are bound to slip into convenient rationalizations and blind spots about ourselves. These blind spots can hurt our Christian witness if not corrected, so we need godly friends to help us see areas that are not what God wants them to be.

Do you have someone in your life to tell you the truth about yourself? We all need that objective opinion of true friends who want to see us prosper. If you don't have a "truth teller" in your life, it's time for a change. Ask the Lord to bring a person to you who will value you and your reputation highly enough to give you honest feedback about your reputation, habits, etc. Accept and invite constructive criticism from a trusted friend. Ask God to reveal blind spots that are hurting your effectiveness for Him.

The message for today: Wounds from a friend can be trusted... (Proverbs 27:6)

Prayer: Dear Heavenly Father, Help me to look at myself honestly and improve in those areas You touch.

November 8 – Give Up Your Rights

Nevertheless, not my will but Thine be done…
(Matthew 26:39)

I have a friend who spent time in and out of jail on drug charges. Try as she would, she couldn't help herself, and three times she ended up in jail – a convicted felon.

She was at the end of her rope. She knew she was going to die if her life didn't change. She told me that somewhere deep in her "sanctified soul", her "heart of hearts", she knew Jesus was the only answer, so she invited Him into her heart. She made no deals and struck no bargains with Jesus; she simply said, "I can't hold on any longer. Lord Jesus, save me." And He did!

She knew she would have to return to the drug-infested neighborhood she had left, but this time Jesus would go with her. When she was released, she leaned on Jesus and said, "No!" every time she was offered drugs. She prayed daily for God's strength to keep her, and she saw that she was getting strong in the Lord to stay off drugs!

What made the change work? She told me that once she decided in her will to stay off drugs, she did. It was not an external change because she returned to the same neighborhood, but it came from a conscious surrender of her will to the will of God. After He got her will, nothing else could shake her!

God had waited until she yielded her will up to Him, and then the battle with drugs never needed to be fought again!

The message for today: Jesus has only the best for you. Surrender to His will.

Prayer: Dear Heavenly Father, I give You my whole life. Do with me as You will.

November 9 – Hear that Thunder?

And Elijah said to Ahab, Go up, eat and drink, for there is the sound of abundance of rain. (1 Kings 18:41)

When things are dry in our lives and there hasn't been any "rain" for some time, we get discouraged. In prison, it is like a perpetual drought with only clouds and darkness, but those storm clouds produce something we need in our lives – spiritual fruit.

Elijah was in a tough situation. The wicked king and queen, Ahab and Jezebel, hated him because he stood for the Living God. He spoke, and it didn't rain for 3 years! Then in I Kings 18:1, he appeared before King Ahab and told him that there would finally be rain.

Elijah went back up to Mt. Carmel after talking to King Ahab and "bowed himself down upon the earth and put his face between his knees". He waited for rain, and his faith paid off. God sent rain – beautiful, wet, needed rain! The drought was over! Crops could once again be grown and vegetation could spring forth!

In your darkest and driest hours, Jesus is there to provide much-needed spiritual refreshment to change your life. When you least expect it, He will show up. It may be in the form of a Christian friend, a court date, or even a release date, but God will show up! He has promised it.

When the thunder storms of life show up, they are God's way of showing you that the "abundance of rain" (a blessing) is coming.

The message for today: Have you felt the refreshing rain of the Holy Spirit in your life today?

Prayer: Dear Heavenly Father, I ask You to give me peace and faith in the midst of my storm.

November 10 – Please Hurry!

The fruit of the Holy Spirit is...patience.
(Galatians 5:22)

Many times prisoners get impatient when they pray for quick answers to prayer and don't get them. They want to give up because God didn't come through when they thought He should.

God tells us to display the fruit of the Holy Spirit in our daily lives. One part of that fruit is patience. As we grow in Christ, and our minds are renewed daily in the Word, patience starts having its "perfect work" in us. James 1 tells us that the "testing of our faith works patience".

The Amplified Bible makes James 1:2-4 very clear about our attitude toward patience. It says,

> "Consider it wholly joyful, my brethren, whenever you are enveloped in or encounter trials of any sort or fall into various temptations. Be assured and understand that the trial and proving of your faith bring out endurance and steadfastness and patience. But let endurance and steadfastness and patience have full play and do a thorough work, so that you may be people, perfectly and fully developed with no defects, lacking in nothing."

The message for today: Don't let patience be a missing "fruit" on your tree of Christian character.

Prayer: Dear Heavenly Father, Help me to endure steadfastly and trust You in trials.

November 11 – Love in Action

Little children, let us not love merely in theory or in speech but in deed and in truth (in practice and in sincerity). (I John 3:18)

I John 2:5-10 talks about the love of God that should show through us toward our brothers and sisters in this world. John tells us that if we say we have Christ in our hearts and do not show love, we are liars.

A group of missionaries went on a trip to England in the cold winter months. One man named David, in poor health, decided to go and help the street people. When he saw their condition, he was brought to tears. He sat down beside one homeless man who was shivering and starving. David went to his car for food and a blanket and tried to feed the man, but he was too weak and cold to eat, so David sat down under the blanket with him for a long time until help would finally come. After several hours, David and the man both froze to death.

Being a true believer in Jesus Christ means more than just talking. It means doing. David will receive a crown in heaven because of his faithfulness to the God he loved. He died trying to help another human along the road of life.

God so loved that He gave. You, as a prisoner, can give to others, too. If you give other residents God's unconditional love, they will definitely notice something different about you – Jesus – and they'll listen when you talk. Since God's love is incredible, ours should be, too.

The message for today: God is love...show someone "God" today.

Prayer: Dear Heavenly Father, Please forgive my selfishness and unwillingness to act out Your love.

November 12 – Food for Thought

If any man's work shall be burned, he shall suffer loss:
but he himself shall be saved; yet so as by fire.
(I Corinthians 3:15)

It was a usual church service in our prison when one of our dear sisters stood up and asked a hard question of the visiting pastor. "What if I am saved and I continue to sin? Can I lose my salvation?"

The pastor pointed us to Ezekiel 18:20-24 as part of his answer:

The soul that sins, it shall die...but if the wicked man turns from all his sins and keeps all My statutes and does that which is lawful and right, he shall surely live; none of his transgressions which he has committed shall be remembered against him; for his righteousness which he has executed, he shall live.

Have I any pleasure in the death of the wicked? says the Lord, and not rather that he should turn from his evil way and return to his God and live? But if the righteous man turns away from his righteousness and commits iniquity and does according to all the abominations that the wicked man does, shall he live? None of his righteous deeds shall be remembered.

These scriptures tell us that the righteous man's deeds will not be remembered, but he will still go to heaven "by the skin of his teeth." II Timothy 2:19 says, "The Lord knows them who are His" so no one can accurately judge who is saved and who isn't. That's God's job alone.

The message for today: If you are "saved" and keep sinning with no remorse or change, you are not saved. No change – No Christ.

Prayer: Dear Heavenly Father, Help me to choose righteousness and not choose sin with its consequences.

November 13 – Costly Merchandise

The kingdom of heaven is like a man who is a dealer in search of fine and precious pearls, who, on finding a single pearl of great price, went and sold all he had and bought it. (Matthew 13:45, 46)

Pearls are very costly because they are produced in oysters by placing a single grain of sand inside their shell. They hate the irritation of the sand, and they produce a substance which covers the sand so they cannot feel the pain, namely the pearl. As you might guess, it takes much time to produce a fine pearl.

When God created us, He made us as beautiful as a fine pearl. We are marvelous in His sight, and He loves us so much, even if we are not aware of it.

Adam sold the pearl of innocence that God had given him, and we all inherited his sin nature. Many of us have sold our "pearls" of virtue for immorality and compromise. Our salvation cost Jesus His life on Calvary, so we are worth more to Him than we could ever imagine. He sold all His heavenly possession to buy salvation for us. How blessed we should feel!

Jesus said that the kingdom of heaven is like a man who is a dealer in search of fine and precious pearls; and then when he finds one, goes and sells everything he has to buy it. That's what Jesus did for us.

The message for today: Jesus is the Pearl of Great Price. Treasure Him today.

Prayer: Dear Heavenly Father, Thank You for Jesus and His great sacrifice for me on the cross.

November 14 – God's Great Faithfulness

It is because of the Lord's mercy and loving kindness that we are not consumed, because His tender compassions fail not. They are new every morning; great is Your faithfulness. (Lamentations 3:23, 23)

Lamentations comes from the world "lament", which means to express grief or sadness. When the Babylonians invaded Jerusalem in 586 B.C., Jeremiah witnessed unimaginable horrors. Solomon's temple was reduced to ruins. With it went, not only the center of worship for the Jews, but the heart of the community. There were no food, no rest, no peace and no leaders left in Jerusalem. But in spite of all that, the prophet found a reason for hope.

Jeremiah said that because of the Lord's mercy, they were not consumed. He expressed his gratitude for God's faithfulness and unfailing love.

Prisoners can be comforted in any bad situation, because we know that God knew about our plight before the foundation of the world. He is our answer to the problems we face daily.

Faithfulness today is becoming a lost virtue. When someone tells you they are going to do something, it is almost a sure thing that they will not keep their word. In former days, I can remember a man's handshake being his promise that the thing would get done; but today legal contracts have to be drawn up, and sometimes force must be used to get people to keep their word.

How good to know that we have a God who is faithful to His promises. Not one of them will fail!

The message for today: God is as good as His Word, and it never fails.

Prayer: Dear Heavenly Father, Thank You for Your great faithfulness to me every day!

November 15 – A Home Run

Jesus said, "Come, be my disciples and I will show you how to fish for people." (Matthew 4:19)

Rick Warren, in his book, Four-Base Model, summarizes our Christian lives by comparing them to a baseball playing field. Check yourself to see where you are in the game.

1. **From Home Plate to First Base –**

   This was the day you gave your heart to Jesus and accepted Him as your Savior. You said, "Lord, I want to be on Your team – not the devil's." Your life started changing radically.

2. **From First to Second Base –**

   You started reading the Bible and praying. You had a real desire to hear God's Word preached, and you longed to learn more about Jesus and His power.

3. **From Second to Third Base –**

   You wanted to do something for God because of your new interest in helping others. You found yourself becoming kinder and more loving. Jesus was molding you through Christian leaders and mentors in your life.

4. **From Third Base to Home Plate –**

   When you reached this part of God's playing field, you were now "walking in the Spirit". You went from an unlearned, incompetent child of God to a soul winner and leader. You got a glimpse of God's power working through you and in you.

The message for today: God needs you on His team. Have you signed up yet?

Prayer: Dear Heavenly Father, Thank You for placing me on Your team and using me to win souls.

November 16 – Who are You?

Prove by the way you live that you have really turned from your sins and turned to God. (Matthew 3:8)

Each of us can help others succeed, even in prison. We can say we have no influence on anyone, but that's not true. Because we do count in God's "bigger picture", it is time we start taking responsibility for our role on this earth.

Success in the Christian's life is "the fulfillment of the life mission God has given me". That's all well and good, but how do we find our life's "mission"? Let's go to Jesus' example of living.

Jesus had two facts which He settled when He was goal-setting before His earthly ministry ever began. We need to do the same thing.

1) He knew "whose" He was
2) He knew "who" He was

When you accept Jesus as Savior, you know "whose" you are. You now belong to God. You are no longer your own. You have been bought with a price. Therefore, glorify God in your body, which is God's. (I Corinthians 6:19, 20)

When you study God's Word and get addicted to it, you start to know "who" you are in Christ. When you know "who" you are, you start taking leadership of your own life. When you take control of yourself, Jesus starts showing you where He can use you by placing desires and dreams in your heart. What a beautiful cycle!

The message for today: Invest your life in the lives of those around you – no matter where you are.

Prayer: Dear Heavenly Father, Show me how to be successful and influence others for You.

November 17 – Great Results

Choose you this day whom you will serve...
(Joshua 24:15)

Think about this saying: "You are perfectly aligned to get the results you are currently getting."

Even if you are in prison, you can be happy and at peace with yourself and the world. No matter what shape your life is in, if you are not doing something to better yourself, then you "are perfectly aligned to get the results you are currently getting".

We are as close to God as we choose to be. We must choose righteousness to get right results. If we choose sin, we get sin's consequences – an exact result of what we are aligned for.

Speaking of changes from within, my friend, who was recently released from 5 years of prison, said that her parole officer keeps trying to catch her slipping up and failing. She is called in for random drug and alcohol testing to see if she has "failed" yet; but because my friend has been born of God's Spirit, she is no longer tempted to break the rules. Her parole office will never trick her again because she has been changed from within. She is "perfectly aligned to get the results she is currently getting"!

If there is something in your life that is producing bad results, ask God to help you change it. He can help you change bad habits and thinking by His wonderful Holy Spirit's power. You just have to give Him a chance to work by working with Him. He can then re-align your entire life! It happened to me.

The message for today: Be perfectly aligned to Jesus.

Prayer: Dear Heavenly Father, Help me to learn where I need to change, and then help me to daily work on my life.

November 18 – Our Greatest Fear

I will never leave you or forsake you. (Hebrews 13:5)

Mankind's greatest fear is dying, because when we die, we are separated from everyone. Even when you are incarcerated, there is still hope because there is still life.

No one wants to face death and its reality. Because of this, we are afraid to really invest ourselves in meaningful, close relationships; and we are not motivated to fully carry out God's purposes for our lives.

Jesus, however, came to earth to conquer death and the fear that goes with it. Through His death and resurrection, we are given His promise of everlasting life with Him. Hebrews 2:14-15 says, "Since the children have flesh and blood, He too shared in their humanity so that by His death He might destroy him who holds the power of death, that is, the devil, and free those who all their lives were held in slavery by their fear of death."

Someday we will all die because of Adam's sin nature being passed on to us. "As by one man, sin entered the world and death by sin…" (Romans 5:12), but the verses go on to say that, by the same token, as by one man (Jesus Christ), all can be made alive – forever! (Romans 5:15-17)

As we grow by reading and memorizing God's Word, we will become secure in the fact that we might be separated from those we love someday through death, but we can never be separated from our wonderful Lord, Jesus Christ!

The message for today: Live life to the fullest for Jesus. Don't let your fears keep you in slavery.

Prayer: Dear Heavenly Father, Thank You for saving my soul and making sure that I will never be out of Your sight.

November 19 – Love's the Greatest!

*They who trust the Lord shall not be in want
of anything. (Psalm 34:10)*

Someone has said that love is stronger than death.

In the movie, Ghost, Patrick Swayze always said, "Ditto", when Demi Moore said, "I love you"; but at the end of the move when the bright white light shines and he knows it is time to go to heaven, he looks back and says, "I love you, Molly. I've always loved you." Demi Moore replies, "Ditto". He then says something so profound, "It's amazing, Molly, the love inside. You take it with you!" He tells her that he believes we can actually take the love we knew on earth to heaven with us!

Love is a good thing because God is lov e. Human love (touched by God's hand) is our most treasured possession on earth. Jesus said that the two greatest commandments were, "Love God and love people." (Matthew 22:37-39)

What kind of love do you have for others? Write your own answers to the three statements below where my underlined words are:

My deepest dream is to: <u>work with people who need Jesus and help them change their lives and be successful for the Lord.</u>

I want my grave stone to say: <u>"A servant of Jesus Christ who made an eternal difference in people's lives."</u>

The one thing I was placed on earth to do is: <u>to lead people to Christ and to disciple them.</u>

The message for today: Don't leave this earth without love. Make a difference in somcone's life.

Prayer: Dear Heavenly Father, Teach me Your compassion for others.

November 20 – Learning New Things

All these events happened to them as examples for us...
(I Corinthians 10:11)

Many prisoners don't grow in Christ because they can't watch Christian TV or have regular Bible teaching. They only read the New Testament when they need a word from God. They don't like to read the Old Testament because they say they can't understand it and it is boring. This leads to a weak faith, unless they read and study on their own.

Paul only had the Old Testament when he wrote his portions of the New Testament. He had been taught it by his teachers in Hebrew school, so he knew about the Israelites and their failures and doubting God, even after He had led them through the Red Sea on dry ground! We are the same type of people, because we forget so soon the miracles we have seen God do in our own lives.

Paul told us that we can learn much from the Old Testament and its teaching. He said that the events in the Israelites' lives served as examples to us who read about them. In I Corinthians 10:11 it says that "these things befell them as examples and warnings to us; they were written to admonish and fit us for right action by good instruction..."

God is the same today as He was in the Old Testament. Let Him teach you the whole counsel of God as you daily read a portion of the Old Testament.

The message for today: Ask God for a clearer understanding of the Old Testament.

Prayer: Dear Heavenly Father, Thank You for giving us Your Word. Help me to understand it better.

November 21 – Believing God

Did I not say that if you would believe, you would see the glory of God? (John 11:40)

In Genesis 22:1-14 God tested Abraham to see if he would obey Him in the deepest of trials, because He was going to make him the father of the Jewish nation, through which Jesus would be born. He had a great calling, so God chose a great testing, and Abraham passed!

Isaac was Abraham's and Sarah's only son, but God did something strange. He asked Abraham to take Isaac and sacrifice him on an altar! God asked Abraham to kill this boy of destiny! What a seemingly terrible and strange request!

Abraham obeyed God and got up the next morning, took Isaac, the wood, a knife and his servant to Mt. Moriah. He told the servant to stay behind because he and Isaac were going to "worship", but they would return. What faith!

Isaac asked where the lamb was for the sacrifice, and that is where Abraham said, "God (Jehovah-jireh) will provide Himself a sacrifice" (Genesis 22:14). Isaac was obedient when Abraham asked him to get on the wood of the altar. Abraham was so obedient that he got out the knife to kill Isaac, raised his arm…and God intervened! He called to Abraham and showed him a ram in the bush.

If you are going to be used greatly of God, He will bring you to your breaking point, but He will also show up in the nick of time when he sees your faith!

The message for today: Steel must be tested to its breaking point to be used for great bridges and ships.

Prayer: Dear Heavenly Father, As you test me to my breaking point, teach me that You can be trusted totally.

November 22 – The Anointing of God

See how God anointed Jesus with the Holy Ghost and power, who went about doing good. (Acts 10:38)

The anointing (God's mighty touch on us) accomplishes several important things in our lives. If you know Christ, you are anointed with the Holy Ghost and power, whether you know it or not. The secret is to use the anointing and watch God work through you. Even in prison, you can practice the four results of your anointing:

- The anointing helps you to be diligent for God. If your life is sold out to Jesus, you will be diligent (conscientious).
- The anointing brings great, eternal results. As you press in with God, you will see Him start to use you amazingly.
- The anointing gives you a desire to give to the Lord. Selfishness begins to go as you walk in your anointing from God. Since God holds first place in your life, you tithe at least 10% of the money, time, and talents He has blessed you with.
- The anointing helps you to walk in love and harmony with others.

Our faith in God is walked out and evidenced in our everyday life when we walk in our anointing from God. The anointing is God's umbrella over us to protect us and use us effectively in His Kingdom.

The message for today: The anointing breaks every yoke of bondage. (Isaiah 10:27)

Prayer: Dear Heavenly Father, Help me to find out how to use the powerful anointing You have given me.

November 23 – Making a Difference

But you – keep your eye on what you are doing; accept the hard times along with the good; keep the message alive; do a thorough job as God's servants.
(II Timothy 4:5)

The saddest thing that can happen in our lives is that we live and die without ever having influenced anyone for Jesus Christ. I heard a poem about the time between our birth and our death. It made me think. I pictured a 73-year-old lady's grave stone, which said her name and 1930-2003. What did she do during those years between 1930 and 2003 to influence others for Jesus? Only the Lord knows and only He will reward her for her efforts for Him.

I would hope that my eulogy would be something like Paul's. He said that he had accomplished three things in his life in II Timothy 4:7 –

He fought the good fight of faith
He finished the race
He kept the faith

Let's strive for the same kind of faith as Paul. What the world counted "gain", he counted "loss" so that he might gain Christ (Philippians 3:8), and he did!

I want the time between my birth and death to win the admiration of heaven so that I will know on my dying day that I have not run the race in vain.

The message for today: Take others to heaven with you.

Prayer: Dear Heavenly Father, Use me in Your Kingdom to "live Christ" and influence others for You.

November 24 – Be a Light

*There was a man sent from God, whose name was John.
The same came for a witness, to bear witness of the
Light that all men through Him might believe.
(John 1:6, 7)*

When we get off track in our lives and end up in prison, we seem to think that God can no longer use us. Satan makes us forget God's special purpose for us.

John had a special purpose in God's plan – to bear witness that The Messiah, Jesus Christ, was coming to die for the sins of mankind and make a way for us to go to heaven. He was the forerunner of Jesus, and he did his job well.

My grandmother once told me a story about when she was growing up in Jamaica. She said that there was no electricity in the country side where she lived. The only job she could get was that of a maid in a rich man's home, but she did it willingly to help the family survive. Some nights she would come home after dark; and far away on the distant hillside where she lived, she would see the little light burning brightly on the front porch of her home. Her mother made sure that it was on so it could guide her daughter home safely. My grandmother said that it gave her a secure feeling of love to see that light welcoming her.

The message for today: No matter where you are today, let others see Jesus in you.

Prayer: Dear Heavenly Father, Help me to burn brightly for You.

November 25 – Imitate Jesus

Be ye therefore followers of God as dear children, and walk in love as Christ also hath loved us, and hath given Himself for us an offering and a sacrifice to God for a sweet smelling savor. (Ephesians 5:1, 2)

I read a verse in III John, verse 11 and it reminded me of my childhood. It says, "Dear friend, do not imitate what is evil but what is good. Anyone who does what is good is from God. Anyone who does what is evil has not seen God."

Growing up as a child, I remember our neighbors, who used to take me with them to visit their relatives in the country side of Jamaica. They had a niece named Linda, and her husband was a drug dealer. Even as a child, I remember their huge expensive home and beautiful cars. I remember saying how much I would like to have all those nice things, even if I had to be a drug dealer to get them.

Through the years, I didn't think much about Linda and her husband; but I always remembered what I had said. I got involved with drug dealers because I wanted to imitate those sinful people. I ended up in prison because I chose the wrong lifestyle and priorities.

I became a Christian in prison, and I learned that Jesus was the One I wanted to imitate for the rest of my life. For that reason, I praise God for sending me to the only place where He could get my undivided attention!

The message for today: God has no greater joy than to see His children walking in truth!

Prayer: Dear Heavenly Father, Thank You for getting our attention through any means You must use to make us more like Jesus!

November 26 – A True Transformation

God…who hath delivered us from the power of darkness and hath translated us into the kingdom of His dear Son… (Colossians 1:13)

I used to live in the Jamaican neighborhood of North Gully. There were many homeless people, who lived under a small foot bridge; but the city council bought that area, and the homeless people had to move.

One man decided that he would do something about his condition, so he took a shower at a mission, got some clean clothes, and started looking for a job. By God's grace, he was hired by a local furniture store, and his life turned around. He became one of the best employees the furniture store ever had! All he needed was a chance to succeed. The man decided to become a furniture maker and became very good at his trade. It was then he realized how much he had missed when he lived under the bridge with no purpose in life.

Colossians 1:13 says that God has delivered us from the power of darkness.

God has not only delivered us from Satan's power, but He has translated (transferred) us into the Kingdom of God through Jesus Christ. It is as if we were "homeless" and Jesus gave us a chance to become someone of value. He can deliver you from your homeless state, too, and transfer you into His Kingdom. If you haven't already, invite Him into your life today.

The message for today: Ask God to change your life.

Prayer: Dear Heavenly Father, Help me to live like the child of the King.

November 27 – God's Timing

And Saul said, "I know that you shall surely be king and that the kingdom of Israel shall be established in your hands." (I Samuel 24:20)

Have you ever had someone who was jealous of you and caused you all sorts of trouble? David had King Saul, who hunted him down like an animal because of his intense jealousy.

God took Saul's kingdom from him because of his disobedience, and David was anointed as king. Everything seemed fine until Saul decided to kill David. He hunted him down for ten years and still couldn't kill him because God was watching over him.

It must have been a tough time of waiting for David, but he did the right thing by trusting God to protect him and get him to the kingly throne; and finally it happened. The blessings that David received were awesome because he refused to be disobedient to the Lord's command not to hurt King Saul.

Are you in prison, waiting for something from God, and it's just not happening? Are you trying to make things happen instead of letting God take the lead? All of us take matters into our own hands at times, and that is not God's best for us.

If you are waiting today to be released from prison, it might seem that the wait will never be over; but trust me, my friend, in God's timing, you will be free. He knows the perfect time for our trials in life to be over, but His teaching must come before your release.

The message for today: God is able to deliver you from anything.

Prayer: Dear Heavenly Father, Help me to patiently wait for You and not give up.

November 28 – Do Unto Others

And you set yourselves to become imitators of us as of the Lord Himself, for you welcomed our message in spite of much persecution, with joy inspired by the Holy Spirit. (I Thessalonians 1:6)

I have come into contact with hundreds of prisoners over the years. I have watched many people embarrass themselves as they acted in total rudeness and disrespect for others, and I have prayed earnestly for them to change.

Sometimes we look at people and think that they will never change. We look at their bad points and don't ever stop to consider what they would be like with Jesus in their hearts.

I heard a poem that stuck with me. It goes like this:

There is so much good in the worst of us
And so much bad in the best of us
That it doesn't pay any of us
To talk about the rest of us!

God has a way of turning His chosen ones around. I marvel when I look at how I used to act and how I act now. My highest goal is to tell prisoners about my Jesus and how He can change their lives.

Are you praying for someone to be saved, and all you see is bad in them? Ask the Lord to show you their good points and how you can treat them with respect until they finally get it.

The message for today: Treat a person the way you know they can become, and someday they will become that person.

Prayer: Dear Heavenly Father, Please forgive me for only looking at the bad in people. Help me to love others the way You loved me when I was just like them.

November 29 – The Power to Change

...not in your own strength, for it is God who is all the while effectually at work in you, energizing and creating in you the power and desire both to will and to work for His good pleasure and satisfaction and delight.
(Philippians 2:13)

Philippians was written by the Apostle Paul while he was in prison in the city of Philippi. Ironically, the theme of the book is "Rejoicing". How could he have the power to rejoice in jail?

The hardest thing I ever did was to rejoice when I was put in prison. The environment was terrible; the noise level was terrible; and the sin level was terrible. I could see nothing good about my surroundings. But one day Jesus reached into my prison cell and saved my soul. He took me out of the "miry clay" and set my feet upon a rock, steadied my steps and established my goings. (Psalm 40).

Paul, from prison, told us to "Let this same attitude and purpose and humble mind be in you which was in Christ Jesus: Let Him be your example in humility" (Philippians 2:5). Jesus was willing to leave His beautiful heavenly throne next to God and come to the "prison" of flesh and blood where we live. He stripped Himself of all privileges and rightful dignity to assume the guise of a servant in that He became like us and was born a human being. Now that's a prison sentence!

The message for today: Let Jesus influence your incarceration.

Prayer: Dear Heavenly Father, Thank You for Jesus becoming a man in order to save me from my sins.

November 30 – God Really Cares!

I can do all things through Christ who strengthens me.
(Philippians 4:13)

I never thought much about God caring about me until one day in jail when my little table fan wouldn't work. It just refused to run, and I was frustrated and angry.

I considered my fan unimportant to Jesus, and I overlooked praying about it. A fellow prisoner had given it to me, and I used it while sitting at my desk, praying and reading God's Word. One day I took the fan apart to clean it; but try as I would, I could not get it back together properly. I would really miss that fan! Never once did I think that Jesus would care about a fan.

One day I was sitting at my desk praying, and almost by accident I put one piece of the fan on another, and it clicked into place! I heard a strange sound; and as I looked up, the fan started running perfectly! There was Philippians 4:13 right in front of me, keeping me cool! I could do all things through Christ, who strengthened me (and gave me the perfect combination of parts for my fan!).

Paul tells us in Galatians 2:20 that we must live "by the faith of the Son of God who loved us and gave Himself for us." We must use the same faith that Jesus used while He was here on earth, and it works!

The message for today: When things in your life take a turn for the worse, turn them over to Jesus.

Prayer: Dear Heavenly Father, Thanks for caring about the little insignificant things in my life.

DECEMBER

December 1 – Don't Tell Anyone

A talebearer reveals secrets, but he that is of a faithful spirit conceals the matter. (Proverbs 11:13)

In school one day, Sharon told her friend Annie that she really liked James a lot, but she asked Annie to keep it a secret. By the end of the school day, the rumor was all around school about Sharon and James! She ran home, crying her eyes out. For weeks, she avoided Annie and James.

Through a thoughtless and cruel act, Annie hurt two reputations and was responsible for building walls that blocked a good relationship from ever starting. She hurt her own reputation, too, because she was a "talebearer" – a gossip. Sharon would never trust her again with a secret.

Gossip is one of the most sinful and selfish acts we can engage in. It robs others of their honor and places them in positions of mockery. It never builds a person up; it only destroys. Gossip casts doubt and puts other people down.

God favors the person who keeps silent when a friend tells them a secret. Trust is one of the most powerful forces on earth, and every good relationship has trust as its main component. Our relationship with God also has trust as its main cornerstone.

The message for today: When tempted to gossip – don't.

Prayer: Dear Heavenly Father, Help me to be worthy of others' trust and confidence.

December 2 – Knowing God's Will

Give thanks in all circumstances, for this is God's will
for you in Christ Jesus. (I Thessalonians 5:17-19)

God wants us to know how to discern His perfect will.

Here is a formula, which I call SCCI – P, and it works when you are praying about a confusing decision:

S - Scripture. What does the Bible say about your decision?

C - Circumstances. Look at what's happening in your life right now. Do the circumstances show that you should move in another direction or stay where you are?

C - Common Sense. I heard a saying once that "Christians should not check their brains at the door when they get saved," and it applies to us when we are making important decisions.

I - Insight from the Holy Spirit. Listen for God's still, small voice, and go with your deepest heart desires, not the surface emotions that Satan puts in your way.

P - Peace. Even if scripture, circumstances, common sense, and insight from the Holy Spirit are there, if you don't feel a deep-seated peace in your heart about your decision, don't do it.

The message for today: Even if you get lost and miss God's will, He will find you!

Prayer: Dear Heavenly Father, Help me to consult You every time before I just do something quickly.

December 3 – Make the Connection

*Love not the world, neither the things that are
in the world… (I John 2:15)*

For years I never understood how I could keep myself pure from the sins of the world without disconnecting from the world. When I first went to prison, I thought if I could stay alone and not interact with anyone, I could keep from sinning; but that didn't work for long.

God started teaching me that, even though I was in the world, I was not of the world. I had to show the other prisoners that I had a God worth serving, and I couldn't do that by staying away from them all the time.

Jesus was not a recluse who thought He was too good for "sinners", and He openly was judged by the "religious" people because He hung with sinners. He was not outwardly disconnected from people, but He remained inwardly disconnected from them at all times.

Jesus concentrated His spiritual energy on God, His Father. He prepared daily to go out among people by spending quiet time with God before He spent time with people. His outward impact on others was awesome because He never allowed anything to take the place of His inward preparation time with His Father in heaven.

The message for today: Make up your mind to be interested only in what God is interested in, and you will remain at peace, even in prison.

Prayer: Dear Heavenly Father, Teach me to connect to others with Your heart, mind, and interests.

December 4 – Windshield Wipers

Learn to do right. (Isaiah 1:17)

The following story made me know that anyone can understand God's forgiveness of sins.

One rainy afternoon I was driving with more caution than usual, because it was raining hard. My five-year-old daughter, Casey, spoke up from her relaxed position in her seat and said, "Mom, I'm thinking of something."

When I heard those words, it usually meant that she had been pondering something in her little mind for awhile, and now she needed to talk about it. I was eager to hear some "words of wisdom" out of the "mouths of babes", but I was amazed at what I actually heard.

"What are you thinking, Casey?" I asked.

"I'm thinking that the rain is like sin, and the windshield wipers are like God wiping it away."

"That's really good!" I said. "Do you notice how the rain keeps on coming? What does that tell you?"

Casey didn't hesitate a moment with her answer, "We keep on sinning, and God just keeps on forgiving us!"

Isaiah 1:18 is one of my favorite verses, and it reminds me of this story of Casey when God says, "Come now, and let us reason together. Though your sins are like scarlet, they shall be as white as snow; though they are red like crimson, they shall be like wool."

The message for today: What can wash away my sins? Nothing but the blood of Jesus!

Prayer: Dear Heavenly Father, Help me to choose to be holy as You are holy.

December 5 – Will It Be Worth it?

Rejoice in the Lord always, and again I say, rejoice.
(Philippians 4:4)

A Christian man had a struggle in answering God's call to return to Liberia after leaving for many years. He had seen his father executed and his mother die from contaminated drinking water. How could he return, especially after he himself had spent time in prison, and was shot and beaten by the Liberian government officials? His wife had been diagnosed with mental illness during that terrible time, too.

All he had were terrible memories that haunted him every time he would think about his country, so he told God all the reasons that he couldn't go back to Liberia.

One day a woman approached him and asked, "When you come to the end of your life and meet Jesus face to face, and you tell Him how you spent your life, will what you're doing now seem worth it?"

He pondered her question for a long time that day and came to the conclusion that, although Liberia was a dangerous country, there was no place on earth more dangerous than being out of God's perfect will. He left for Liberia the next month!

With all this man had been through, his life verse was…Philippians 4:4…rejoice in the Lord!

The message for today: If God brings you to it, He'll bring you through it.

Prayer: Dear Heavenly Father, Help me to be in the center of Your will and trust You fully with my future.

December 6 – Don't Try This on Your Own

Trust in the Lord with all your heart and don't lean on your own understanding... (Proverbs 3:5)

Have you ever wondered if God has a mission for you, a prisoner?

Throughout our lives, we pray and pray to be used of God in some great work for Him; but most of us don't become great in the eyes of the world. I have discovered a secret to my life-long quest of knowing God's will: I'm in it right now! If I seek the Lord with all my heart and strive to live for Him every day, I'm exactly where He wants me. He can always change my lot in life; but for now I'm right where God wants me.

Let God unravel the future for you. You can do it on your own, but it won't have His stamp of approval on it, and life will not be fulfilling.

> *If I cannot unfold a rosebud,*
> *this flower of God's design,*
>
> *Then how can I have the wisdom*
> *to unfold this life of mine?*
>
> *So I'll trust in Him for leading me,*
> *every moment of my day.*
>
> *I will look to Him for His guidance*
> *each step along the way.*
>
> *For the path that lies before me,*
> *only my Heavenly Father knows.*
>
> *I'll trust Him to unfold each moment,*
> *just as He unfolds the rose!*

The message for today: Let go and let God.

Prayer: Dear Heavenly Father, Help me to trust Your hand to lead my future.

December 7 – Get Help Quick!

Call unto Me and I wi ll answer you and show you great and migh ty things wh i ch you do not know. (Jeremiah 33:3)

When we repent and turn our lives over to Jesus, He helps us to become obedient. The devil has to flee because Jesus paid the price for our sin. Everything seems to be going along well until we start trying to handle things ourselves. God knows we will fail in our Christian lives, so He has provided us a lawyer (Jesus Christ), who mediates between us and God.

God also sends angels to guard our paths in prison. When Jesus was in the wilderness for 40 days being tempted by Satan, He endured much suffering. But when the temptation was over, God sent angels to minister to Jesus. (Matthew 4:11)

Jesus created the angels before the foundation of the world. There is the same number of angels today as there were millions of years ago. As the world's population grows larger and larger, the number of angels stays the same; so someone has said that Satan is extra busy and has to work smarter to hurt Christians in this day and age.

Hebrews 1:14 tells us that God's angels are ministering spirits (servants) sent out in the ser vice of God for the assistance of those who are to inherit salvation. Before you were born, God knew you would accept His Son, Jesus, so He assigned you one or more "ministering spirits" – angels – to watch over you during your whole life.

The message fo r today: God has given His angels a special charge over you to accompany, defend and preserve you... (Psalm 91:11).

Prayer: Dear Heavenly Father, Thank You for always being there when I call.

December 8 – Celebrate God's Love!

Bless the Lord, all His works in all places of His dominion; affectionately, gratefully praise the Lord, O my soul! (Psalm 103:22)

Even as a prisoner, I have so much to praise God for! King David had the same response when he wrote Psalm 103. Sometime when you are a little down in the dumps, read this psalm out loud and see how many blessings you can pick out of the verses. Here are a few that I found:

1. He forgives our sins and heals our diseases (103:3).
2. He preserves our life and crowns us with love and compassion (103:4).
3. He satisfies our desires with good things (103:5).
4. He works justice for the oppressed (103:6).
5. He made known His ways to Moses and revealed Himself in history (103:7).
6. He is compassionate and slow to anger (103:8).
7. He does not treat us as our sins deserve (103:10).

Leslie Weatherhead summarizes why we should praise God all the time:

I believe that each individual is precious to God and that a divine, undefeatable purpose is being worked out in every life — a life that goes on after death. A thousand things happen to us which are not "the will of God," but nothing can happen to us which can defeat His purposes at last.

The message for today: Gratefully praise the Lord in all things and meditate on His love for you!

Prayer: Dear Heavenly Father, Help me to love You supremely in this life and "better after death."

December 9 – God's Always on Time

The humble will see their God at work and be glad. Let all who seek God's help live in joy. For the Lord hears the cries of His needy ones. (Psalm 69:32, 33)

How long has it been since you have seen God at work in your life? Many times we look at the wonderful answers to prayer in others' lives, but we see none of our own, and it's discouraging. Satan makes us think that God cares about everyone but us, and that is a lie! God loves each of us with the very same love!

The story of Jesus raising a woman's dead son in Luke 7:12-15 shows His genuine concern for each of us. The woman probably had been praying fervently for her only son to get well, but his sickness kept getting worse, and he died. It looked as if she would live the rest of her life alone, but Jesus showed up! Usually, in a Christian's life, when things look the worst, Jesus shows up!

The passage tells us that when the Lord saw her, He had compassion on her and said to her, "Do not weep." Then He touched the casket. Out of unspoken authority, the pall bearers (and the demons of hell!) stood still. Jesus said, "Young man, arise from death," and the young man sat up in the casket and began to speak! Jesus then returned him to his mother. Wow! The passage says that "profound and reverent fear seized everyone, and they began to recognize that Jesus was God!"

The message for today: Jesus hears your cry, prisoner, and He will show up when you least expect Him!

Prayer: Dear Heavenly Father, Thank You for Your great love!

December 10 – Do You Have Joy?

What joy awaits us inside Your holy temple, Lord!
(Psalm 65:4)

The word "joy" gives us the thought of delight and pleasure. When you meet a Christian with true joy, you know you have met the "real thing".

The psalmist said in Psalm 65:4 that true joy awaited him inside the Lord's temple. We can't expect to live on the periphery of fellowship with Jesus and be joyful at the same time. Psalm 91:1 says that we must "live" in the secret place of the Most High in order to remain stable and fixed in our lives.

If you meet someone who is sad all the time, you can conclude that they are on the throne of their life, and Jesus has been pushed off. He doesn't take first place. If He did, their joy would be overflowing, even amidst the sadness they might be experiencing.

Even in prison, your joy can be full because it doesn't originate with your circumstances. Meditate on these verses today, and start smiling:

God places the lonely in families. He sets the prisoners free and gives them joy! (Psalm 68:6)

Oh what joy for those whose disobedience is forgiven and whose sins are put out of sight! Yes, what joy for those whose sin is no longer counted against them by the Lord! (Romans 4:7, 8)

The message for today: Joy is contagious.

Prayer: Dear Heavenly Father, Help me to know You so well that joy will flow from me.

December 11 – Blessed and Highly Favored

The officials sent messengers to bring Jeremiah out of prison. (Jeremiah 39:13, 14)

People make mistakes and they always will. The officials in Jeremiah 38:6 took Jeremiah from his jail cell and put him in a huge unused water reservoir. It was full of mud and Jeremiah would have died if he were left there long. But God provided a man called Ebed-melech to go to the king and represent Jeremiah. He told the king that it was not fair to do this to the man of God, and the king responded favorably. God was watching over Jeremiah, and caused the king to order his release from the reservoir.

In Jeremiah 40 God even provided a man named Nebuzaradan to give Jeremiah food and money and release him from prison for good. God just kept showing up every time His child cried out!

God loves you, prisoner, and He knows right where you are today. As you start seeking Jesus Christ and obeying Him, you will see God's hand working on your behalf.

Jeremiah was greatly loved by God, just as you are. He carried out his purpose and was rewarded with freedom. In Isaiah 39:11 King Nebuchadnezzar told Nebuzaradan to find him and look after him well. Jeremiah's faith caused everyone to respect him and his words from God – even in prison in a foreign land!

The message for today: Seek Jesus and watch Him turn your life around.

Prayer: Dear Heavenly Father, Thank You for choosing me to be Your child. Help me to serve You faithfully and see Your hand on me.

December 12 – Make Jesus Happy!

Now when Jesus heard this, He marveled at him, and He turned to the crowd and said, "I tell you, not even in all Israel have I found such great faith as this!" (Luke 7:9)

Jesus rejoiced when he saw people exercising true faith! The story in Luke 7:1-10 shows that Jesus cares about all the details of our lives. A Roman Centurion's servant, whom he respected and highly valued, was at the point of death. When the Centurion heard of Jesus, he sent messengers to Him, asking Him to just "say the word" and he knew his servant would be healed. He explained to Jesus that he was a man with authority, who only had to speak a word, and people obeyed. So he understood that Jesus, also being a man of authority, could do the same thing. What faith!

When the messengers returned to the Centurion's home, they found the servant totally healed! Jesus honored the man's faith highly!

How impressed is Jesus with our faith? Do we see answers to prayer on a consistent basis? Are our needs met consistently?

One of my favorite verses is II Corinthians 9:8. It says, "And God is able to make all grace abound toward you, that you (always having all sufficiency in all things) may abound to every good work!"

The message for today: God is able…but we must exercise the faith.

Prayer: Dear Heavenly Father, Thank You for Your grace in supplying all my needs.

December 13 – The Real Jesus

If any man preach any other gospel unto you than what you have received, let him be accursed. (Galatians 1:9)

I heard a preacher telling about his spiritual journey to finding out who Jesus really is.

"Growing up in Mexico as a Roman Catholic, the primary image of Jesus for me was the crucifix, Jesus hanging on the cross. I believed that Christ was still suffering for my sins every time I participated in Mass.

Later in life I became a Jehovah's Witness, and they began demolishing my Catholic belief system; so I believed them. They told me that Jesus died only for a select few, the 144,000 anointed JW's. Jesus only played a small role in my new faith. Now I worshiped Jehovah only – not Jesus.

In the early 70's, I heard the Gospel, and I accepted Christ as my personal Savior. I was labeled a Jesus freak. I saw Jesus as a carefree, wandering Preacher of L—O—V—E.

Somewhere along the way, I became connected with a fundamental Baptist church, and my view of Jesus changed again. I learned that He was the sacrifice for my sins; He arose from the dead, and now reigns in heaven. Basically, though, I thought of Jesus only as my Savior, not really my Master.

My last 'journey' took place when I started seeing the Jesus of the Bible, Adonai – my Master and LORD. The Bible came alive, and so did I! I now live Christ, and I've done a complete turnaround."

The message for today: Learn to know the Jesus of the Bible.

Prayer: Dear Heavenly Father, Help me to know Jesus and the power of His resurrection instead of a religious system.

December 14 – I Messed Up!

*Like a father pities his children, so the Lord pities them
that fear Him. For He knows our frame; He remembers
that we are dust. (Psalm 103:14)*

God is merciful and gracious to us, in spite of the fact that
we are not perfect. Read the following story and smile:

Jennifer left work at the flower shop and went across town
to open a bank account. Her bank had moved across town, and
now it was not near her work. After giving the bank all the
needed information, Jen thought to herself, "They treated me
so nicely! I'm going to send them flowers."

When she got back to work, she started getting a fresh
flower bouquet ready to send to the bank; but in the process,
she found out that her aunt had just died. Now she needed to
send two floral arrangements. She wrote out the cards, but she
put them on the wrong arrangements.

The card that went with the funeral arr angement read,
"Congratulations on your new location!" The one that went to
the bank said, "You are sadly missed."

Fortunately, Jen's aunt was a Christian, so she in fact did go
to a "new location", and the bank just thought that she missed
them since they moved! All worked out well.

We all make mistakes, but God doesn't. He keeps all of our
records perfect because He is perfect. I would like to receive a
flower arrangement and a card from God that says, "Well done,
thou good and faithful servant."

The message for today: God makes my way perfect because He
is perfect.

Prayer: Dear Heavenly Father, Thank You for understanding all
my flaws and imperfections and still loving me.

December 15 – Death and Life

Death and life are in the power of the tongue.
(Proverbs 18:21)

Many prisoners speak words that hurt others and cut them to the bone. They don't even realize what they are doing until the damage has been done. Many parents also "teach" their children how to be rude and cruel with words because they are the only examples that the children have when they are growing up.

One mother tearfully told a story about her son and how much she hurt his feelings. One day she told him to tie his shoe strings, and he said, "I can't because you said I will never learn to do anything right." She quickly realized that her words had put a curse on that little boy's future. Had she not corrected herself, she would have created an adult with low self-esteem and a failure "tape" that would play every time he tried to do anything new. From that moment on, she determined to positively influence her son's opinion of himself.

Sometimes we learn the lessons of how to be kind too late in life; but most of the time God allows us to correct the damage we have done – with words. An apology can make the difference between the life or death of a relationship.

The message for today: Speak life and see the rewards in this life.

Prayer: Dear Heavenly Father, Help me to exercise the gift of encouragement instead of the curse of discouraging others.

December 16 – As Good As New

The Lord says, "I will make my people strong with power from Me! They will go wherever they wish and wherever they go, they will be under my personal care." (Zechariah 10:12)

Prisoner, God offers you hope. In Zechariah 9:11, 12, read what The Message Bible says:

"And you, because of My blood covenant with you, I'll release your prisoners from their hopeless cells. Come home, hope-filled prisoners! This very day I'm declaring a double bonus—everything you lost returned twice over!"

If God gave this promise to the Israelites, His chosen people, He also gives it to you if you will repent and completely turn your life over to Jesus.

Read Zechariah 10:6…

"I know their pain, and I will make them as good as new. They'll get a fresh start, as if nothing had ever happened. And why? Because I am their very own God. I'll do what needs to be done for them." (The Message)

It might be hard to believe that God could actually give you a fresh start, but He's the God of second chances. He is waiting for your surrender, and He will go into action for you.

The message for today: Give God the chance to prove Himself to you.

Prayer: Dear Heavenly Father, Please do what needs to be done for my release and help me to live for You.

December 17 – Spiritual Power

When I think of the wisdom and scope of God's plan, I fall to my knees and pray to the Father. (Ephesians 3:14)

When you know someone well, you know what makes them happy or sad, fearful or peaceful.

Paul couldn't express how much he loved Jesus. I was reading The Living Bible, and I immediately saw in Ephesians 3 the five things Paul prayed from experience for his friends in Ephesus. You can pray these five power resources for your friends in prison, too.

1. Inner strength through the Holy Spirit (Ephesians 3:16)
2. That Jesus Christ would be more and more at home in their hearts as they trusted Him (3:17)
3. Spiritual roots that go down deep into God's great love (3:17)
4. Power to understand the width, length, height, and depth of God's love (3:18)
5. That they would experience the love of Christ (3:18)

Paul assures us that God's power is at work in us and He is able to accomplish infinitely more than we could ever ask, think or hope! (Ephesians 3:20)

The message for today: Give God glory for what He can do in your life and those you pray for.

Prayer: Dear Heavenly Father, Help me to pray Paul's five-fold prayer for _____ so that they will change and become more like You.

December 18 – Sorry, I'm Not Interested

*Because of that Cross, my interest in the world died long
ago, and the world's interest in me is also long dead.
(Galatians 6:14)*

As I look back over my life, I see God's finger print all over it.
He has walked alongside me and has replaced fear with power,
love and a sound mind. As I've sought Him, the old things that
caused pain have died off. Satan just can't keep them alive,
because my sadness and lack of focus have been replaced with
joy and purpose in my life. Even as a prisoner, I could see God's
love for me.

Your friends might have disappeared when you started
getting serious about serving Jesus, but look what you have
gained. I have found that we are the happiest when we are "sold
out" to God – not when we are lukewarm and half-baked
Christians.

Paul prayed that the Ephesians would begin to understand
the incredible greatness of God's power in them as believers in
Jesus Christ (Eph. 1:19). Paul reviewed their life by saying,
"Once you were dead, doomed forever because of your many
sins. You used to be like the rest of the world, full of sin, obeying Satan…and following the passions and desires of your evil
nature. But God, so rich in mercy and love, made you new creations in Christ so that you could do the good things He
planned for you long ago!" (Eph. 2:1-10)

The message for today: Submit yourself to God. Resist the
devil, and he will flee from you! (James 4:7)

Prayer: Dear Heavenly Father, Help me to turn my eyes upon
Jesus so that the world will have less appeal to me.

December 19 – You Can't Disobey and Walk in God's Blessings

Saul and his men captured King Agag and kept the best of the sheep and cattle, the fat calves and lambs – everything in fact that appealed to them. (I Samuel 15:8, 9)

King Saul had a problem with totally obeying God. He would go so far and then fail. In I Samuel 15 God told Saul to do a harsh thing – destroy every single person in the nation of Amalek, including all the animals. People today would judge God and say He had no right to kill a whole nation of people; but remember, He's God – we are not. The Amalekites opposed Israel when they came from Egypt, and God had to judge them.

Saul's job was to destroy every living thing, but he just couldn't bring himself to kill the king and some of the best animals. Samuel, God's prophet, was upset! When he found Saul, he couldn't believe his ears when Saul said, "May the Lord bless you. I have carried out the Lord's command," but Samuel asked him, "Then what is all the bleating of sheep and lowing of cattle I hear?"

Saul insisted that he had obeyed the Lord! He said he spared the animals for a sacrifice to God. Samuel replied, "What is more pleasing to the Lord: your burnt offerings and sacrifices or your obedience to His voice?" Because Saul's obedience was incomplete, God removed the kingdom from him.

The message for today: Being unwilling to hear God in one area can make us unable to hear Him in other areas.

Prayer: Dear Heavenly Father, Help me to obey You in every area of my life.

December 20 – May I Have Your Attention Please?

But I will reveal my name to my people, and they will come to know its power. Then at last they will recognize that it is I who speaks to them. (Isaiah 52:6)

It takes hard times for us to turn to God. There is an old saying, which proves that there is a "God-shaped vacuum" in each of us. A person can claim that they are an atheist (one who denies there is a God), but "there's no such thing as an atheist in a fox hole!"

In World War II the fox-hole saying originated when men found themselves in ravines (fox holes) with the enemy shooting down their comrades all around them. Many an "atheist" was heard praying, "God, help us!"

In Isaiah 52:6 God told the Israelites that He would reveal His name and His power to them if they would only call on Him as Sovereign Lord.

Are you in hard times now? Has being in jail or prison about "done you in"?

Satan wants you to think that there is no hope for you, but he is such a liar! Today, do what Isaiah 52:1, 2 says to you, "Clothe yourself with strength and rise from the dust". God's there waiting. Give Him a chance.

The message for today: Let Jesus into your "God-shaped vacuum". He's the only One who can satisfy your empty soul.

Prayer: Dear Heavenly Father, I come to You, asking You to reveal Yourself to me today.

December 21 – What Did You Say?

And the whole earth was of one language and of one accent and mode of expression. (Genesis 11:1)

Mankind decided one day (in his pride) to build a tower that reached to the sky, so the people made bricks and started building. Genesis 11:4 says that they wanted to make a name for themselves and stay together forever. The Lord came down to see the city and the tower which they had built. When He saw it, He said, "They are one people and they all have one language; and this is only the beginning of what they will do. Now, nothing they have imagined will be impossible for them" (Genesis 11:6). God then said to Jesus and the Holy Spirit, "Let Us go down and confuse their language, that they may not understand one another's speech."

Can you imagine God creating every language at one time? I laughed as I thought about a French man asking a Spanish man at the Tower of Babel for a hammer!

Genesis 11:8 says, "So the Lord scattered them all over the earth, and they gave up building the city and the tower." The city was called "Babel" because the Lord had confounded their language and made them "babble" to each other.

The message for today: Be very, very careful when you get ideas that don't include God.

Prayer: Dear Heavenly Father, Help me to include You in all my plans.

December 22 – How Do I Look?

My little children, of whom I travail in birth again until Christ be formed in you... (Galatians 4:19)

Gandhi said the following of Christians:

"I've got the impression that they were just a group of worldly-minded people going to church for recreation and conformity to custom. I have the highest admiration for the Christian life and for the Christ of the Bible. And I might have become a Christian if I could have seen one."

One of India's greatest leaders might have become a Christian if only he had seen Jesus Christ in action through one of His followers! What a sad commentary for those of us who call ourselves "Christian".

How about you? Whether you are incarcerated or free, people are watching your life. They may not realize that they are watching, but they are.

When I walk into a room, the Holy Spirit goes with me and illuminates my very being. Every morning I pray the following prayer: "Father, I ask that You will bless every one with whom I speak and every one who speaks to me." As I go through the day, I see Him answering that prayer over and over again as I stay close to Him.

The message for to day: Let's pray for Jesus Christ to be "formed" in us as we grow day by day in the knowledge of Him.

Prayer: Dear Heavenly Father, Help me to be a "sweet savor" of Christ every day.

December 23 – One Day at a Time

This is the day that the Lord hath made; let us rejoice and be glad in it. (Psalm 118:24)

I have found that my attitude makes the difference as to how I will handle each day. Will I awaken and be mean, or will I praise the Lord for the ability to get out of bed? I play a game with myself sometimes when I want to complain. I do an alphabet of blessings. Try it sometime. It changes your whole outlook on things – even in prison. Just speak God's blessings quietly to yourself.

"A" – Thank You, Lord, for the "Air" I breathe.
"B" – Thank You, Lord, for the "Bible".
"C" – Thank You, Lord, for "Christ", my Savior.
"D" – Thank You, Lord, for "Day" and night.

On and on I go until I get to "Z". (I find that, by the time I get to "H", I usually feel 100% better than I did when I started.)

Nehemiah 8:10 says that "the joy of the Lord is our strength". When Satan can steal our joy, he can steal our strength. Counting our blessings (one by one alphabetically) forces us to concentrate on the good things our God has provided for us.

The message for today: Joy helps us rise above our circumstances.

Prayer: Dear Heavenly Father, Help me to set my mind on "things above" – not on things here on earth. (Colossians 3:2)

✝
December 24 – Elizabeth's Baby

Now Elizabeth's full time came that she should be delivered; and she brought forth a son. (Luke 1:57)

Elizabeth was John the Baptist's mother. God had chosen her to give birth to the "forerunner" of Christ. John was born three months before Jesus Christ,. The Savior of the world. God's timing is so perfect and amazing!

Luke 1:58 goes on to say that Elizabeth's neighbors and cousins heard how the Lord had shown mercy to her, and they rejoiced with her in the birth of her son, John. Her husband Zecharias was overjoyed, too, because he knew that the Messiah (Jesus) would soon arrive.

In Luke 1:68-80 Zecharias was given a glimpse of Jesus' ministry on earth, and he spoke it out for everyone to hear:

"Blessed be the Lord God of Israel for He hath visited and redeemed His people and hath raised up a Horn of salvation for us in the house of His servant David... that we should be saved from our enemies and from the hand of all that hate us... to remember His holy covenant. And the Child shall be called the Prophet of the Highest...to give knowledge of salvation unto His people by the remission of their sins... to give light to them that sit in darkness... to guide our feet in the way of peace."

Truly, Jesus Christ is all that He says He is! He leads us to repentance by His goodness and helps us to be sanctified and fit for His use. Praise You for coming to earth, mighty Lord Jesus!

The message for today: Christmas is nothing without Christ.

Prayer: Dear Heavenly Father, Thank You for sending Your only Son to earth for me.

December 25 – It's Christmas!

Christ first came down to the lowly world in which we live. (Ephesians 4:9)

Today is the commemoration of the day of Jesus' birth as a human being. Ephesians 4:9 says that He came down before He went up again. I can't understand how much humility it took to leave the glories of heaven and actually be born of a woman into this sinful world, but Jesus had a plan to save us from our sins.

Jesus is the same One who also ascended higher than all the heavens so that His rule might fill the entire universe when His task of dying for us was finished. (Ephesians 4:10).

Jesus gave gifts to His newborn church also. Ephesians goes on to say that He provided apostles, prophets, evangelists, pastors and teachers to equip God's people to do His work and build up the church. He wants unity and knowledge to overshadow every group of believers. (Eph. 4:12, 13)

When Christian prisoners are alive and well in Christ, they help create unity and peace among the other residents. Jesus Christ is held high as each person does their own special work and helps others to grow, one person at a time.

We can give the greatest Christmas present back to Jesus today by turning ourselves completely over to Him, and He will give us the best present of guiding every step we take!

The message for today: Use your gifts and talents to build up and strengthen God's kingdom.

Prayer: Dear Heavenly Father, Help me to renew my heart and mind daily as I read Your Word and seek You. Help me to give myself away for Your purposes.

December 26 – Incredible Love!

See what an incredible quality of love the Father has given us that we should be permitted to be called the children of God! (1 John 3:1)

The world cannot define love accurately because it does not know the Author of Love, Jesus Christ. As I read 1 John, my heart is full of how much God loves us! His quality of love is so far above human love that I stand in awe of Him as I grow in Christ.

Just read from The Amplified Bible with me and put yourself into the verses as the recipient of God's mighty love:

> *Beloved (that's you and me!), we are even here and now God's children; it is not yet disclosed or made clear what we shall be, but we know that when He comes and is manifested, we shall, as God's children, resemble and be like Him, for we shall see Him just as He really is.*

> *And everyone who has this hope resting on Him, cleanses himself just as He is pure. (1 John 3:2, 3)*

Before we can love others as they ought to be loved, we have to experience and learn God's love. Do you know His love yet?

As prisoners with poor role models, many of us have doubted God's love and are not included in God's family because of fear. If you are not born of the Spirit of God yet, why not end this year by asking Jesus Christ to be your Savior? Go to the February 28 devotional and review how you can become a child of God.

The message for today: There's no other love like God's love.

Prayer: Dear Heavenly Father, Please show me Your love as I seek You.

December 27 – Breakthrough

Seek ye first the kingdom of God and
His righteousness... (Matthew 6:33)

People go to prison because of problems and habits they can't control. It seems to be an unending cycle, unless Jesus Christ enters the picture.

In her book, *Looking Back Between the Cracks,* Verna Bradley (a former prisoner and three-time convicted felon), shares some insight about the life of a drug addict.

My grand daddy died...and my mama's father had passed on my birthday the same year...I was only 18 years old. After experiencing these deaths, I felt like "a little girl in a great big world". My life was empty and shallow...I didn't know which way to turn. People started to talk about me and judge me, which hurt me so much. I hated their small character and attitudes. My attitude got bad, too. I left home and lived life "to the fullest". I was dipping and dabbing in drugs and alcohol in my feeble effort to hide the pain I was going through from years of unresolved conflict within myself. (Upon This Rock Publishing Co., 2001, p.31)

Jesus is your breakthrough today for all that holds you captive. Ask His help, and you will get it.

The message for today: It doesn't matter what the question is. Jesus is the answer!

Prayer: Dear Heavenly Father, Please bring someone across my path to disciple me so that I can change my life to one that counts for Jesus Christ.

December 28 – Priorities

I applied myself to seek and search out, by human
wisdom, all human activity under heaven.
(Ecclesiastes 1:13)

A high school teacher picked up a large, empty mayonnaise jar and proceeded to fill it with golf balls. He then asked the class if the jar was full. Everyone said it was.

The teacher then picked up a box of pebbles and poured them into the jar. When he shook the jar, the pebbles rolled into the open spaces between the golf balls. He asked the class again if the jar was full. Everyone said it was.

Next he picked up a box of sand and poured it into the jar. Of course, the sand filled up every other space not filled. He asked once again if the jar was full. Everyone said it was.

Next the teacher poured water into the jar and asked the same question. Yes, it was full!

"This jar represents your life," the teacher said.

"The golf balls are the important things (your spiritual life, health, children, and friends)"

"The pebbles are the other things that matter (your job, house, etc.)."

"The sand is everything else – the small stuff."

"If you put the sand in first, there would be no space for the golf balls and pebbles."

If you spend your time, energy, and money on things that don't matter (the sand), your life won't be fulfilling.

The message for today: Set your priorities in life. The rest is just "sand".

Prayer: Dear Heavenly Father, Please show me how to put You first and everything else second.

December 29 – The Blessing

The Lord bless you and keep you; the Lord make His face to shine upon you and be gracious unto you; the Lord lift up His countenance upon you and give you peace.
(Numbers 6:25)

I pray for six things to happen in your life in the coming year.

1) I pray that the Lord will bless you (with every spiritual and physical blessing He has for you).
2) I pray that the Lord will keep you (in all your ways and everywhere you go).
3) I pray that the Lord will make His face to shine on you (in divine appointments and unexpected favor from others).
4) I pray that the Lord will be gracious unto you (by giving you excellent health and love from others).
5) I pray that the Lord will lift up His countenance upon you (make you aware of His wonderful presence in your life every day).
6) I pray that the Lord will give you peace (the peace that passes all human understanding).

Why not memorize this blessing from Numbers 6:25 and pronounce it on Christian friends who need encouragement.

The message for today: Use God's Word to give hope to someone today.

Prayer: Dear Heavenly Father, Use me to help others know that You love them.

December 30 – Where Did the Time Go?

Let Your face shine on your servant; save me for Your mercy's sake and in Your loving-kindness. Let me not be put to shame, O Lord, or disappointed for I am calling upon You…(Psalm 31:16, 17)

Another year is almost over! Take time to think about your victories and defeats in prison. You need both to make you grow.

There is an old song about a lighthouse, which guides ships and keeps them from destruction. I remember one line that says, "If it weren't for the Lighthouse, tell me, where would this ship be?" I think of that line in my own life. Jesus is the Lighthouse of our life. He keeps us on course when the world and its temptation take us off course.

The psalmist asked for God's mercy and loving-kindness to be upon him and to keep him from shame and defeat. The only way we can successfully run our lives is with Jesus guiding and directing us at all times.

If you have had a good year, rejoice! If not, consider what it could have been like without Jesus by your side. Why not make a list of the positive things that did happen and dwell on those things?

Psalm 31:23, 24 gives us some good advice for the coming year: "O love the Lord, all you His saints! The Lord preserves the faithful and plentifully pays back him who deals haughtily. Be strong and let your heart take courage, all you who wait for, hope for, and expect the Lord!"

The message for today: God longs for your companionship in the coming year!

Prayer: Dear Heavenly Father, Thank You for bringing me through this year by Your grace.

December 31 – Ten, Nine, Eight, Seven…

I am hard pressed between living and dying. My yearning desire is to depart and be with Christ, for that is far, far better; but to remain in my body is more needful and essential for your sake. (Philippians 1:23, 24)

Every day of our lives brings us another day closer to seeing Jesus! Sometimes that makes me happy and, to be honest, sometimes it makes me sad. Paul had the same feeling. He wanted so much to go "home" to be with Jesus, but he also wanted to stay and continue his ministry here on earth.

As this year winds down tonight at midnight, what is your heart saying? Are you ready to go to heaven if Jesus would call you? This is perhaps the most important question you could ever answer. Matthew 24:44 says, "You also must be ready therefore, for the Son of Man is coming at an hour when you do not expect Him."

I love the old hymn that says, "Some glad morning when this life is o'er, I'll fly away…to my home on heaven's distant shore, I'll fly away."

My friend, if you know our Lord Jesus as your personal Savior, I'll meet you someday over on that distant shore. Can you imagine what it will be like to see Him face to face and thank Him for all He's done for us? Wow! See you there!

The message for today: Is your house in order for the coming of the Lord?

Prayer: Dear Heavenly Father, Help me to watch carefully, for I know neither the day nor the hour when the Son of Man will come.

Notes

ORDER FORM

TwoWays to Order!

By Internet (credit cards only): www.prisondevotional.com

By Mail (credit card or money orders):
Message Publications
P.O. Box 220
Holly Springs, G A 30142-0004

Book Prices:	
1-10 Copies	$11.95
11-25 Copies	$10.95
26-100 Copies	$ 9.95

Use this form for Mail Orders:

Bill to:

Name:_____

Address: _____

Address: _____

City: _____

State:_____ZIP: _____

Phone#(_____) _____

Send to:
❑ Same addresss as above   ❑ Address below

Name:_____

Address: _____

Address: _____

City: _____

State:_____ZIP: _____

Phone#(_____) _____

Number
of Books: _____x $ _____ each = $_____
(see book prices above)

Shipping and Handling (see below) $_____

Total enclosed/charged: $_____

Payment Method:
❑ Money Order or Cashier Check

❑ Visa   ❑ MasterCard

Credit Card Number:

Expiration Date _____ / _____ (mm/yyyy)

Signature:_____

(All prices quoted in U.S. funds. Postage rates are per address.)
Please submit a separate order for each additional mailing address.

USA First Class

# of Items	Shipping
1	$2.85
2	3.85
3-6	6.00
7-9	10.50
10-12	14.00
13-16	15.00
17 & Over	+$1.00 per book

Canada Air Mail

# of Items	Shipping
1	$3.50
2	4.50
3	5.50
4-6	9.00
7-8	10.50
10 & Over	$1.25 per book

Postage rates are per address

Europe/South America

# of Items	Shipping
1	$6.75
2	9.25
3-5	11.50
6 & Over	$3.50 per book

Cut along dotted line